PRAISE FOR *HELLO, BEAUTIFUL!*

'It's a book of beautifully crafted, free-flowing vignettes...
[Rayson] takes centre stage with a sharp, economical style,
skipping vividly between juicy anecdotes, shards of
remembered conversation and moments of reverie.'
Australian

'This is a book that welcomes readers generously into its author's
secure and stimulating private world—and makes us wish, as we
reluctantly close the final chapter, that we could be there for real.'
Adelaide *Advertiser*

'Rayson's vignettes are perfectly constructed and she is a
virtuoso of self-deprecating humour.' *Sydney Morning Herald*

'Beautifully structured and articulated, not to mention
hilarious…Rayson reels you in with her storytelling.'
Australian Book Review

'With a playwright's unerring ear for dialogue, these gems
of stories are crafted and delivered with humour and insight…
It was a pleasure to read such a refreshing take on the genre of
memoir, written with skill, warmth and optimism. Like every
good theatrical experience, you are left wanting more.'
Good Reading

'With her coolly curious eye and facility for dialogue, Rayson
has chronicled key moments in the nation's social history…
Hello, Beautiful! is a scrapbook of Rayson's family foibles,
thoughts and simple dreams.'
Big Issue

Hannie Rayson is a playwright and screenwriter. Her works, which include *Hotel Sorrento*, *Inheritance* and *Life After George*, have been performed around Australia and internationally. She has received two Australian Writers' Guild Awards, four Helpmann Awards, two NSW Premier's Literary Awards and a Victorian Premier's Literary Award. *Life After George* was the first play to be nominated for the Miles Franklin Literary Award. Hannie lives in Melbourne with her husband, Michael Cathcart.

HELLO, BEAUTIFUL!

SCENES FROM A LIFE

HANNIE RAYSON

TEXT PUBLISHING MELBOURNE AUSTRALIA

textpublishing.com.au

The Text Publishing Company
Swann House
22 William Street
Melbourne Victoria 3000
Australia

Early versions of some chapters appeared in the *Age* ('Leaky', 'Hair', 'Let Me Eat Cake', 'Staging a Wedding', 'Pigeons', 'Jack Goes to Paris', 'Greece', 'Walking the Coast to Coast', 'The Butterfly House'), *HQ Magazine* ('The Fruit Shop', 'Real Class', 'Billy Crystal and Me', 'Staging a Wedding', 'Seville', 'Blood Ties', 'The Good Citizen', 'Making a Splash', 'Falling from Grace in Japan') and *Good Health Magazine* ('Next Doors', 'The Golden Mile').

First published in 2015 by The Text Publishing Company
Reprinted 2015

Book and cover design by WH Chong
Cover image by Simon Schlüter / Fairfax Syndication
Typeset by J&M Typesetting

Printed and bound in Australia by Griffin Press, an Accredited ISO AS/NZS 14001:2004 Environmental Management System printer

National Library of Australia Cataloguing-in-Publication entry:
Author: Rayson, Hannie, 1957–.
Title: Hello, beautiful! : scenes from a life / by Hannie Rayson.
ISBN: 9781922182128 (paperback)
          9781925095128 (ebook)
Subjects: Rayson, Hannie, 1957–.
          Women dramatists, Australian—Biography.
          Australian drama—Women authors.
          Women authors—Biography
Dewey Number: 920.72

This book is printed on paper certified against the Forest Stewardship Council® Standards. Griffin Press holds FSC chain-of-custody certification SGS-COC-005088. FSC promotes environmentally responsible, socially beneficial and economically viable management of the world's forests.

This project has been assisted by the Commonwealth Government through the Australia Council, its arts funding and advisory body.

To my father and mother,
who taught me how to love.

Do I contradict myself?
Very well then I contradict myself,
(I am large, I contain multitudes.)

WALT WHITMAN, 'Song of Myself'

CONTENTS

Prologue

I AM a playwright. I have spent thirty years pretending to be other people. I lie on the floor in my study and try to imagine I am someone else. It's exhausting. Right now I am a dying man with drug-resistant tuberculosis. Earlier this morning I was his angry daughter and after lunch I plan to be his Asian wife. Often I am everyone at the same time.

My imaginary people are always spitting the dummy. They cheat, they fight and they lie; they're cruel and they betray each other. The more scandalously they behave, the better for all concerned. I develop an affection for most of my characters. Even the racists and the bigots.

There's no place for shy people on the stage. You have to be a talker to earn a place in one of my plays. You have to be volatile. You have to *emote*.

Which means *I* have to emote. And sometimes I emote for hours on end. I feel like that guy in the circus who runs up and down the line of sticks keeping the plates spinning.

Not even an actor has to do that much *emoting* in one day.

I look out the window in the morning and I see women in trim navy suits walking to work in running shoes. I envy them. I wish I worked in a bank. I wish I could count out fifty-dollar notes, with my finger in a rubber thimble, and say to people, 'Big weekend coming up? Got any plans?'

*

My plays are never about me. But for reasons I cannot explain, I have woken up and found *myself* interesting.

I do not have to think of nine hundred people sitting in the dark in the Playhouse Theatre wanting *drama*. I just have to imagine you, tucked up in bed, wanting something companionable and consoling. Iris Murdoch said literature should never console. I think that's bollocks.

My women friends have big jobs. They have families. At night when they climb into bed they read two pages of the novel on their bedside table and fall asleep. The next night they have to reread those two pages. They creep forwards slowly, page by page, until Saturday. Then, because they are optimists, they buy another novel.

An idea began to take shape. I could write those two pages. That would be manageable. But once I started, I found I had more to say.

Some of these stories began their lives as articles in the *Age* or *HQ* magazine. All of them have been reworked with a simple rule: everything has to be true. More or less.

I have filled gaps in my memory with the odd imagined detail and renamed some people. I have omitted information that was clogging up the story. I may have taken a real event and put it in a different context, to protect the identity of my friends and family. But my poor mum has had to cop it on the chin. And the fact that my father is dead doesn't make me feel any breezier about questions of disloyalty to him. In fact, it has made me more mindful about what I write about him. He has no right of reply.

I have a lot of writer friends. They agonise about writing about their families, the betrayals of confidences. My mother was clear about this when I was younger. 'When you're more mature, you will wake up one day and find us interesting.' I hope she still feels that way.

I was aided in this endeavour by a camphorwood box my father gave me when I was sixteen. In it, I have kept every piece of writing I have scribbled since I was a teenager.

What I didn't do was put words in other people's mouths. I may forget what people were wearing or where they sat or precisely when the event happened. But I rarely forget what people say. In that respect I will always be a playwright.

Other people can do the ranting and shouting for a while. This is my year without drama.

1

Robinson Street

I WAS born in Brighton. Some people call it *Brarton*. Others call it—the horror—Bayside. Brighton is about twenty minutes by train from the centre of Melbourne on the Sandringham line. It sits on six kilometres of foreshore on Port Phillip Bay. It has historic sea baths, where we learned to swim, iconic bathing boxes on Dendy Street beach, great wealth and Shane Warne.

My husband, Michael Cathcart, says, 'Hannie grew up in Middle Brighton—insulated from the rest of the world by all the other *types* of Brighton.' But he is so very wrong. Our house was in *East* Brighton and people in *East* Brighton were different. Back then, in the 1960s.

These days, the women double-park their SUVs and dash between school drop-offs, the gym and the gourmet deli. They are the yummy mummies, with designer toddlers and toy dogs (spoodles, groodles or cavoodles), shopping in Church Street in their post-work-out *active wear* from a sportswear shop with a sign out the front that reads:

Run Girl Run!
Run like Ryan Gosling is waiting for you at the finish line.
Go get him girl!

They have coffee dates at the Cosmopolitan Place, which is the least cosmopolitan place imaginable. It specialises in sandwiches and Devonshire teas. There is a dress shop called Sweet and Vicious. Another one along the street is called Very Very.

I ask my son, 'Very, very *what,* do you reckon?'

'Very, very *white,*' he says, rolling his inner-city eyes.

Outside a salon dedicated to blow-drying hair (you can have a blow-dry party for sixty dollars a head) there is a poodle in a car with its paws on the steering wheel.

'Look!' I say to my son. 'Even the poodles drive BMWs.'

Our family left Brighton in the mid-seventies. We scraped it off our shoes and none of us have set foot in it again. That is, until last week, when I got in my car and drove down the Nepean Highway to have a look at my old house.

It's 1962. We live in Robinson Street on the corner of Parker. My parents have christened me Helen but I can't get my tongue around it. Helen Rayson. I call myself Hanna Basin. My version sticks. I become Hannie.

We are not wealthy. We have only one servant: our mother. She makes our beds, washes our clothes and sews on our missing buttons. My dad sells real estate. One night at dinner he tells us he's sold a house to a lady who says he's the most handsome real-estate agent in Brighton. We gag on our crumbed cutlets.

My mum loves my brothers and me to bits, and never whinges about having to do housework. There is no permission, at this stage, for a housewife to feel trapped. The American feminist Betty Friedan has not yet published *The Feminine Mystique*: the world has yet to hear about *the problem which has no name*.

In Brighton, we have a more pressing problem, and his name is Harry Smith.

Once a fortnight, on a Monday, Harry pulls up in his pale-blue Hillman Minx. I watch him from high up in the massive cottonwood tree out the front of our house. I am five years old, wearing my brown stretch pants and green jumper that I have chosen from Straws Drapery specifically for camouflage and detective work. I spend a lot of time in trees.

Harry makes a dash up our path, bent over as if he's been caught in a sudden downpour. He is clutching a ledger and a leather bag to collect the rent money for Sir Gilbert Dyett, who owns our house. Sir Gilbert is the president of the RSL and has a considerable portfolio of investment properties, houses he built after the war. He lets these houses cheaply to ex-servicemen. Wally and Maur next door have got one. Mac and Belle, over the road. The Keens. And Ralph and Little Lynnie.

On many occasions when Harry Smith knocks, my mum will have to hide in the hall cupboard because we don't have the money. My mother doesn't hide because Harry is a mobster who will cut off her little finger—Harry is a short fellow with a comb-over who lives with his mother—but because she is ashamed of being skint. However fair and decent Sir Gilbert may be about his rental policy, if you haven't got the money, what can you do? You keep quiet, never suspecting that all your neighbours are in the same boat.

On Sundays, Sir Gilbert strolls down our street wearing a black hat and black coat, surveying his estate and patting small children on the head. I was never patted.

When my parents arrived at Robinson Street, there were market gardens behind the back fence. Gradually, my father added sleep-outs and extra rooms to our place, and new houses sprang up around us. First there was Major Darcy next door. Then Betty and Alan moved in with their kids.

Then Di and John, who nip over to our house for fondue parties on a Saturday night. These gatherings involve frying cubes of meat into brown frizzled lumps, and dancing to Herb Alpert and the Tijuana Brass. My dad loves parties. The whole side of our house is lined with empties: brown beer bottles waiting for the bottle-o to come and load up his truck. He hands over cash in exchange for empty bottles—which Mum finds embarrassing, but handy.

My brothers are students at the high school at the end of our street. My oldest brother is involved in school drama: he is the lighting and sound man. We host large cast parties after his plays. Mum lets the kids drink beer from jam jars after we run out of glasses and cups.

No one worries about gatecrashers or hooligans. The only person displaying antisocial behaviour is me. I am vomiting. I am eleven, and my brother's eighteen-year-old friend gives me a small glass of crème de menthe and asks me to marry him. I have been schooled in not hurting people's feelings, but am sick with anxiety about having to say 'yes'. It never occurs to me that he might be joking.

Two houses down, Hilda and Harry Keen keep three malevolent pekingese. They are small and they know how to hate. My dog hates them back. When we walk past the Keens' house, the pekingese run back and forth behind the wire fence, yapping and slathering and smacking into each other. My dog bounds up and down, shamelessly flaunting her freedom. She thinks those pekingese are schmucks. I wonder why Hilda keeps them, what pleasure there could possibly be in patting them and peering into their dark, disgruntled souls.

By any measure, Hilda and Harry should be riding high, as they are the ones who bring glamour to our street. They have a daughter, Janis, and she is the closest anyone in Robinson Street has ever come to celebrity. She is in the Channel Nine dancers. She wears an Alice band and has perfect white hair turned up at the bottom like Patty Duke.

I am more interested in Little Lynnie, who lives two doors down from the Keens. Little Lynnie is taller and older than me. Her mum, Rita, has flown the coop and Lynnie is looked after by her dad, Ralph, a leathery bloke who heads off to work each day with a brown Gladstone bag. When he isn't wearing a blue singlet, he wears a short-sleeved white nylon shirt with an impressive crease down the arm. Who knew men could iron? They are Catholics, and their house smells of grilled chops. My mum seems to think Ralph is doing a pretty good job under the circs, but she worries about who will advise Little Lynnie when she gets older and bleeds and needs a brochure.

Our street is overpopulated with boys: Kenny, Terry, Johnny, Jimmy, Timmy. Apart from Lynne and me, the only other girls are the Bagwell sisters from Parker Street. Mrs Bagwell always seems to be running a mop over the floors, at which point everyone has to clear out. She shoos us off like cats, deaf to complaints that twelve-year-olds may not want to play with four-year-olds: 'If you can't play together, don't play at all.'

I have a foot in and out of the Bagwell group dynamic, preferring to nip back home alone and play National Velvet on my dad's wooden sawhorse, galloping in the Grand National Steeplechase, watched by Martha and Herbert, Winna and goofy old Teddy.

Several doors down, towards Curly Street, are the Fowlers. They have a daughter, Eileen, and a lumpy son, Brian. (Forty years pass before I learn that Eileen is not actually Mrs Fowler's daughter. She's Brian's, but Mrs Fowler is raising her as her own. *Fascinating.* Why didn't I know that? Childhood is wasted on children.)

Finally, and directly opposite us, there is Louie Rigutto and his wife, Mrs Rigutto. Their daughter, Jemma, turns twelve and takes me aside to make a special announcement: 'Now I'm twelve, I can't play with you any more, Hanna Basin.' I nod solemnly, enjoying the immense gravity and drama of the situation. But I am over there an hour later.

Lou Rigutto is a concreter. The Riguttos' drive and front garden are lovingly concreted except for small circles of earth, where Mrs Rigutto grows rosebushes. Lou's front fence is an artwork: a wall of concrete, reinforced by six decorative tree stumps. Each stump has brown concrete bark festooned with the knobs of lopped-off branches. The top of the stump is a diagonal slice exposing the bright pink rings of the fallen tree. His sawn-off trunks sprout from front fences across the suburbs of Melbourne. They are a paean to concrete's taming of the land.

In our street, neighbours take other people's kids to the footy. My brothers mow neighbours' lawns and paint their fences. The dads build billycarts and bonfires. Everyone comes out for Guy Fawkes Night. One day, Johnnie Bowden's dad takes my brother to General Motors to see their new computer. It is as big as a room.

These are neighbourly times.

＊

Forty years after leaving Brighton, I find myself driving slowly down Robinson Street at eight-thirty in the morning. I feel a creeping sense of despair. They've pulled everything down. There is nothing—*nothing*—of my childhood left. The street is swaggering with oversized faux-modernist mansions, flat-topped, multi-roomed boxes with white pebbles in the front and manicured plants. Some look like boutique resort hotels, with palm trees straight out of the Queensland tropics.

I can't find Hilda and Harry's wooden house, with its cyclone-wire fence. Or Stan Stewart, the SP bookie's place. Or Lorna Laslow's Californian bungalow with all the cars in the front yard. (Lorna had mental problems, according to my mum, and someone in the next house along was rumoured to be the first woman in Australia to have her skull cut open. She also had mental problems. There was a lot of it about.) Surely that pink stately home can't be Lorna's?

I get out of the car and walk across the road to my house. Gone. In its place, two massive units cover the entire quarter-acre block. There is a speedboat on the nature strip.

A black car passes, turns around and roars back, squealing to a stop in front of me. A man leaps out and marches over.

'What are you doing here?' he demands.

'Well, what are *you* doing here?' I ask after a moment's hesitation, baffled by his aggression.

'I live here,' he says defiantly.

'I used to live here.'

He looks me up and down, stabbing the air with his chin. 'You used to live here?'

He grunts, deliberating about whether to make a citizen's arrest. Any moment now he will demand to see my identity papers and search my handbag.

The man leaps back in his car and drives away.

I look around. I feel as though unseen people are watching me through the chinks in their plantation shutters. Someone, I feel sure, is going to ring the cops.

I hate this place. I get in my car and drive away.

I drive to Church Street and go into the real-estate agency. I tell a white lie. 'I am thinking of buying a house here,' I say. 'We live in Sydney, so I don't really know what sort of a suburb this is. What sort of people live here?'

The real-estate agent leans forward cheerfully. 'Pretentious bitches!' she says.

I laugh.

'Oh, there are some nice people, too,' she concedes. 'You'll find people like you. Good, solid, old money.'

I can't wait to tell my mum. Old money (good or bad) did not set up house in *East* Brighton.

I walk down to the Middle Brighton Baths. I used to come here every summer, practising for swimming certificates, running along the hot wooden piers in my bikini, eating icy poles and flicking towels, getting bombed by boys. Heaven.

In the public toilet on the foreshore someone has scratched a message on the metal toilet-roll holder: 'Have a nice poop.'

My father enjoyed a brief period when he did make money. Mum calls it the 'fat years'. During that time, they sent me to Melbourne Church of England Girls' Grammar school, and Dad bought a Daimler. I hunched down in the back seat, determined never to be seen in it. My credibility as a socialist was blown by that wretched vehicle.

By his own admission, Dad was good at making money, but not much good at keeping it. When he could no longer coax his good luck back, his heart gave out.

Had my dad lived to accompany me on this nostalgia trip, perhaps he would have liked the new Robinson Street. He was a real-estate man, after all. He approved of development. He liked progress.

One thing I know: he would be proud that his daughter was passing as old money.

2

Bruce, Honestly

HE LIKED a drink, my dad. He prided himself on having a big thirst. Sometimes he reckoned he could drink out of a dirty sock. That's how thirsty he got. He could get quite lyrical about his thirst. It spoke of manhood, Australianness and an appetite for life. He'd take a long swig from a glass of beer and collect white froth on his upper lip. Then he'd wipe it off with the back of his hand and say, 'Aah. Needed that.'

He was like a parody of a beer advertisement.

He liked to 'call in' after work. This meant going to the RSL. He'd call in for an hour or so, then show up for tea at home with a frozen chook. He was always winning chooks or meat trays. He was lucky like that.

My dad was a Melbourne Bitter man. Anything else was cat's piss. He'd be happy to discuss the finer distinctions of the various beers at length. Sydney beer gave you a hangover. Foster's gave you wind. And that new Courage beer was for pansies and public servants.

These days, there's not much social cachet to be garnered from being a man who can hold his grog. No one likes a one-pot screamer, but we no longer have a special place in our hearts for boozers. The bloke who could 'drink you under the table' used to have a status that hovered between footballer and poet laureate.

That was my father: a legendary drinker. No matter how much he drank, he never appeared to be drunk. He tobogganed into a party mood or else he slid into a slush of sentimentality. Somewhere between these two states he would leap up and make speeches. He liked talking out loud.

My father was the kind of man who would walk into the bar of a country pub and shout everyone a drink. If he were spending his last dollar he would never let on.

My mother tells how, at the end of the war, she went down to Station Pier in Port Melbourne to welcome him home. Three thousand, two hundred Australian and New Zealand servicemen were hanging off the decks of the RMS *Andes* when it docked. My father was first off the ship. While all the other troops were marshalled into coaches and taken to the Caulfield racecourse for the official demobbing procedures, my dad just walked away. The war was over and he'd had enough. Mum looked up and there he was, walking down the pier towards her in his navy-blue Burberry and air-force forage cap. Her handsome airman was striding back into her life after three years of flying planes in England.

He bounded into peacetime like he conducted all his affairs: no plan, no parachute, no regrets.

He was too impatient for university or job training. Instead he embarked on a series of entrepreneurial projects. He and his father bought a consignment of army surplus tinned cabbage and took it to a dilapidated shop they rented in Hoddle Street in Collingwood. There was a shortage of tins in the aftermath of the war, so they prised the lids off and dumped the cabbage down the outside dunny. Then they sold the tins to a paint company.

Many years later, when I lived in Collingwood, I'd always have trouble with the sewerage. Every time I shelled out a hundred bucks to the plumber to unblock the drains, I held my father personally responsible.

Later, he called himself a manufacturer's agent. He had business cards and letterheads made up, and sold knives, household goods, wooden sleepers, fluorescent lights.

By the time I came along, my father was working in real estate and auctioning houses on the weekend. I remember going with him on Saturdays. He'd stand out the front of suburban houses and preside over gripping dramas, in front of big crowds. Eager buyers competed ferociously, bidding and outbidding, pushing up prices in an electrifying crescendo.

'Are you all done? Are you all finished?' he'd shout, at which point he would retreat inside to consult with the vendors.

Later, driving away, he would sigh, 'Not a single bloody bid!'

They don't let auctioneers do that these days. It's against the law. Back then, it was considered an essential part of the art.

When I was a little girl, I leapt into bed with him every morning squealing excitedly, 'Punishment! Punishment!' He would sit quietly reading the paper, ostensibly ignoring me, and then suddenly he would lunge. The covers would be thrown aside, the newspapers tossed and I would be tickled into a yelping, squeaking, gasping hysteria.

I suspect he envied the easy intimacy I shared with my mother once I reached my teenage years. But he didn't know *how* to be interested in me. I remember one day, after a torrid teenage rampage, I managed to convey the idea that he wasn't the only one in this house who had worries.

He stared at me. This was a revelation.

'What could you possibly have to worry about?'

That I could be an individual with a *psychology* seemed utterly implausible.

My smug seventeen-year-old self wrote in her diary that he did not know the difference between being *interested* and *interesting*. 'He always opts for the latter, which is why he doesn't have friends—just audiences.'

As I grew older, I began to feel nauseated by his sentimentality. The grog watered down his robust personality into a slop of neediness. 'You know I love you, don't you? I know I don't say it to you often enough.' (Yes, you do.) 'I know I should say it more often.' (No, you shouldn't.)

'And I love you, too,' I would say frostily, like a schoolteacher, gathering my books to indicate that class was dismissed. But he would grasp my wrist and pull me back down to my seat at the kitchen table, and the toe-curling outpouring would continue.

My dad was fulsome on many topics that divided people in the 1960s. In the great Holden-versus-Ford debate, he was a Holden man. He loved Bob Menzies. He loved his family, and he was scornful of anyone who worked in the public service. He was self-made. Working for The Man was soft. He started businesses. He worked hard. He failed. He tried something else. He made money. He lost it. He believed in Risk. His children have all imbibed this philosophy.

He was also an ardent believer in the superiority of Melbourne over Sydney, an argument he relished having with my Uncle Marty, who lived in Maroubra. Marty had been a bomber pilot with the No. 32 Squadron in New Guinea. When Marty's plane went down in Townsville, he fell out of the sky and into the arms of my mother's pretty sister, Nurse Margot. They were in love from the moment they clapped eyes on each other in the hospital to the day she lay on her deathbed and commanded God to take her away. Marty was waiting patiently for her in heaven.

One hot January, my father bundled us all into his golden Holden and we drove up the Hume overnight to have a holiday in Maroubra with the Laws. Margot and Marty lived in a big house on a cliff. They had a pool out the front. We would spend every day perfecting bombs in that pool. 'Look at me, Mum,' my brother would shout, as he leapt into the pool for the hundredth time. 'I can do a curly one!'

The Pacific Ocean smashed at the bottom of the cliffs and great plumes of water rose up in the salty air. Back in Melbourne, our cases smelled of it for weeks afterwards.

One day, while we were up there playing with the Laws' alsatian, Roly, my father ran out of money. He couldn't afford the petrol to get us back home to Melbourne. So he and Marty went to the pokies at the St George Leagues Club. With his last ten quid, my dad won enough to fill the car, fill his wallet and take the Laws out for a counter tea. No one but my mother knew of our perilous financial situation, because my father always acted as if he were loaded.

Everything about him was impetuous. One winter's night he came home and said to my mother, 'It's cold. I think we should go to

Hayman Island.'

'When?' she asked.

'Tomorrow,' he said. 'I've bought the tickets.'

My brothers were always being inveigled into his impulsive schemes. He arrived home with a dishwasher one night. When the boys came home from a party at midnight, Dad made them climb under the house with a torch and a hacksaw. He couldn't work out how to connect the water. At 3 a.m. they were still lying on their backs under the floorboards, sawing through metal pipes, making threads and attaching tubes. Dad had long since gone to bed.

He made his most harebrained decision on a Sunday afternoon. He announced that we were going to convert our living and dining rooms into one big room. The rooms were joined by double-doors. In the front room was a roaring fire, and Dad thought he could heat the whole house if he opened the space. My brothers were deputised to remove the doors and the plaster.

Peter was twelve. David was fifteen.

Dad wanted to remove not just the doors, but the entire wall. And he imagined it would take 'about half an hour'.

Recently, my brother Peter was at our house for dinner.

'What was he thinking?' I asked.

'He wasn't,' said Pete. Then he reconsidered. 'He was thinking, "Let's get it done now, and we'll have people over for dinner tomorrow night."'

They bolted a six-by-two Oregon beam across the room for support, and Dad proceeded to cut the supporting studs off with a bow saw, the sharpest one he had. He cut the first two away with no trouble. On the third stud, the saw jammed. Dad was not to be defeated. He hacked away. He chiselled. He sawed some more. Until, at last, he had wrenched the stubborn thing free.

Peter and David looked up. The ceiling was sagging.

Peter was sent up into the roof to investigate while David and Dad stood there, holding up the house with their arms. Peter called down through the manhole. He had found the post (or tom) that held up the roof. It was swinging. The stud removed with such gusto had supported the entire weight of the roof.

Dad was unfazed. They'd work out something.

Then my brother David had a brainwave. He ran outside and got the car jack. The boys jacked up the stud my father had severed. Then they relocated the main roof tom to a more stable support.

The car jack remained in place for many weeks until Dad got a flat tyre, prompting him to rethink the pesky problem in the lounge room.

A few years later, Dad took Peter to the Brighton Police Station to sit his driving test. After answering questions about road rules and completing the parking test, Peter got in the car. Dad sat in the front passenger seat. The driving tester sat in the back. He leaned forwards and told Peter to drive up Wilson Street, past the primary school.

Dad made polite conversation with the driving tester. It turned out he was in the market to buy a house. Never one to miss an opportunity, my dad seized the moment.

'Turn right at the lights, Pete.'

He had a few properties the driving tester might be interested in. What followed was a tour of all the three-bedroom houses my father had for sale, spread over several suburbs. The two men got out. They inspected the properties. They talked. They got back in.

'Head for Sandringham, Pete,' my father directed. 'Got a ripper of a place on Bay Street. You familiar with Bay Street, Joe?'

By now, of course, he was on first-name terms.

Back at the police station, my brother had to ask whether he'd passed his test. Dad and the driving tester had completely forgotten.

There are countless stories of my father's hijinks and practical jokes. My favourite is the time Dad leapt out of his car at the lights when the man in front had cut him off.

My father rapped on the window.

'Victoria Police.' He flashed his membership of the Real Estate Institute of Victoria. 'Licence please.'

The intimidated driver handed it over.

'I'll take this, thank you. Now on your way.'

He thumped the roof of the car decisively and the compliant driver took off.

The next morning, my mum made him post it back.

On another occasion Dad was pulled over for running a red light by a police officer on a motorbike. He had just driven through an intersection. He apologised to the policeman: 'Officer, I'd seen you in my rear-vision mirror. To stop suddenly may have endangered your safety.' The policeman accepted this and waved him off. My father got back in the car and promptly drove over the policeman's bike.

As the sixties came to an end, we stopped being a family who sat at the dinner table with a brown bottle of beer. My parents made a sophisticated shift into wine appreciation. But not just any wine: after a brief flirtation with Porphyry Pearl and Mateus Rosé, which came in hourglass bottles encased in raffia, they settled on Blue Nun.

I've since discovered that Mateus Rosé, the wine I associate with hippy peacenik folk singers, was among the brands of wine stockpiled in the vaults of Saddam Hussein's palaces.

What with their Saturday-night fondue parties and their occasional visit to the French restaurant *Froggies*, where they ordered frogs' legs, I thought my parents were impressively *with it*.

At Christmas dinner in 1969, my father sat at the head of the table, about to tuck into roast turkey. He raised his glass of Blue Nun and said to his assembled family, 'Well, I wonder what the poor people are doing today?'

My mother gently chided him. 'Bruce, honestly.'

I sat there in a fug of shame and confusion. My father was a generous man. And yet, for nice and decent people, which we told ourselves we were, such a sentiment smacked of a breathtaking lack of compassion. We were, after all, better than poor people. Not more fortunate. Superior. And we deserved to raise our glasses and congratulate ourselves.

Even though we were often riding by the seats of our pants, we were not *them*. Not poor. Not *peasants*, which was a word I heard him use viciously about certain people who *rented*.

My mother commented a short while ago that of all the children I am the one most like him. This was startling to me.

When I asked her why, she said simply, 'You're a risk taker.'

'The boys have taken risks.'

'Measured risks.'

I tried to detect a tone of disapproval, but I couldn't hear one.

Given that his risk-taking landed her in the shit, or anxious about being in the shit, it was magnanimous of her to be so free of judgment about me.

Recently, I asked Peter to give Dad a mark out of a hundred on his performance as our father. 'One hundred,' he said, without hesitation.

'Who out of us three is most like him?'

'Me,' said Pete.

As evidence he cited Dad's shoes. Slipping his large and oddly shaped feet into our father's worn brogues, Peter found that they fitted like soft leather gloves.

'All the values I think are important I learned from him,' my brother said. 'Open-heartedness, generosity, having a shot. He taught me the right things to do.'

Peter took a sip of wine. 'He was the best dad you could ever have.'

After my father died, my mother invited each of us three children to look through his stuff and take whatever we wanted. There were his golf clubs and cufflinks, his leather satchel and suede jacket—the accoutrements of a middle-aged man. There were also the contents of his den. Hilariously, we used the word 'den' without irony. Men of my dad's generation furnished these musky rooms with leather chairs and dark wooden shelves on which they kept globes of the world, German beer mugs, backgammon sets and often a collection of leatherette *Reader's Digest* classics. There was nothing there for me.

All I wanted were my father's handkerchiefs. My mum handed over a pile of neatly ironed squares. They reminded me of my father's hands, strong and big and warm.

Rushing out of the house this morning, I realised I didn't have a hankie. I dashed back inside and went to my wardrobe. There were no handkerchiefs in the socks and undies drawer. I looked in various bags and washing baskets. Nothing.

I have cared for this diminishing pile of handkerchiefs for thirty-three years. They have accompanied me all through my life, just as I hoped they would. I have carried them in glittery purses when dainty white ones would have been more appropriate. I have carted them across the world in backpacks and suitcases.

Standing on my front step, I want to sob. How could I have been so careless?

3
My Diary

ON 4 October 1971, I had an epiphany.

After our dinner of grilled lamb chops—it was Monday—my mum and I went outside into Robinson Street to look at the full moon. My dog, Pebbles, wiggled out too. She was as excited as I was.

It was a cold night, still and black. The moon hung over the back fences of East Brighton. It was a perfect yellow orb, framed by Vi White's gum tree and the McWilliams' cottonwood. It seemed to light a path down Robinson Street and into my future.

I know this because I recorded this revelation neatly in My Diary. I have not been much of a diarist. The record of my life is mostly written on undated scraps of paper, chucked into the box. I now have no idea whether I hated Geoff Morgan in 1965 or when I was at high school.

In her memoir, *Bonkers,* the comedian Jennifer Saunders says that all of her diaries were written 'in remarkable detail for the first couple of weeks of January'. That is true of me, too. There is not much in this book that happened between February and December.

But in 1971, I had a proper diary, and wrote in it properly. My Diary is a small, gilt-edged book bound in orange-and-yellow floral cloth. It has a satisfying brass lock. For the past four decades, it has sat patiently in my camphorwood chest. Unread until now. *Tonight marks a turning point*, I wrote. *Tonight I have discovered something that will affect my whole life. (See pink page.)* I was fourteen years old.

The pink page is folded into the pages of My Diary. I stuck it in with sellotape, which has now gone brown and lost its stick. I recognise the paper. It came from my father's work at the real-estate agency. It is a listing sheet of a property for sale. This particular house (listing No. 2425/5) is a simple weatherboard with an iron roof, in Newport. Very handy to all facilities, including rail (5 min). Three bedrooms, $11,000.

Our family's fortunes rose and fell on these pink pages. We had wads of them at home. We used the backs for notes and lists and shopping.

On that particular moonlit night, I came in from the cold, took one of these sheets, cut the Newport house in half and wrote on the back in biro:

> God has cleared the way and shone a torch on the path I must take. I will [underlined three times] be a journalist and I will strive to make the best possible use of my life however hard and demanding it might be.
>
> I want to write and write I will!!

I am certain that I didn't tell my mum about God and the torch.

She was impatient with God and anything to do with religious fervour, the paranormal, and girls having epiphanies.

I knew that I faced a hurdle. Life in my family was making me well adjusted. This is a serious problem for any would-be writer. But instead of doing the obvious and creating a more iconoclastic personality for myself, I accepted my fate as a good and dull girl, in an ordinary family.

This did not diminish my determination, but it vanquished any notion I had that I could be the subject of my writing. It didn't worry me: I knew that other people were infinitely more interesting. I didn't need to be the protagonist. In fact, an interest in myself would impede progress. I was a watercolour hanging behind a cupboard. My friends and the people to whom I was most attracted were painted in vibrant oils.

I felt no regret at this lack of star power. When all my friends at university were trying to be different from everyone else, I was trying to be the same as everyone else. Not because I was a conformist. I was a spy.

I believed that to write well that I had to stop talking and start listening. What I wanted was to slip into other people's heads unnoticed. To find out what it was like to be them.

I realised also that a curiosity about the world would lead me out into it. To be a person with an interesting, but troubled, backstory might mean a life marooned at home in my study, stuck with myself, analysing the murky depths of my own psyche.

The comedian Wendy Harmer had a business card that read:

> Wendy Harmer
> Adventuress

I thought that was brilliant. This was what writing could mean: a passport to adventure.

My little orange-and-yellow diary is lying on our kitchen table. My husband picks it up.

'Can I have a look?'

'Under no circumstances.'

Despite the many references to my longing to be a writer, two things are clear from the diary. The first is that I don't actually do much writing; the second is that my teenage reflections display absolutely no talent for it.

My diary is prima facie evidence of self-delusion on a grand scale.

Moreover, on my first glance through it, I thought these were the daydreams of a girl of seven. To my horror I realise that in these pages, I am a teenager.

No one has ever read a single scrap of paper from my camphor-wood chest. This is writing about my life, which is separate from notes I've made for my plays. Those are kept in filing cabinets, and in boxes on top of wardrobes.

'Please?' begs MC, clutching my old diary to his chest.

I capitulate. He sits opposite me at our kitchen table and reads aloud:

> October 5. I want to be friends with Sue. She's really nice but I think Meg wants to sit next to Jo and she probably thinks I'm pushing in on her and Sue's friendship. What to do?

'Stop!'

I can't stand it.

He doesn't stop. He reads the entries for one whole summer: the scores of the tennis games I played with my best friend, Jan Batty, almost every day on the high-school courts.

> Beat Jan 6:5 after being 5:0 down.
> Got beaten 6:5 *etc*.

I write of my early morning bike rides alongside the milkman and his horse. There are records I made with Jan of suspicious numberplates and nefarious goings-on in the hood: *Mr Montgomery's car is parked two hundred yards from his house. Suspicious.* There are minutes for the club meetings of Skateboard Inc. in the Battys' shed. I describe the hot endless days when Jan and I lay around in our bikinis at the Middle Brighton Baths. There's the announcement of our dogs' wedding (Pebbles wore a lace tablecloth, Rebel sported a bow tie that belonged to Jan's dad, Bob Batty, a bank manager in Bentleigh). Also documented are our excursions to places of interest, like the National Mutual Life building in Collins Street, which I rated as *very* interesting.

On 12 January: *Rode to Moorabbin Airport with Jan. (Hope to get a story.)*

Despite several searches in the camphorwood chest, I cannot find a story about the airport. What was I hoping for? Surely at fourteen I was beyond *Five Go Missing at Moorabbin*.

When I talk to other writers—particularly male writers—it seems that even as children they were shaping their stories with a beginning, a middle and an end. By the time they were teenagers they were asking themselves about *incident*. What happens next? And after that? Where is the most efficacious spot for that *reveal*? How do I finish this story?

I never thought about plot or structure. When I went in pursuit of a story, I was seeking a *feeling*. All of that summer in 1971, I wanted the *feeling*. I didn't describe it as such in the diary, but I know that was what I was looking for: a kind of sacred experience. A moment of exquisite clarity. A glimpse of understanding. A moody and romantic air of tragedy. A sweet, pensive sadness. The moment when the real becomes the poetic. Forty years later, I still have the yearning.

When Michael reads me these reports from my past, I try desperately not to be the judgmental older sister to my little-girl self. I feel as though I should embrace the little girl, find within me a warm and indulgent love, like a mother to a daughter. But, in truth, I think she's a dickhead.

I can see her trying too hard.

I can see her trying to be a grown-up.

I can see her exposing an earnestness that makes her diary seem *inauthentic*.

I am mad at her. She lurches between being mortifyingly immature and humiliatingly over-achieving.

Who in their right mind would think there was a story to be discovered at Moorabin airport?

I am reminded of something MC said to me in a park one Sunday morning. 'These fathers are yelling at their sons because the boys are exposing personality traits their fathers are working overtime to disguise in themselves.'

The fourteen-year-old girl in this diary is exposing personality traits that 'the mother' is working overtime to disguise. Am I the mother to my younger self?

My husband is chortling away. He loves the diary because he

loves the little girl. I sort of get this, because when I look at a boyhood photograph of him riding his tricycle in the garden, I could weep with tenderness.

I tell my friend Ailsa about finding my fourteen-year-old self an irritating over-achiever. She is so *inauthentic*, I moan. Ailsa says, 'Don't you think that part of the authentic experience of being fourteen is trying to be twenty-one?'

At the kitchen table, I say to Michael that I could not possibly include the crap from my adolescent diary in this book.

'You are still the same person,' he says. 'You still alternate between swotty enthusiasms and a life of complete fantasy.'

This idea that I don't live in the real world riles me. Sometimes when my husband ambles down the hall after work, he calls out, 'How's it going on Planet Hannie?'

It is true that when I'm writing a play I spend weeks at a time with my imaginary friends: they live inside my computer. I have photos of them on the wall above my desk. Not the actors, but faces I have cut out from magazines or newspapers. Pictures I've spotted online. I stare into their eyes and imagine what they are feeling. I try to figure out how they would talk. I give them licence to run amok and they do. They surprise me with their decisions and passions and mistakes.

Sometimes, the postman delivers mail for some of them—letters I open on their behalf. ('Dear Lyle, Thank you for your inquiry about our financial planning services. I have enclosed our brochure. Please feel free to ring me at any time.')

This is Lyle from *Inheritance*. He was up to his neck in debt and he needed help.

Living other people's lives is my job.

Jan Batty and I met at kindergarten and we saw each other almost every day for the next fifteen years.

Back then, she was my best friend in the whole world. My twin sister, stolen at birth by the Battys.

Mr Batty and my dad were two different species of father. Jan's dad was reserved, gentle and asthmatic. Mine was garrulous, authoritarian and hearty. Whereas Mr Batty was treasurer of the Sunday School at the Brighton Presbyterian Church, mine thought the Sabbath was a great day for selling real estate. You felt that Bob Batty did things to the letter, whereas my dad was always thinking of ways to get around the letter.

After university, Jan became a naturopath and joined the practice of Ruth Trickey. They were Batty and Trickey—presenting an obvious branding problem for pioneers of alternative medicine.

Jan and I were both the youngest in our families. I think this was the aspect of my upbringing that shaped me the most. There are ten years between me and David, the oldest. We were a family who gathered ritually at the table for dinner. There was lots of talk: it was hard for me to get a word in edgeways. My father talked the most, then my mother (my dad often derided her views, even though she was smarter than him). My brothers filled the remaining space.

It's said that kids in poor families learn to eat quickly or else miss out on dinner. I learned how to shape a brief, well-timed anecdote. I learned how to do perfect imitations of teachers, neighbours, other kids' mothers. I learned how to deliver a killer punchline.

Or, at least, to recognise the spot where a killer punchline should go, if I could only think of one.

All this was aided by a holiday my parents took in Fiji. My father returned with a present of a duty-free cassette recorder.

I spent hours making radio plays, writing the scripts, doing all the voices.

But I was also developing a modus operandi for being in the world. It was a way of deflecting attention: if I find myself too interesting, I'll miss what everybody else has to say. But what's more, I'll miss exactly *how* they say it.

*

At this time, the person I most wanted to be was the Irish novelist Edna O'Brien. This was not only for literary reasons. I wanted her *style*. I had seen her on TV, on *This Day Tonight* with Bill Peach. She was sultry and sexy and smart, with a seductive Irish lilt. She didn't lean forwards and try to impress herself on you. She sat back and reeled you in.

When other girls at school were modelling themselves on Dusty Springfield, or Stevie Nicks, or Ali McGraw, I was experimenting with how to be cool Edna. I resisted adopting an Irish accent in public, but, home alone, I got that down pat.

I recently emailed the novelist Charlotte Wood, a friend of mine, to ask whether she related to this idea that writing was about an elusive yearning: trying to induce a certain *feeling* in oneself.

She wrote back in the subject box: Oh YES YES YES absolutely YES.

Coincidentally, she quoted Edna O'Brien, from an interview in a very old *Paris Review*:

> When I say I have written from the beginning, I mean that all real writers write from the beginning, that the vocation, the obsession, is already there, and that the obsession **derives from an intensity of feeling which normal life cannot accommodate.**

Charlotte provided the bold. She also responded to this idea that writing was a kind of spiritual yearning:

> I have discussed this with other ex-Catholic friends—we got all sort of juiced-up on sacredness and holiness through religion as children, and then when you realise it's all shit, you are bereft. Then you discover ART and it's all there!! What you seek is transcendence, and communion, and a sort of sacred plane of experience, just for a little while.
> Sigh. What a lovely thing to talk about.

Unlike these ex-Catholic girls, I was not inducted into religion from an early age. I had to go looking. I used to joke that I turfed Jesus out when I discovered boys, but this is glib and untrue. I lost interest in religion when I could induce the same feeling of transcendence through my own creativity.

For most of my teenage years, I was effectively an only child. Even though both brothers stayed at home until they got married, by 1971 they were off being adults.

Jan and I were now at different schools, but we hung out together after school and most of the weekend. We were both obsessed with the idea of owning a horse. My father capitulated to the extent that he bought several rolls of horse-patterned wallpaper with which he covered my bedroom walls. He had now discharged all fatherly responsibilities in the horse department.

One night, Jan and I were sitting up in single beds in my room, reading horse magazines, when she gasped and pointed. There, on the horse wallpaper, was a massive huntsman spider, scuttling sideways across the wall, like a giant hairy crab. I screamed out for my father. He ambled into my room and stood nonchalantly with his back to the wall. 'What spider? I can't see any spiders.'

Gagging with anxiety, I spluttered, 'There.'

'Where?'

Eventually, he turned around and smashed the thing with the heel of his hand.

My mother had a different method of spider disposal. Balancing with one leg on my bed and one on the chest of drawers, she would slam a glass jar over the spider with a steady hand. Then, she would expertly slide a piece of paper between the wall and the rim of the jar, shake the spider down and snap the lid on. Out it would go into the garden for humane release.

I have adopted this practice myself, not because of any considered environmental or Buddhist philosophy, but because it demonstrates what a marvellously capable and level-headed woman I am. Disposing of spiders in this cool and fearless way makes me feel at one with Xena, Warrior Princess.

Mrs Batty was of the same mind: live and let live. She believed that the Lord God had made all things bright and beautiful. If you asked my mum where spiders came from, she would have said the garden. End of story.

When Jan was fifteen, her mum died. It was so awful and sad and huge. Her mother was gracious and kind. Marge Batty and I were born on the same day (31 March) and I always felt safe with her.

I went to the funeral. In 1971, there was no expectation that children should face these things. We were insulated from death. But I knew I must be there with my best friend.

Mum had promised Mrs Batty that she would always look out for Jan. Our friendship remained steadfast for the next three years, but something had happened to her that I couldn't know. Or fix.

I so cleaved to my own mother I could not imagine life without her. I experienced separation anxiety when I stayed overnight elsewhere, even at the Battys'.

Jan had now been transported into a parallel world that was deep and unknowable. She was remarkably normal thereafter, but there was a chasm. It was called grief and we never broached it.

Many years later, Mr Batty married his housekeeper, Topsy. She was an earthy, jolly and strong mother of five. Between them they had ten children. Everybody loved Topsy.

These were the fat years. Dad put a pool in our back garden. One hot day, my brother David returned from work in the city. He opened the back gate and, seeing he had an audience, walked directly into the pool in his suit and sunglasses.

According to my diary the new pool was quite a feature that summer.

> Moz and Paul came round and got up to their usual pranks. I
> got chucked in as usual with clothes on. Went to Poppa's Pizza
> with Mum and Dad. There was a boy I know from school

there. Victor Wells. Mum reckons he was eyeing me. What a bull-artist she is!!! Still frightfully keen on writing. I'm as definite as ever.

In my play *Hotel Sorrento,* there is an excoriating passage about ordinariness, which one of the characters reads aloud from a fictitious novel, *Melancholy*. In this moment, I am suturing my own sense of ordinariness onto the national psyche.

'There was something very ordinary about Helen,' I write. Note that I use my own name.

> Ordinary and sensible. She had an ordinary face. People would stop her in the street. 'Don't I know you from somewhere?' It used to happen a lot. She'd shimmer with pleasure, shrugging it off for our benefit, of course, but inside she held on to that hard little nugget of hope that there was something distinctive about her…A permissible vanity. After all what good would it do to know that you were indistinguishable from a thousand others…

This is me. At least once a week someone, somewhere, says, 'Don't I know you from somewhere?' 'Haven't we met?'

They don't say, 'Aren't you Peter's sister?' 'Judy's daughter?'

They don't have any specific idea of how they know me. They just know me.

What is that all about?

The play continues, 'This is a country which honours ordinariness above all else. She might have taken heart that she'd always be cherished for it.'

I have written fourteen plays. None of them and all of them are about me.

When I first met MC, he asked, 'Why are all your plays about people who don't have fathers? Or you kill the father at interval?'

In my life, my own father, of course, died at interval.

I can honestly say I had never before made the connection.

4
Leaky

ONE OF the great mysteries of my childhood was the phenomenon known as 'women's problems'. Chippy McConville's mother had them and they necessitated a 'lady's operation' followed by a spell in the country.

We kids rode our bikes to the Moorabbin tip and caucused. My theory was, if Chippy's mum had a problem, it was most likely to be Chippy's dad, and a spell in the country without him would be just the ticket. I didn't want to ponder the landscape under Mrs McConville's apron.

Then my own mum had to go into hospital. This was quite exciting for me and my brothers, as my father was now in charge of domestic operations, and this meant a trip to the Chinese restaurant. Every suburb and country town in Australia has at least one of these. Some have names redolent of Imperial China, like the Golden Dragon or Jade Palace. Many have Chinese names like Wing Hing, Lau's Family Kitchen and Ching Wah's Wodonga. And some are funny, like Pu Pu Hot Pot, My Dung and Nin Com Soup.

The Chinese takeaway in Brighton was called the Hob Nob. (There was rarely anyone in the Hob Nob, so I'm not sure what networking opportunities they were promoting.)

In those days, if you wanted Chinese takeaway, you brought your own saucepans. We took two—one for fried rice, and one for chicken and almonds.

I still remember the glory of that meal. Driving home, nursing one big aluminium saucepan wrapped in a tea towel. The fried rice at my feet. Knees warm. The smell of toasted almonds and soy sauce filling the car. Heaven.

My poor mum languishing in the Brighton Community Hospital on a drip: did we give her a thought?

At the Moorabbin tip, Jim Turner was adamant that, whatever the nature of the problems that specifically afflicted women, he was certain it involved the removal of some form of tubing. Kenny from over the road concurred. He also volunteered that some girls use tampons and others don't. The reason for this is that some girls are leaky.

I shrugged, feigning boredom with the conversation, and rode off on my bike over the bobbly landscape of the tip. The prospect of leakiness was disquieting, to say the least.

Shame was always hovering over my childhood. The disgrace of being ignorant. The apprehension that my strong little brown body might malfunction and ooze foetid substances. The dread of being mocked. Sex and mockery were almost inseparable when I was growing up.

'Hey, you! Beautiful!' a boy would call out on the tram. I would look up. 'Not you, you idiot.' Schoolboy laughter would rattle around the compartment.

It occurred to me to counter Kenny's derision about female plumbing with information I'd gleaned from Jan Batty's home health encyclopaedia, *Vitalogy* (1930 edition). Men leak too. They have *nocturnal emissions.*

In *Vitalogy*, there were several pages devoted to the grave consequences of 'self-pollution'. It was an unnatural and degrading business and, to illustrate the dire consequences of indulging in such an activity, there were colour plates of gaunt and wasted sufferers who looked more like prisoners of war than victims of their own hand. These men leaked due to their own lack of moral fortitude.

Few, perhaps, ever think, or ever know, how many of the unfortunate inmates of our lunatic asylums have been sent there by this dreadful vice. Were the whole truth upon this subject known, it would alarm parents, as well as the guilty victims of the vice, more even than the dread of the cholera or small-pox.

Jan Batty and I sniggered our way through many a rainy Saturday afternoon reading *Vitalogy*. But the impediment to putting Kenny in his place was the word 'nocturnal'. I wasn't confident. In my mind, it was associated with possums.

I was deputised to go and pack a bag with some clean undergarments to take to my mother in hospital. This involved going to the top drawer, where she kept her 'smalls'.

In the early sixties, the concept of 'smalls' was a most inappropriate euphemism. 'Smalls' were, by and large, enormous, even those of trim ladies like my mum. On washing day, you saw the full extent of their voluminosity.

The 'smalls' drawer contained many mysterious and magnificent feminine items. On Saturday night, when there was steam and singing from the bathroom and the sweet smell of lavender talc in the air, a strange rubbery construction came out of this drawer. Mum stepped into it, shimmied it over her knees, then heaved and hoisted it over thigh and buttock, until it snapped shut around her waist.

Any recalcitrant rolls spooling over the top were tucked in. Stockings were held up by suspenders, front and back, and a white petticoat crackled as it was pulled over the elasticised substructure.

Then came the frock.

Thus equipped with a flat, hard tummy and perky breasts, my mother was ready to serve shrimp cocktail and apricot chicken followed by Coffee Velvet to Dad's work colleagues from Arnold and Scott Real Estate. (One colleague was an impeccably groomed German called Nick Orff.)

I've often thought that the women's movement made too much of bra-burning. The panty girdle was the much more sinister force.

Being oppressed by men and capitalism was one thing, but the panty girdle denied women a more basic human right: access to oxygen. The elastic structure impinged on the diaphragm to the extent that it was impossible to breathe and talk simultaneously.

It has occurred to me that the bimbo phenomenon—light-headedness, breathless banter, gasping and giggling, so characteristic of movie stars like Marilyn Monroe—was merely evidence of slow asphyxiation.

My mother emerged from the hospital with her tubing intact. She was, however, minus a gall bladder.

My father decided to bake a cake to welcome her home. I can see him now, wearing Mum's apron and standing at the kitchen bench, squinting at the recipe book. He held aloft two eggs and read out the instruction: 'Separate two eggs'. He stared from the book to the eggs. *Separate* two eggs. He placed two eggs side-by-side on the bench— then moved them apart.

When my mum got back on her feet, we made the journey down to Mr Maynard's to stock up. He had a small grocery shop in East Brighton, where he wore a white coat and accessed most of the produce by ladder. Most things needed to be scooped from a tin, weighed and wrapped neatly in white paper, secured with sellotape. It could be a time-consuming business, so I had plenty of opportunity for idle eavesdropping.

Mrs Polk and Mrs Hyde were in the shop and I discovered that Mrs Polk found it very embarrassing to carry toilet rolls in her shopping basket. Mrs Hyde was able to bury her pride on the toilet-paper issue, but drew the line at displaying anything 'more personal'.

I wondered what could be more personal than doing poo. Then I remembered those pre-wrapped items in brown paper that you bought at the chemist.

I wonder how Mrs Polk and Mrs Hyde would cope these days, standing at the check-out, dividing their purchases from the next person's with a thin block of wood. You can't help your eyes darting over the stockpile of the man directly in front. What could he possibly be doing with all that processed sliced cheese?

There is a shop near the Queen Victoria Market where you can buy toilet rolls in slabs of fifty. One Saturday morning, my husband staggered out with one balanced on his shoulder, like a labourer going off to build a wall.

My mother never buys anything in bulk. She thinks it encourages waste. Anyway, who has enough left over from the weekly housekeeping to spend on extras? And where would you store it?

We always had the smallest jar of Vegemite in our cupboard. When I went to other people's houses, I was shocked to discover you could buy it in huge jars. Vats of Vegemite. I didn't fancy it. The toast crumbs in there might be a decade old.

The Vic Market is a very sociable place on a Saturday morning. We are always running into people we know. Our massive toilet-roll purchase is balanced precariously on our trolley. There is barely room to squeeze in a Dutch carrot.

'Good morning! Hello!' I am pushing the trolley up the aisle, smiling and nodding. Michael is caught up in conversation with a man he went to university with. He is just near the entrance to the deli, in a place we call 'Deserted Husbands', where men wait when they've lost their wives.

He is taking no responsibility for this humiliation.

Of course, it is not the *fact* of it. It's just toilet paper.

It's the implication that apparently, some people need an awful fucking lot of it.

Some people must be very, very…leaky.

5
Soup

I WANT to write a few words in praise of soup.

In my first year of acting school, I shared a house in Carlton with three lumpy boys, all university students. One autumn Saturday, my mum came over for lunch. Well, *with* lunch: she brought a pot of pea and ham soup, a loaf of white bread and a fluffy honey sponge. The boys slurped two helpings of soup, ripped into the bread and cheese and homemade pickles, then sliced off large slabs of sponge cake, which they washed down with mugs of tea and exclamations of hearty gratitude. They eulogised my mother as a culinary deity and compared her favourably with their own mums, who were clearly too lazy to bring pots of soup to the needy. After they loped off to their rooms, my mum sat down with a very satisfied sigh and said, 'I don't know how you can *resist* feeding them.'

I was twenty-one, a feminist and an actress. A girl like me did not *feed* anyone, even herself.

These days, the prospect of ladling out soup to hungry university students is so appealing to me it borders on the pathetic. The desire to be a source of nourishment runs deep. It became more intense after my son left home. I had to quell the impulse to run around 'a little something' to his apartment. My son reassured me, 'You never need to repress the desire to bring food to this house. Be very clear about that.'

'What if you're having sex?'

'I won't answer the door.'

The American writer Nora Ephron says the only reason mothers of teenagers should get a dog is so that when they get home from work they'll have someone there who is pleased to see them. This is true, but it's amazing the transformation that occurs when teenagers eventually move out and have to fend for themselves. Even the most irascible, the most densely grafittied teenager, when offered a pot of homemade soup is not going to snatch it off you and sneer, 'What do you want, you pain in the arse?'

Sometimes, if a little offering is called for, when tending to the sick, I might consider taking a cake. But cakes, unless they are plain and un-iced, speak of a desire for affirmation on the part of the baker. There's also the risk that the recipient will turn up his or her nose and make you feel like a fatty-boom-bah for making one. Or else the patient is lactose-intolerant or gluten-affected or they wheeze if they come in contact with vanilla extract. Cake brings out the allergies in people. Soup brings out people's better natures.

I am my best self when I'm cooking soup. Capable and calm. I rarely think, 'I should be writing', which is not true of almost every other activity. Writing is an affliction. It is for the selfish and the insufferable. Soup-making is a job for the angels.

When we were sick in bed as children, my mother would come to the door with a tray and say, 'Could you take a little nourishment?'

I would rally my wan and ailing self to sit up and take a few sips of soup.

Her mother did the same. Now I am doing it.

I would like to be able to tell you that I am a well of comfort for the sick. But when sick people are too sick to eat, I lose interest in them.

The actor Ronald Falk made a very astute comment about soup, during rehearsals for my play *Inheritance*.

Of all my plays, *Inheritance* was the most fun to rehearse. It is a family saga about two eighty-year-old twin sisters named Dibs and Girlie. These feisty old girls are embroiled in an argument over who should inherit their family farm. Ron played Farley Hamilton, the curmudgeonly old patriarch on his last legs.

Ron was standing on a chair in his underpants while Monica Maughan, who played his wife, pinned up a pair of trousers she'd bought at Kirby's garage sale for fifteen dollars. The stage manager called for a lunch break. The lighting guy carried in a bowl of pumpkin soup from the Melbourne Theatre Company canteen. Ron, still in his underpants, peered down at the bowl and scowled, 'The problem with soup is that every mouthful tastes the same.'

Every time I have a bowl of soup, I think of Ron Falk and I ask myself, 'Am I happy with this unerring sameness? This unremitting soupiness?' And unless I've had to eat it for four days in a row, including breakfast, my answer is always yes.

Soup is like a best friend. Most people are not looking for capriciousness or unpredictability in their chums. Most of us want a hearty and velvety friendship, characterised by comfort and intimacy, trustworthiness and contentment. A good soup delivers all of this.

I am thinking particularly of Tiamo's minestrone on cold and rainy days in Carlton, when the windows of the café fog up and the air is thick with garlic and parmesan. Or my mother's heartwarming vegetable and barley soup (always made with her own stock). The Vietnamese chicken and tofu phở from *I Love Phở* in Victoria Street in Richmond is brilliant at eight dollars a bowl. Even in summer, when the temperature soars and one is in need of punkahs and cool refreshment, soup is a stalwart companion. My friend Caroline Baum makes a divine gazpacho and Charlotte Wood's chilled leek, pea and cucumber soup is legendary.

And I haven't even mentioned my cousin's bouillabaisse, which she serves with grilled bread and a garlicky mayonnaise with saffron and cayenne pepper. One mouthful of this broth and you are wandering the ports of Marseille reckless with desire and danger.

A great soup doesn't even have to be homemade. Some of the best days of my life have been accompanied by Rosella tomato soup in a tin. One of those days was 21 July 1969. I was twelve and Neil Armstrong walked on the moon. Buzz Aldrin did, too. This was an historic moment in East Brighton because Joan Jedd, Pam Turner, Lauren Williamson and Andrea Garraway—my school friends from Brighton High—were allowed to leave school in the middle of the day to come over to my house to watch telly. There was no precedent for this anarchic breach of school protocol.

The five of us sat clustered around the TV in our grey tunics and thick winter tights as Neil climbed down from the spacecraft and took his one giant leap for mankind. We spooned in mouthfuls of tomato soup. I remember feeling sorry for the guy who had to stay in the command module, Michael Collins. He had to drive around the block while the other two got to dash into the shops. He said this great thing: 'You cats take it easy on the lunar surface.'

As Neil rammed the American flag into the lunar surface, we sipped that smooth tomatoey elixir and ate our buttery English muffins, and I thought to myself: life does not get better than this.

Last week my neighbour Dora stopped me in the street and told me that her father had had a massive stroke and was in intensive care. Dora is a bank executive and lives in a cute doll's house over the road from us. She is very beautiful and stylish.

She has a small baby and she has to make trips to hospital to see her dad, so at this moment, life is tough for Dora. I have made a pot of minestrone. I wonder if it might be intrusive or hokey to take it over to her. I wish it wasn't just plain old minestrone. I wish it was cream of artichoke and pear, or something similarly sophisticated.

There is an old Yiddish saying: *troubles with soup are easier to bear than troubles without soup.*

So I take a deep breath and knock on her door, pot in arms. It is a bit awkward, because we are both shy. She thanks me, and I scurry back across the road.

After a few days, I see Dora in the street. 'Wait,' she says and hurries inside. She returns with my pot. 'That was the best minestrone I have eaten in my entire life.'

I feel like I've won a prize. I've won the ANZ Soup-Making, Good Neighbour Medal.

I go back into my house, and feel all warm and Yiddish.

6
Hair

I AM having a coffee at Marios. Almost every man in the café is bald. Some are bald by design, but most have been depilated by middle age. The man at the next table rubs a thoughtful hand across his pate. I feel as though I know him.

I stare.

This is my Number One Bad Habit. It has irritated every boyfriend I've ever had. 'It's just plain rude,' they say. And they're right. It *is* rude. But I forget. I get lost in the interesting conversations other people are having.

But in this instance I'm not eavesdropping. I'm scrutinising the bald man, because I think he might be Graeme Gavin from high school. I put Graeme's hair on this man's head. I take off his navy jumper with the faux-suede elbow patches and help him into a Brighton High uniform: grey blazer, grey pants, white shirt. I can't quite remember what tie we used to have. Was it red and yellow?

When the makeover is complete, the man looks up from his paper. I look away hastily and play with my phone. Yep. It's him.

That crusty, sun-spotted dome is shocking and ironic. The only way Graeme Gavin distinguished himself from the masses at Brighton High was his hair. It grew down to his shoulders in brown waves. Graeme's luxurious locks were his revolutionary flag—a statement of defiance that he waved in the face of conservative suburbia.

And conservatism fought back. Our headmaster—a short-haired moralist—paraded Graeme and three other *long-haired louts* before the cameras while a local barber applied shears to all four teenage heads. Graeme got his picture on the front page of our local paper.

He became a hero, his head a battleground for the struggle between generations.

The next day, at school assembly, he stood at the microphone and told us that his hair—he held aloft a fistful of his severed tresses—was a *symbol*.

We were totally into symbols. We scoured Ingmar Bergman films for clocks without hands, faceless men and wild strawberry patches. What did they all mean? Death, loneliness, sex. We especially loved anything with halved figs or mangoes or pears. Things that were *moist* or *luscious*. We also liked snakes, lighthouses and trains.

And now, before us, was Graeme, brandishing his hair-symbol. It was as if Che Guevara had come to East Brighton.

We gave him a standing ovation. We stamped and clapped and hooted. They could cut his hair, but they couldn't stop it growing back. It was growing now! Graeme was not like the men of our fathers' generation. Their short-back-and-sides, their hair oil, their Brylcreem—these transformed natural hair into conformist helmets, each one a *symbol* of repression. It was their way of locking up their thoughts, of toeing the line. Graeme's locks were tendrils of consciousness. *Our* consciousness. His hair, our hotline to the cosmos.

Like every girl in the hall that morning, I was smitten.

But I was also cautious. Boys of the Graeme Gavin type were like rock stars: reckless, invincible and capable of terrifying scorn towards girls like me. Girls whose report cards read, 'Helen is always pleasant and courteous. She is a valuable member of the form.'

The following Friday lunchtime, Daddy Cool came to our school. The band set up on the stage, in the hall. Senior boys from the Theatre Club fixed orange and pink gels to the lights. The place looked like Festival Hall. Joan Jedd and I went to the girls' toilets and I released the two bunches of hair that sat on either side of my head. She teased my hair with her comb, and we both hiked our grey tunics over our belts so that they just covered our knickers and showed off our legs. Everyone in the whole school turned up, even the teachers. Even the shorn Graeme Gavin, who leaned against the wall, nonchalantly sucking a paddle-pop. We danced like wild creatures to 'Eagle Rock' and 'Daddy Cool'.

As I waved my arms in the air, I hoped that Graeme might spot me in the crush and recognise a fellow rebel. I hoped that, in the flicker of the disco ball, I would be unrecognisable to Graeme as 'a valuable member of the form'.

For ninety minutes, Brighton High was the coolest place on earth.

That was more than forty years ago, and for most of that time I have had my own problems with hair.

Initially, the difficulties were operational: how to effectively remove it from legs and underarms. My mother was of no help. Until recently, when her granddaughter gave her a voucher for a manicure, she had never been inside a beauty parlour. Her skin-care philosophy was straightforward: splash your face with water in the morning, swim in the sea, walk in the fresh air, be happy, and rub a bit of Nivea into your legs and elbows at night. Oh, and Oil of Ulan. How that soft, pink cream in a glass bottle reminds me of my mother.

But as for a bit of unwanted hair—she didn't worry about it.

I was on my own. I tried depilatory creams and lady razors and wax strips. All unsatisfactory, mostly due to the time outlay and the boredom factor.

How many hours a day was a woman expected to spend on grooming? And with only one bathroom for five people, my beauty routine involved a lot of fending off my brothers.

'Go away. Go and shower under the hose.'

Moreover, all this depilation and shaving and waxing was accompanied by the anxiety that hair removal encouraged massive, uncontrollable regrowth. Was I wilfully transforming my legs into an old-growth forest?

At school, none of us ever discussed pubic hair. As far as I understood, hair that grew in that locality was fixed. But among my friends,

I expected a bit more collegiality when it came to information-sharing about the issue of leg hair.

We year 10 girls spent many hours sitting on the warm concrete at recess or lunchtime, sunning our legs, so I had a lot of time to contemplate this vexing problem. How did Angela Wade achieve her beautiful, smooth legs? All my attempts to find out were fruitless.

> H: How do you get your legs like that?
> A: Like what?
> H: You know. Smooth?
> A: I dunno. They just are.

That was patently bullshit. She was one of three Wade girls and they were all *smooth*. Clearly, *their* mother understood something that had passed my own mother by. This much was certain: brisk walks in the fresh air did not give you creamy, supple skin.

For that, you needed *products*, preferably ones that came from Paris.

I learned this later, when I got talking to Mrs Wade at the school fete. She was on the coathanger stall. 'You have to invest in your face,' she told me.

That's how I learned about Babs of Bentleigh, House of Hair and Beauty.

But nothing was simple. I worried about vanity. Instead of committing myself to a concerted program of nagging to get my mum to pay for me to visit Babs, I shot myself in the foot, trying to weigh up whether it really mattered. Surely people (boys) would see what a nice person I was. Inside.

What a fool.

Our Italian teacher had serious underarm hair. She wore sleeveless summer dresses, and when she returned our Italian homework, she stood before the class calling each name aloud. She raised her arm and hurled inferior work into the bin at her feet.

'R-rrarbish to the rrrarrbish!' she used to declaim.

We were riveted. She was everything we expected from an Italian: excitable, fascist and hairy.

Later, when I was at university, my boyfriend would untuck the sheets at the bottom of my bed and expose my legs.

'What have we here? Do these belong to the human family or are they from the plant kingdom?'

I suffered on.

By the time drama school rolled around, hair on girls was no longer a matter of vanity. It was much more. It was *ideological*. Hair was natural. Hair was beautiful. (Who were we kidding?) More importantly, these were our bodies and we must not subject our decisions about *our* bodies to the pleasing of men.

The first time I heard about 'the male gaze', I was sitting cross-legged on a mission-brown carpet in my friend Hilary's flat in Mitford Street, St Kilda. We opened up hot fish and chips in white paper and laid it out on her coffee table. I don't remember there being chairs. But what Hilary lacked in furniture, she compensated for with her knowledge of feminist film theory. She dipped her chips in tartare sauce and explained that women were objectified in film because heterosexual men were in charge of the camera.

I thought these were the most exciting fish and chips I had ever eaten. Hilary knew about Marx and Althusser and Freud and Marcuse. She was reading *The Women's Room*. It was the first time I'd ever heard of 'false consciousness' and gender power 'asymmetry'. We talked endlessly about fucking men, how much we loved it.

She was brilliant, fiercely articulate, beautiful and hilarious. Moreover, she sprinkled vinegar over her chips—an entirely novel concept. I became a convert.

But did she shave her legs?

'Of course.'

'But aren't you simply conforming to norms established to benefit men, thereby reinforcing the power of the gaze to reduce the woman to an object?'

Hilary flipped open her Benson and Hedges packet, lit a cigarette and drew in a luxuriant draught of smoke.

'Do you like hairy legs?' she asked on the inward breath.

'No, I hate them.'

She blew two perfect smoke rings.

'So do I. I *fucking* hate them.'

That confirmed it. We were destined to be best friends.

Two weeks later I met a nurse at a party. She told me that hair growth in women could be directly correlated with the intensity of their orgasms.

Simply stated, hairy girls have the best orgasms.

Medical research has been slow to catch up with this important revelation. I once mentioned it to a doctor, who thought it was preposterous.

But honesty compels me to say that she was pale and hairless.

And although I would not wish to appear boastful or smug, ever since I learned of my good fortune from the nurse at the party, I have not whinged about having to get my legs waxed. It's only an hour, every six weeks. A very small price to pay, in my book.

At Marios, I am trying to frame the words to introduce myself to Graeme.

'You won't remember me, but I was there in the hall that day, when you held aloft a tuft of hair…'

No.

You know how some middle-aged men still look like boys? They wear a vaguely hurt expression, as though they have never quite got what they wanted from life. Graeme—bald Graeme—looks that way.

I feel around for my purse in my handbag, and as I stand to make my way over to pay for the coffee, a woman pushes open the glass door to the café.

She is wearing a tight-fitting, scooped-neck jumper and a tight red skirt. She looks like a cartoon from *Pix* magazine, circa 1963: round tits, round bum, perfect red lips and wavy blonde hair.

She walks directly across to Graeme. He stands. She puts her cute little plump arms around his neck and they smooch. Right there in Marios, in the window, for all to see.

They sit, heads together, and she talks ten to the dozen. Graeme is totally into her. Graeme is lost to me.

I walk across to their table. I am committed now.

'Excuse me, I'm sorry to interrupt, but are you Graeme Gavin from Brighton High School?'

Graeme looks up. 'No. Sorry.'

'Oh.' I can feel a slight rush of heat. 'You look…I thought…Beg your p—'

I start to back away.

'But you did go to Brighton High, didn't you?' his girlfriend chips in.

'Yep.'

'Oh!' I perk up. 'What's your name, then?'

'Graeme Lodge.'

I introduce myself. He doesn't remember me. I don't remember him.

'Do you remember Graeme Gavin?'

'No.'

'He was the guy who was, like, this big radical. Famous for his long hair.'

Graeme's girlfriend starts to laugh. I plough on.

'Do you remember when Daddy Cool came?'

'Sure.'

I take a deep breath and tell him briefly about the headmaster and the barber and the local paper.

'I remember that story doing the rounds, but it wasn't at our school. Can't have been. We had that woman principal by then. Miss Brennan.'

I bid my farewell and go over to the counter to pay for my coffee.

Graeme and his girlfriend resume their private talk.

There is something I have to know. I take another deep breath, and push back through the tables.

'Sorry. Just one last thing.'

A tiny flicker of incredulity passes over Graeme's face.

'At the Daddy Cool concert, did you lean up against the wall eating a paddle-pop?'

Graeme's girlfriend is biting her lip to stop herself from guffawing.

'Look, I'm sorry,' says Graeme. 'I really can't remember.'

Of course not.

I push open the café door and slip out into Brunswick Street.

7

Two Weddings and a Funeral

ONE HOT Saturday in December 1972, my oldest brother, David, married a pretty scientist, Barbara, in the Victorian border town of Wodonga. We went swimming in the Hume Dam on the Murray River before the ceremony. The bride arrived at the church in a dusty red Fiat 125 with a surfboard on top. She climbed out of the car, wearing a white dress with fresh blue cornflowers at her throat. Her hair was still glistening wet. I thought she looked glorious.

Waiting outside the church was a choir of fifty tiny children wearing white cassocks. They were recruited from the local primary school, where the bride's mum was the principal.

David and the best man (my other brother, Peter) wore the same outfit: a red-check shirt under a skin-tight navy-blue tank top, with tight navy pants. The whole ensemble was offset by a wide, white leather belt. They looked like a Monkees cover band.

I went for a sort of eccentric gypsy look, which I created myself: a gaily patterned peasant skirt, a skimpy black singlet and, on my head, a red kerchief, which I am now prepared to concede was a mistake. At the time, I thought I looked countercultural: a bit Joan Baez, a bit Joni Mitchell.

My husband stares at a photo. 'You look like a demented Ukrainian peasant.'

In the same photo, my mother looks amazing. She is wearing a full-length halter-neck dress with a tight black bodice. The skirt is patterned with large black-and-white diamonds the size of bathroom tiles. She looks like a sixties pin-up girl.

Back at school on Monday, Angela Ackland, Joan Jedd and I

were in the girls' changing rooms, slipping into our sports clothes. Angela probed for details. She had very strict rules about wedding protocol. She had specific views about who should escort the chief bridesmaid from the ceremony to the reception, who was responsible for the distribution of hymn books and buttonholes, and the importance (often overlooked) of matching luggage for the honeymoon.

She clicked her tongue disapprovingly about the whole fiasco. In Angela's world, brides did not go swimming with their grooms on their wedding day. And they certainly did not show up at the church with long blonde hair still wet from a swim—even if they were beautiful and looked like Peggy Lipton, the hippy undercover cop in *The Mod Squad* on TV.

Proper brides had their hair done in a salon, with copious amounts of spray to keep everything just so. The men wore black suits with a sprig of lily-of-the-valley in their buttonholes. I'd seen the wedding photos of Angela's favourite cousin from Bairnsdale. That was how you did it.

One year later, Peter married a Catholic he'd been dating since she was sixteen. He used to pick her up after hockey practice from the Star of the Sea in his green Volkswagen. (The Star of the Sea was the same convent where Germaine Greer was educated.)

For this wedding, each member of the groom's party wore a purple suit and a pale green shirt, matched with a purple-and-white-striped tie.

Mum and I are looking at the photos. She insists the suits are pink. They are not. They are purple.

'If you say they were wearing pink suits, it sounds gay.'

'I don't care what it sounds like,' snaps my mother. 'Those suits are pink.'

She calls my son over. 'Jack, what colour is that?'

He is not getting drawn in.

Later, he says to me, 'Between Grandma Judy and you and Dad—who is off-the-scale stubborn—what chance have I got? I am drowning in stubborn!'

My brother had to work hard to convince our parents that his bride's Catholicism and her attendance at Mass were within the range of normal behaviour. The Catholic Church did not get good press in our house. Dad suspected the Catholic priests of paedophilia. (He held the same suspicions about scoutmasters. My brothers were not allowed to join that particular organisation.) Mum thought Catholicism was mediaeval and oppressive. So Peter had an uphill battle to get them to rejoice at the whole 'marrying-in' business.

My parents did not single out the Catholic Church for special suspicion. They regarded all religions as equally fanciful, but in 1970s Brighton you were less likely to come across a Muslim or a Sikh.

By then, sectarianism was on the wane: we now forget how riven an older Australia was by the Catholic/Proddy divide. In some quarters, the antipathies were intense.

MC's father used to say that you could tell a Catholic by his eyes. When he was a boy at Lilydale Primary School in the 1930s, he got into a fight with a Catholic boy in the playground. He slugged the boy and made his nose bleed. Upon hearing of this triumph in the playground, my father-in-law's dad was so proud he gave his son two shillings.

As late as the sixties in some places, Catholics were not allowed to go into Protestant churches. So if a Catholic man married a woman in the Presbyterian Church, his family couldn't attend the wedding.

'You'd never put a Mick in charge of anything,' Uncle Jack said. 'They're in the grip of the priests.'

My dad would nod sagely. 'Always got on in the public service, the Micks.'

Presumably, this demonstrated that Catholics were not capable of being self-made men. They did not have the mettle to deal with Risk; they were merely salary men who did what they were told.

It occurred to me recently to wonder what Catholics thought of Protestants. I rang my friend Bob Gott, who was educated by the Christian Brothers.

'It was not only that Protestants were disagreeable,' said Bob.

'They were actually damned. And we were taught all about what they'd done to Catholic martyrs. So we knew that a Protestant was the type of person who would cut off your nipples.'

After his years in Catholic churches, 'When I go into a Protestant church, I still think they look as if they've been burgled.'

If my parents were suspicious of Catholics, the bride's family were exempt. They welcomed us with the kind of largesse that my dad approved of. They had a table-tennis table and big bottles of Coke and Fanta in their downstairs fridge. They always had potato chips. You could help yourself.

Betty and Noel were business folk, hotel brokers. They lived in a big house in Brighton, with a vast living room that sported a luxurious peach-coloured wall-to-wall carpet. But the carpet stopped short of the wall by about thirty centimetres, where a water-filled trough ran around the entire perimeter of the room. This was an in-floor fish tank: a lap pool for goldfish.

Every Christmas, my dad performed a little ritual. He took orders for hams from friends and relatives. A few days before Christmas, he drove to the Mayfair ham factory in Footscray to collect the booty. Then, he would drive around dropping off hams and stopping for a little refreshment at each house along the way.

By the time he got to Betty and Noel's, he was so refreshed that he slipped on the stairs inside the front door and fell flat on his face. The ham flew out of his hands and plopped into the fish tank. When Betty and Noel came running to see what all the commotion was about, they found my father on his hands and knees, scrabbling about in the water.

On Sundays at noon, Dad loved to watch Killer Kowalski and Abdullah the Butcher in action on World Championship Wrestling, and we'd join him on the couch for the entertainment. Before the wrestling, a strange gnome-like man named Bob Santamaria presented a very short program called *Point of View*. It was a sort of propaganda show for Santamaria's mixture of Catholicism, puritanism and fear of dissent. If we tuned in for the wrestling too early, we had to put up with this queer fellow with the quavering voice, banging on about the dangers of North Vietnam, the secret and subversive agenda of the Whit-a-lem government and its godless tolerance of aberrant secks-uality.

We thought he was a nut.

Another nail in the Catholic coffin.

My brother's strategy for bringing the families together and nipping any potential conflict in the bud was to promote his girlfriend's family priest as a punter and genial boozer. It seemed to work. My father grudgingly gave the priest the benefit of the doubt and in due course he was appointed to do the honours at the wedding. At my mother's suggestion, the venue was the 'multi-faith chapel' at Monash University. My mum favoured this ecumenical centre because of Peter's connection with Monash—he'd done his economics degree there—and because the chapel had no overt religious imagery. Even the cross was detachable, a fact that, midway through the ceremony, struck me as hilarious, causing me to shake with uncontrollable laughter, which spread to the other bridesmaids.

It was around this time that I embraced the Lord Jesus Christ myself, much to my parents' dismay. I stuck a pink iridescent sticker on my bedroom door that read 'Jesus Is Alive'. My mother wrote underneath: 'and living under the bed'.

Undeterred, I went to the Brighton Church of England and took confirmation classes.

That's when my parents became alarmed. They feared that I'd joined a cult. The Brighton Church of England was the first step on the slippery slope towards Jonestown and Kool-Aid.

But I was undaunted. I tried to convince my mother that she, too, should take Jesus as her saviour.

I always got tangled up in my attempts to explain what it all meant. It was a mystery, I told her. You had to make a leap of faith.

'I'll say,' said my mother.

My one and only modest advance was when I told her that believing gave me joy.

Joy. She was thoughtful. 'I would like to experience joy.'

But I could never get her to join the dots between joy and Jesus.

I can't remember now how I was joining the dots myself. But I do remember that the music and the majesty transported me to a place of awe.

Later, my best friend Jan Batty and I signed up for a Uniting Church youth group and went on church camps. Kids used to come around to our house and talk earnestly, sitting cross-legged on the floor. My mother found it unnerving.

'What do you talk about all the time?' she wanted to know.

My father just wanted to ban it.

As I noted in my diary in March 1973, he said, 'All this loving each other. It's unhealthy.'

By then at Youth Group, Jesus had pretty much dropped off the twig and been replaced by an obsession with *human relationships*.

We did our share of *good works*. After Christmas 1974, we suspended our scheduled camp activities and walked the streets, raising money for the people of Darwin, who had just had their homes flattened by Cyclone Tracy. But our good works mostly involved intense teenage encounters, trying to help each other work out our problems with our parents or our own adolescent conundrums.

We told each other that God is love, and this translated neatly into caring for people, which I was very keen on.

My parents approved of this, as long as I didn't care in a churchy way.

My diaries during this period are consumed with questions of how to be good. Moral. Ethical. I began to shape the idea that I would be a social worker. I would devote my life to serving the poor. My mother was unconvinced of the wisdom of this. Poor people are depressing and often tedious, she counselled. Are you sure this is what you want?

I wanted to understand the ways of the heart, I knew that much. Being close to people—this was next to godliness, in my sixteen-year-old mind. I still believe it. Understanding the world through eyes other than your own is the most powerful and subversive act a human being can engage in. I learned that at the Uniting Church youth group.

I see now that my religious phase, my three-year flirtation with psychology at university and my compulsion to write were all activities through which I sought the same end: I hoped they would explain the human race to me.

In any case, religion came and went.

My mother, on the other hand, has never wavered from her belief. To this day, she remains the most stubbornly rationalist person I have ever known.

To illustrate: Mama (my mother's mother) died in Sydney. The next morning, my mum flew up from Melbourne to be with her three sisters, Nancy, Margot and Joan. Night fell and it was decision time. One of them had to sleep in Mama's bed—the bed in which she had died not fifteen hours earlier. Nancy, Margot and Joan blanched.

My mother thought this fuss was ridiculous. It was just a bed. *Honest to goodness*. She took her case from the hallway, lugged it into the bedroom, put on her nightie and went to bed.

In my mother's world, when a person dies, that's the end of them. Ashes to ashes. No hocus-pocus. Everything else is superstition.

At three o'clock in the morning, when Mum was fast asleep, a black cat jumped on her head.

She nearly dropped dead herself, from fright.

In the morning, upon hearing of my mother's experience, her three sisters nearly died themselves—from laughter.

But from Mum's point of view, there was nothing oogy-boogy about the event. She had left the window open. A cat jumped in.

Actually, the fact that a cat jumped on her head is totally explicable. My mother cannot abide them. Her loathing is visceral. As a result, she is a total cat magnet.

I so wish I'd been there that morning in Nancy's flat in Rose Bay. Those Bland girls—Nancy, Margot, Joan and my mother, Judy—really knew how to laugh.

Mum is now the only sister left. At Margot's funeral, my cousin told of how her mother, who was ninety, had been at home in her bed and called out with a ferocity that had startled my cousin: 'I want to go and I want to go now!' And go she did. Margot died within the hour.

At the wake, my mother said she wanted to go and lie down. I went upstairs with her and we lay on the bed together. I know Mum is worried about dying. She's frightened that she will not be ready when the time comes.

We lie quietly, staring at the ceiling.

'You know, I've been practising being dead.'

She's pretty funny, my mum.

'Okay. How are you doing that, Mum?'

'I've taken to lying down every afternoon. I go into this deep sleep for a couple of hours, and then I wake up and I think, "That wasn't so bad".'

Postscript

I emailed my mother this story. She corrected my grammar (galling), changed dates and altered certain details that she remembered differently. She crossed out the colour of the suits—purple—at Peter's wedding and wrote PINK in block letters. She added the detail that my religious friends sat *cross-legged on the floor*. This seemed to nail it for her. The cross-legged nature of the proceedings demonstrates incontrovertibly that we were engaged in peculiar behaviour, and she was right to question it.

In addition to her edits, she had written down some other facts I might like to include. The letterhead on the paper she handed me was for Allison Monkhouse Funeral Directors. It was torn from one of those promotional to-do-list notepads.

Item one was already printed:

1. Call Allison Monkhouse for pre-paid funeral information.

This, my mother had ruled out neatly with a black biro.

On Mother's Day, I noted that she had three pads of this paper on her kitchen bench.

'What are you doing with a to-do list from a funeral director? That is macabre.'

'I told you,' she said. 'I went to an information lunch about retirement homes, and it turned out it was sponsored by the funeral parlour. They gave us a little show bag.'

8
Ormond Story

THE YEAR is 1976, and I have finally convinced my parents to let me leave home. I'm in my second year of an arts degree at Melbourne University, and I have just arrived at Ormond, a residential college affiliated with the university.

My brothers are both older than me. David by ten years, Peter by seven. Sometimes older siblings pave the way for the little ones behind. Not in my case, as my brothers both lived at home until they got married. Selfishly, they never rocked the boat. There is no *precedent* for the kind of wild, libertarian break-out that I have in mind.

In the twelve months leading up to my move, I waged a relentless campaign to persuade my father that to live in Ormond was a canny investment in my future. He feared (quite reasonably) that once I'd left home, I would never return.

I am nineteen, tall and willowy, and have earned the nickname 'Legs'. My dad is hoping I might become Miss Victorian Beach Girl. What Ormond College can do to advance this laudable ambition, he cannot fathom.

The family has just moved to Black Rock, which is a seaside suburb twenty kilometres from Melbourne University. I maintain it is too far to commute. My father points out that it is only at the end of the Sandringham train line.

The fees for Ormond are $1200 a year. I get a half-scholarship and my father pays the $600 balance. I promise I will generate all other money.

I own two long Indian embroidered cheesecloth dresses, which are my outfits of choice. I wear them with boots. I also own an array of old ladies' hats, adorned with ornamental fruit and secured with hatpins. Sometimes I decorate them with roses stolen from Parkville gardens. I imagine myself to be in thick with Virginia Woolf, Annie Hall, Carly Simons and Joni Mitchell. Suffice to say, I look excellent.

Women had just recently been allowed to live at Ormond. Previously, female students were only here as maids—I know this because my sister-in-law was one, serving meals in the grand dining hall.

So men run the place, but men run everything in every aspect of my life. The men of the college are divided into two groups: the Men and the Heads. The Men are the jocks, the sporting Adonises and the chubby beer-swilling oiks who fawn over them. They associate with people called Woppo or Gibbo or Balls or Grunt.

The Heads are the intellectual, arty types. Naturally, I am hoping to find a Head—but preferably one whose head is grafted onto the body of a sporting Adonis.

There is a movement led by certain male students at Ormond to revert to a men-only policy at the college. I am incredulous. This is the *seventies*, man! Get with the program! How embarrassing to be such a pack of dickheads.

The promise of feminism is in the air. The seminal texts have been written. We read them avidly, but the movement hasn't quite taken hold. Or at least, it hasn't quite taken hold of me as yet.

There is also a lot of talk about revolution, all different kinds. The sexual revolution is the one in which I am most keen to participate.

I made this little joke at a recent speech I was asked to give at Ormond College. (Apparently, I am now an eminent alumna.) Nobody laughed. Later, I was sitting next to an impressive young woman at High Table. She asked earnestly, 'What was it like to be in the sexual revolution?'

I think she imagined it was like being in the Hitler Youth Movement or the Boxer Rebellion.

I didn't want to embarrass her by saying, 'That was a joke,' so I chewed my bread while I thought about how to answer.

'It was good.'

My parents drop me off in late February 1976 and drive away. The idea that I can do what I like is almost incredible. I can still summon the ecstasy I felt then. I am the heroine in my own boarding-school novel. I am Henrietta in *Summer Term at St Clare's*. I am Wilhelmina in *The Upper Fourth at Malory Towers*. There'll be tricks and japes and midnight feasts. But in this boarding school there are no 'lights out', no cruel headmistresses. And the only person with a key to my room is me.

In those first weeks, as the summer rolls into mellow autumn, I am a schoolgirl in love with the idea of becoming a young woman. I rarely wear make-up. My parents have inculcated the idea that there is a correlation between a fresh face and a quality of authenticity. The highest praise they can bestow on any of my brothers' female friends is to declare, 'She's so natural!' So I strive to be natural, too. It is a philosophy I will carry doggedly into my fifties, with considerably less success.

I am intoxicated by the romance of the buildings, the turreted exuberance of 1880s architecture sitting amid manicured gardens. In my room, with the window open, I can hear the smattering of applause and cries of 'nice one, Simmo' from the playing fields or the *clock, clock* of a tennis match in the late afternoon. I can smell the mown grass. There is an air of quiet studiousness, a sweet melancholy of lonely Sundays.

People swish about in their black academic gowns.

There is a gardener called Frank. We all sing out, 'Hi Frank', as we walk past or swing by on our bikes. Frank always says, 'Good morning', in a way that seems quaintly old-fashioned. At nineteen, I think this all shows what a splendid egalitarian bunch we are— as if we were not actually the sons and daughters of the well-to-do, tousling the hair of the servants.

During Orientation Week at the university, you could fill every minute with activities. (I found the roneoed program in my camphorwood box.) On Wednesday 5 March, for example, you could have wine and cheese with the philosophy students, sherry with the geographers, tea and biscuits with the Lesbian Liberationists, or cider and assorted nuts with the Liberals. You could see a macramé demonstration ('Get Knotted' with Tony Dempsey), take part in a cream-puff contest or a water-bomb fight, or hear Barry Jones in the Public Lecture Theatre. You could compete in a streaking competition (fifty-dollar Bookroom vouchers for the fastest male and female), see *uncensored* Swedish films at the Prince Philip Theatre, or join a Mad Hatter's Tea Party on the Botany Lawns. At 9.30 p.m., the Swedish Club presented Swedish folk songs and dancing. And if that didn't appeal, there was always the Informal Gathering for anyone interested in the Christian Union.

On the first night of Orientation Week, I went to a party at the Master's lodge. The Master of Ormond College was Davis McCaughey, who later became the governor of Victoria. There I was, in the living room of his home with a group of students, one of whom was a fresher who had been drinking beer since six o'clock in the morning. Suddenly, like a character in a sitcom, she keeled backwards. One moment she was making small talk with the Master's wife, Jean McCaughey; the next, she hit the floor with the back of her head. Jean did not bat an eyelid. In her soft Irish lilt, she said, 'Oooh, we'd better get you into bed...' Jean and a pale boy with a consuming interest in insects helped the girl upstairs to sleep it off.

I lay in bed that night staring at the ceiling, thinking, 'There is so much to know and I want to know it all.' I saw sherry parties and wine-and-cheese gatherings stretching into a brilliant future.

In my mind, Ormond was a wondrous place where you could think great thoughts. I can't honestly say that I ever actually had one—but I felt as though it *could* happen.

Life was bursting with possibility.

Two weeks later, my father had a massive stroke. I moved back home to help my mother.

*

Fast-forward thirty-eight years.

I am talking to my mum about what a colossal sacrifice I made, coming home for those months after Dad's stroke. I want her to recognise what it cost me.

She looks at me thoughtfully. 'And you were so useless, too.'

I have this idea that I'd like to meet the person who lives in my room now. This is in McCaughey Court, an octagonal, Romberg and Boyd–designed tower, which was almost new when I lived in Ormond. I slip a note under the door addressed 'To Whom It May Concern'.

I imagine that the person might be a shy Asian girl studying commerce.

Later that day, I get a call from Shireen Tang. She is a vivacious Asian girl studying commerce.

We arrange to meet the next day at the Ormond Reception office at 11 a.m. This is in the main building of Ormond. The imposing Clock Tower dongs melodiously.

Eleven o'clock comes and goes. I call Shireen. She is asleep, naturally.

Minutes later, a gorgeous young woman with long black hair and black-rimmed glasses skips across the vestibule. She is wearing black jeans and boots and a plain V-necked grey sweater. She looks like the cool Asian girl in a TV teen series like *The O.C.* or *Gossip Girl* or *Beverly Hills 90210*. That's if they had Asian girls.

Shireen is eighteen. Her father is a professor at a Singapore university. He has suggested she rein in her socialising. (Like that's really gonna happen.)

She was born in Brisbane and grew up in Singapore. Her parents are from China. This makes her ethnically Chinese, legally Australian and spiritually Singaporean. Her name is Persian.

She tells me this with a slight American inflection.

'I've got that weird international kid accent.'

She tells me she feels like a nomad. 'All my life I've been an outsider. A foreigner. In Singapore, I'm part of the expat community.

In China, when I visit my relatives, I'm the White Kid. In Australia, I'm just another Asian girl.'

But Shireen isn't troubled. She likes the nomadic life. 'In the end, I'd rather spend my life in different places. I have been brought up to feel this way: to be part of an international community.'

I remember myself at Shireen's age. Only the wildly adventurous, the madly religious or the terminally restless entertained ideas of being 'part of an international community'. At eighteen, I'd never been overseas. My parents had only been to Europe once (not counting the war). Air travel was not cheap. Most of us dreamed of having our 'big trip' and then coming home.

I tell her that my fees were $1200.

Her parents have had to find $24,000.

Shireen is well aware of how lives can change in the course of a generation. Had life been only a little bit different, she would be a farm girl in a rural Chinese village. But her dad got a scholarship to study in Germany. He is now a Physics Professor in Singapore teaching optic lasers. His advice to Shireen: 'If you get hungry at College, fill up on potatoes.' That's what he did when he was a student in Germany.

The day we meet at Ormond College, pizza is on the lunch menu. There is a sandwich bar where you can help yourself to every possible sandwich filling. There are trays of salads. Shireen will not have to fill up on potatoes. There is even a café now, with a barista. You don't need to go to Carlton for a cappuccino.

We go back to her room that was once mine, and drink Chinese tea and talk. Being Asian in Ormond College, Shireen says, is to be still in the minority. In her commerce lectures, nearly everyone is Asian. Classes are big, no one knows your name and many of the students struggle with English. So for her, the interesting conversations are occurring at Ormond.

For Shireen, college is the hub around which her university life revolves. My experience was the opposite. It was the university that was the centre of activity. You walked back up the path to Ormond to sleep and eat and have sex. But the student union was where we hung out—for theatre, cinema, every club you could possibly imagine, bands, parties, politics and lectures (occasionally).

So, more and more, if you want to have 'a university experience', you have to have it at College. This is the American system. Despite all the best laid plans for diversity and democracy, rich people will get to have a richer experience. Who would've thought?

9
Diary of the Dumped

MY FRIEND Nell was recently offered a very impressive job by a man named Andrew Macquarie, whom we had both known at university. The night before Nell's first day at work, Andrew rang her from his office and talked rather intimately about his life. Nell found this a tad inappropriate. He asked after her sisters. Then he asked after the people who had shared that house with them in St Kilda.

A house? What house? Nell felt a shiver of anxiety. There was something in the man's voice that suggested...what? A certain right to familiarity? She scrolled through her memories of several student houses. Floor plans. Bedrooms. Nothing presented itself.

It was getting late. She was tired. Andrew became more confessional. Nell was keen to hang up. Then she had a horrible sensation, like iceblocks had been poured down the back of her neck.

The phone rang at my house at 10.30 p.m.

An urgent whisper: 'Did I have sex with Andrew Macquarie? Do you remember?'

Later that night, in bed, my husband is shocked.

'I can remember,' he says, 'the names and faces of every person I've ever had sex with.'

Clearly this is evidence of a superiority of character. A clarity of mind for which a man of his generation should be awarded the Victoria Cross.

Foolishly, I admit that, like Nell, I might also be a bit hazy on certain details. 'University was a fair while ago. And we are talking about an activity that is conducted largely in the dark.'

Eventually, my husband is prepared to concede that, back in the

1980s, there may have been a (nameless) girl in a German youth hostel.

Nell shared my enthusiasm for penises, when it seemed to me most other girls were a bit stand-offish. But, luckily for her, she consulted another friend that night who was able to vouch categorically that never once, not even under the influence of excessive alcohol, had Nell done anything remotely intimate with Mr Macquarie.

These are important assurances when you are about to occupy adjoining offices in a Collins Street tower of power.

Fortunately, I have an aide-mémoire in the form of my large camphorwood box. The occasions when I had sex—and with whom, and under what circumstances—were documented. There will be a memorandum of some sort to jog my memory.

In the box, I've found a manila folder labelled *Marcus McKenna*.

The first piece of paper in the folder is headed:

O God how do you recover from sex like that?

I read on. (Naturally.)

There are no dates on any pieces of paper in this folder, but I have shaped a rough chronology. I put this at around 1976, my second year of university. What follows is a diary of being dumped.

Here is the first entry.

Dear Marcus McKenna,

This is my plan for the night. Do you want to be part of it?

I thought I would have dinner at College and study until 10 p.m., after which I will ride over to your house, bringing a small bottle of massage oil.

You will put the heater on in your room, so it's warm and cosy.

Then I will give you a fabulous massage in which you

will luxuriate and then reach up, pull me down on top of you
and make love like there's no tomorrow.

Offer closes 5 p.m. today. Hurry while stocks last.

I expect Marcus McKenna took me up on it. I remember nothing.

I don't even remember writing this brazen invitation. But there
it is. In the folder, in the box.

The question you must be asking is why is this letter in *my*
folder? Why is it not among Marcus McKenna's memorabilia? The
answer is that it is a photocopy. The invitation itself was a piece of
handmade photocopy art.

Moving on.

The next entry is entitled 'Café Paradiso'.

> Imagine me,
> Of all people—
> a known hater of poetry—
> feeling *compelled*
> to write to you in this way.
> I am undone
> and it's your fault.
>
> I have to tell you
> That I hate being the one
> Who's '*more* involved'.
> But I also hate being the one
> who's '*less* involved'.
> Can we quit mucking about
> And be 'the *same* involved'.

The affair had begun in a messy way. Marcus had a girlfriend,
Penelope. I had listened sympathetically for hours about Penelope's
shortcomings. Privately, I felt he would be happier with me, but his
negotiations in the girlfriend camp were *complicated*.

A diary entry:

> I ride over to Marcus's house. He says, 'Listen, I've thought about this and I don't want anything to happen between us.'

This was a very disappointing development.

> I am nodding in a grown-up way. Of course. I agree. It's hopeless. There has never been a more hopeless scenario.
> I am Emma Bovary, Lady Chatterley, Countess Ellen Olenska. What can happen except disaster?
> I say I understand. I mumble. I say yes, put the skids on. Just don't ring me for a while until you've worked things out with Penelope.

Penelope was a lawyer. Bossy, and good at making decisions. She was five years older than me, and owned stuff like casserole dishes and wine glasses. She lived in Carlton, in a house with polished floorboards and an exposed brick fireplace. She kept smoked salmon in the fridge. After work, she relaxed on a leather couch with her stockinged legs tucked up underneath her, sipping chilled riesling, eating smoked salmon and watching the news.

I was a college student. I owned a bicycle and a vitamiser, which was still in its box at my parents' house, to be retrieved when I eventually became an adult.

To 'do a Penelope' is explained in the diary as putting Marcus in the 'boyfriend compartment' and closing the lid until it is convenient to open it. For compartmentalisers like Penelope, specific times are allocated as boyfriend time: weekends, and one or two nights per week. Being unhappy in your relationship would not, for example, be given consideration during office hours, or during the time allocated to play squash or get your hair cut.

This capacity to *compartmentalise* is analysed endlessly and pejoratively in my diary. Compartmentalising is the behaviour of the emotionally retarded. Men can compartmentalise magnificently, which is why they are the last to know their marriage is on the rocks. The neighbour has to tell them, even when they're reading the note on the table that says, 'I'm leaving, you great Neanderthal dunderhead.'

I, on the other hand, am so emotionally integrated that I can dream about my beloved twenty-four hours a day, seven days a week, even when studying, attending lectures or going to the dentist. Whereas Penelope...

> I say: I will try to *do a Penelope on you*.
> He says: Crikey, you'll need to get into a different tax bracket for that.

I make special mention of this in my diary. I like a man who has a snappy turn of phrase.

> I get up to go. He tells me not to be provocative and vivacious and beautiful. I smile sadly and say goodbye.
> Part of me is looking forward to returning to my lonely room, where I will begin my new life as the tragic heroine: young, poor and provocative, unable to offer my weary lover a sliver of smoked salmon at day's end.
> He kisses me.
> He doesn't stop. I don't want him to stop.
> We don't stop all the way up the stairs to his bedroom.
> We make love.
> Then we both agree. IT MUST NEVER HAPPEN AGAIN.

In the diary, I have dutifully recorded all the compliments, followed by my own commentary in brackets.

> He says I'm lovely. (Does he really mean that?)
> Or worse, worse. Did he feel sorry for me? (Please God

not that.)

I can't afford to yearn, because THIS MUST NEVER HAPPEN AGAIN.

I am reading the diary as though I am this girl's mother. I note how often I write in block letters, the way mad people do in their letters of complaint to the ABC.

While I am fully prepared to acknowledge my own bad behaviour, this boy, this Marcus McKenna, is giving very mixed messages indeed.

> 'We have to remember never to get drunk together. I can't trust myself. Now go!'

If you want my advice, young girl, I'd warn you to be very careful about this man.

I finish the diary entry:

Oh GODDDDDDDDDDDDDDD.

My passion for Marcus McKenna lurched on for weeks, then months.

> THIS IS TORTURE.
>
> Why did you start this? Why did he start this?
>
> He has a girlfriend who he has broken up with, but she needs…what?…tendering. When we don't see each other he misses me dreadfully. *Dreadfully*. But he is impatient with himself for missing me. Why? Why are men so hard to understand?
>
> He needs SPACE. It's complicated.
>
> Despite my frustration with this *thing,* I know that nothing will make me abandon it. I HAVE NO SELF-CONTROL.

Eventually, at Café Paradiso, Marcus makes his choice. He is very sorry. He needs time to work out who he is.

'It's not you. It's me.'

Goodbye. Goodbye. End.

He's decided on Penelope.

At college, I have an American friend, Hank. I tell him that Marcus isn't going back to Penelope. I tell him that Marcus needs time alone to grow as a human being.

My girlfriends and I used to say *grow as a human being*, as though there were some danger of growing as a pterodactyl or a chimp.

Hank says, 'Marcus is going back to Penelope. Trust me.'

Hank is wise and cynical. I decide I don't like him. I wish I hadn't told him about Marcus.

In my diary, I write:

> If I could have three wishes this is what I would wish for:
> That Marcus McKenna loved me
> That Marcus McKenna loved me
> That Marcus McKenna loved me

Days, weeks, months grind on. I long to 'face up to whatever I'm supposed to face up to'. I dream of being a 'whole human being'. I try to enjoy being alone. I try to love solitude. Then I write in pink texta:

TRANSLATE LONELINESS TO ALONENESS

On a slip of paper in my camphorwood box, dated many years later, I find this:

What sustains me is the idea that after I've done my time as a single girl, I'll be independent and desirable and Marcus McKenna will fall in love over again.

With me.

When you read of Nell's dilemma, maybe you felt judgmental. What sort of a person can't remember who they made love to? Is sex so inconsequential, so meaningless to you?

Maybe there is a simple explanation for such lapses in memory. You see a harried and crumpled bloke in the car park. Thirty years have passed since you last saw him. He doesn't look anything like the taut and chiselled boy you made love to, on a foam mattress, in the front room of a terrace house in Carlton.

More importantly, ask yourself this: have I made the most of this one fleeting life? How disappointing to realise that you've lived your life at the pious end of the bell curve.

10

Stop Acting So Small

'Stop acting so small. You are the universe in ecstatic motion.'
Rumi, thirteenth-century Persian mystic

DRAMA SCHOOL was a hotbed of promiscuity. We were all into
it. How could we not be? We were forever sliding and slithering over
each other in the movement studio. Acting was all about 'your human
instrument'—your voice and your body—and this needed tuning.
That required taking your clothes off and putting them back on,
several times a day. We wore leotards, tracksuit pants, running shorts
and stinky old T-shirts, and we crowded into small unisex changing
rooms to switch from one outfit to the other.

We wanted to lay ourselves bare; we wanted to be emotionally
free. Such freedom creates intimacy. And intimacy, as we all know,
has a way of leading to sex.

Personally, I think this is a good thing.

The world needs more loving. And the theatre needs sex.
Sexuality is the engine room of performance. After nearly forty years
of watching actors, I reckon that the best ones work from the pelvis.

I contrast this with bosom acting. Think of those bawdy English
dramas, like the *Carry On* films: the women made their entrances
preceded by their tits, as though the director had told these actresses
to imagine they had headlights on their nipples. This was true
whether the actress had the perky variety or a matronly shelf. I've
often thought that's why English sitcoms had a lot of barmaids. They
were cut off at the waist.

By contrast, Marilyn Monroe shone a mighty light from her

pelvis. She had an animal power that came from deep within her sexual being. Yes, she was 'commodified for the male gaze', but what made her so charismatic was her raw sexual energy. She was giving you her entire body.

The great male actors do this naturally. Their power comes from the groin, and we love them for it. Recently, in New York, I watched a fabulous actor perform in my play *Extinction* at a public reading at the Manhattan Theatre Club. With unselfconscious power, every time he addressed an actress, he turned his pelvis towards her. Every woman in the room was mesmerised. One of the theatre agents whispered to me afterwards, 'I thought things I couldn't tell my husband.' The novelist Anna Funder said, 'I don't know what he's got, but he's got it.'

Turn your pelvis—as if to confront your lover, or your enemy, or your oldest friend—and your whole body is committed to that action. It was that full-bodied commitment our teachers at VCA were trying to unleash in us. We were a 'universe in ecstatic motion'. That line from Rumi was scratched onto the door in one of the girls' toilets. Underneath, in biro, someone had added a quote by Laurence Olivier: 'An actor needs the voice of an orchestra and the body of a god.'

If we didn't have the bodies of gods, we had three years to get them.

In our first week at the VCA, we were photographed standing against a wall marked with a grid. We were photographed like criminals—from the front and from the side. The Polaroid snaps were stuck up on another wall for all to see what a sorry rabble we were: round-shouldered, asymmetrical, swaybacked, overweight or slouching. Some of us had our chins sticking out; others had their shoulders hunched around their ears. We looked like any normal group of people waiting for a train.

At the end of the year, we all lined up against the grid again, for a second set of photographs. The transformation was miraculous. Thanks to our training, we had all grown taller, some by several centimetres. We had unlearned our bad physical habits and returned to 'a balanced state of rest and poise'—the mantra of the Alexander technique. Our bodies had become well aligned.

We were also fitter and slimmer, the result of exercising for several hours every day. I felt intense muscle stiffness for the entire three years I was there. But it wasn't my body that caused me grief. It was my voice.

I have a slight sibilance. A listhp. It's not that noticeable in conversation. But in public performance, when I'm nervous, my tongue seems to thicken and get stuck on the roof of my mouth.

For many years, I lived with a man who stuttered. I watched him make eccentric word substitutions, for fear of getting stuck on words starting with 't', for example. He would never say *television*; he would always say *square box*. This gave him a kind of endearing nuttiness.

I found myself doing the same. Listening self-consciously to my speaking voice. Avoiding words beginning with 's'. This could be managed in private conversation, but when it came to saying lines, it was non-negotiable. Only the laziest actor paraphrases.

Many years later, when I was working in Hollywood, a fellow scriptwriter gave me a stamp with the letters 'AWMF' on it, to use on actors' scripts. It stands for *As Written, Motherfucker.*

We had voice classes every morning. Remedial students like me had to return at night. It was torment. I stared into a small mirror and rolled my tongue up and down for forty minutes, thinking, 'This is now my sixth year of tertiary education and it's come to this.'

Apart from my vocal problems, I was having the time of my life. A rummage through my camphorwood box unearths the drama school's 1979 elective program. I could weep with joy at the choices. You could do everything from circus skills to creating theatre in shopwindows. Mr Trim ran the costume department (true) and he ran classes on making extravagant costumes from op shop raids. We studied improvisation, we made puppets, we learned to perfect British and American accents, we created political theatre (*The Golden Years of Gough*). There were classes in the broad comedic style of the Italian commedia dell'arte. You could even learn the skills of the Wild West: rope-twirling, knife-throwing, buck-jumping and sharp-shooting.

One Friday, I found myself falling from the second-floor balcony after being shot in the chest. I fell magnificently onto a truck below, stacked with mattresses.

The school's boast was that it was training us to turn our hands to all aspects of theatre-making. The idea that actors would sit at home waiting for their agents to phone was anathema to us. This, we told each other, is what happened at NIDA—the National Institute of Dramatic Art in Sydney. Those actors were being groomed to be tools of the industry. We, on the other hand, were being trained as creators. Movers and shakers. We graduates of the VCA would distinguish ourselves by being able to write, perform and produce our own work. Even if we had to perform in schools, community centres and footy clubs, at least we would be working.

To this end, we were also offered electives in every aspect of theatre production, including sound, lighting and stage management. We learned how to raise the money, market the show and clean the theatre afterwards. Those who wanted to be stars were understandably disgruntled.

The dean was a bright-eyed, hyperactive bloke named Peter Oyston. I viewed him with a mixture of awe and love, bemusement and embarrassment. His personal style was usually over the top: the hallmarks of his public speeches were excessive passion and hyperbole. There were occasions when I had to stare at the floor.

But Oyston changed the way I thought about myself. Like all gifted teachers, he could convince you that the key to understanding the universe was his own particular discipline—in his case, the theatre. He made me feel that I was an ornament to the human race.

Years later, when I wrote the play *Life After George*, about a charismatic university professor, Oyston was one of my role models. The director of that show was Kate Cherry. In preparation for the rehearsal period at the Melbourne Theatre Company, Kate and I mused about our own experiences at university and drama school. She had studied in America. We had both had mentors who had thought we were brilliant. Kate laughed. 'Yes, it's marvellous to be marvellous.' That became our catchphrase for the rehearsal period. When I meet clever, shiny young women, I often say it to myself wistfully and, I hope, not enviously.

The greatest lesson Oyston taught me was that Australian culture was in the process of being created. Australian theatre was at the frontier and we were the discovery party. We wanted nothing to do with a second-hand theatre culture where most theatres only showcased plays from America and Britain. Sure, we wanted to see the best from around the world. But we also needed to make our own. To this end, we needed to persuade governments and bureaucrats and audiences that an Australian voice had something unique to say about the human condition. It was not just the British in their drawing rooms or the French languishing in prison cells or the Russians hovering around the samovar who had a monopoly over stories for the stage.

Oyston's grand vision was that graduates would form their own artist-managed companies. He envisioned all manner of theatre collectives emanating from the college and setting up shop in every corner of the country.

This was all very inspiring. But, by my second year, I was having an existential crisis. It dawned on me that I didn't actually like acting. This feeling of being on the wrong train was apparent one day in an acting class. Our teacher was Lindy Davies, an acting teacher with admirers around the world. (Lindy is Julie Christie's personal acting coach.) She practised a technique called impulse work. This involves standing against the wall waiting for an impulse. Once the impulse strikes, you run across the studio to another wall. You are free. You are abandoned. You run and run. You are no longer working from the cerebral or the habitual part of your brain. You are alert and awake and you *react*. You run.

In the three years I was in drama school, I never once had an impulse. I stood against the wall in my leotard, like everybody else. And nothing happened. I wanted an impulse. Everyone else was having one. I thought about faking. But all that happened was that I stood against the wall. Stuck. *Blocked*. Jammed. *Hopeless*.

I dragged my *impulse-less* body to Peter Oyston's office, knocked on the door and blurted out my confession. 'I don't want to be an actor any more.'

He stared at me thoughtfully.

'I want to be a writer.'

He gazed out the window for an interminable period.

'Do you own a typewriter?'

I did.

Then he did something that changed my life. He reached into the top drawer of his desk and rummaged about, leaned across the table and handed me a key.

'That's the key to the front room at the end of the corridor.'

I took the key.

'That's yours. Your room, okay? We need playwrights. Go and write a play.'

And I did.

11
Storming Mont Albert by Tram

IN MY experience, most parents who work in the arts want their children to become accountants or stockbrokers or plastic surgeons. They express a palpable sense of relief if their children show no interest in following in their footsteps.

But not us.

When my son, Jack, decided to enrol in law school, my husband urged him to think again.

'When I dropped out of law school,' Michael told his stepson, 'my world changed from black-and-white to colour.'

'Unlike you,' Jack countered, 'I happen to be interested in what Section 51 of the Constitution says.'

This sounded weird to me. He was a boy who had spent many summers at acting school and seemed particularly unsuited to life in a city tower block.

'You're eighteen,' said MC. 'Just don't wake up one morning and discover you're thirty-four.'

This struck me as truly persuasive. How appalling to waste one's twenties at a desk, toiling in the service of rich pricks suing the shit out of each other.

But Jack was wise. He took no notice of his parents. His twenties have been action-packed—in tower blocks and foreign countries.

This is a sign of a massive generational shift of values. When I was eighteen, I regarded the prospect of working for a corporation as an unacceptable surrender to conservatism and dullness. The concept of alienation was the big topic in the seventies. Capitalism alienated the worker from himself and his own body, and turned him into a machine in service of the enrichment of others.

Which made tower blocks evil as well as nerdy.

And, once I had fully embraced feminist theory, I saw that tower blocks were also phallic and therefore oppressive to women.

Jack's generation has eroticised these urban erections. These days, the smartest and the sexiest university graduates seem drawn to them, flitting across the big foyers in tight skirts or well-cut suits and pressing the high numbers in the lift.

So when we were cautioning my boy against corporate life, what were we campaigning for, exactly? We cannot have wanted him to be an actor, surely. Did we imagine he would be happier dressing up in overalls and dancing across our TV screen, singing, 'Call, call Carpet Call, the experts in the trade'? Or wearing a koala suit and handing out leaflets in the street?

I think not.

Not long after Michael dispensed his stepfatherly advice, he and I were walking along busy Brunswick Street in Fitzroy when we were accosted by a koala. The koala was shaking a bucket, trying to raise money for the Wilderness Society. Michael held up a hand and said, 'Not today, mate.' He then moved to walk around the bear.

The koala stepped in his path. Man and koala did a sort of dance on the crowded footpath, the koala vigorously shaking his bucket. Eventually, exasperated, my husband said, 'Fuck off, bear.'

To which the koala replied, 'Fuck off yourself, Cathcart.'

To this day, we do not know the identity of the impudent marsupial.

There is a fair bit of hubris involved in the parent's assumption that they know their child better than he knows himself. And, equally spurious, that they know a thing or two about the world in which he lives.

In my adult life, my experience of work has been largely confined to the theatre. There's a lot to recommend work in the performing arts. For all its financial and emotional insecurity, the theatre seduces you with its easy (and sometimes deceptive) intimacy. It's also fun.

Like a party. With a purpose.

No one gravitates to a career in the theatre for money. So it should come as no surprise that it is a place where idealism flourishes. The managerial classes are doing their darnedest to wring it out of every other profession on earth, but it remains the lifeblood of this one.

Of course, theatre people don't necessarily wear their idealism on their sleeves. In people over forty, such a display is unworldly. So we disguise it beneath a veneer of jealousy, animus and sulkiness. But for even the most irascible, curmudgeonly, petulant, arrogant and grumpy of our number, there is still a robust and romantic belief that the theatre can influence the way we live. That it can effect social change.

So, the prospect of a job that offers intimacy, fun and idealism— who wouldn't want that for their child?

Ninety-nine per cent of the population.

Perhaps the catch comes with that first breezy phrase—the *prospect* of a job.

When I left drama school in 1979, I walked straight into a full-time acting job. It paid $117 per week—a princely sum. I was a founding member of a community theatre company called Theatre Works. There were five of us, all VCA graduates. I was the youngest and the least experienced actor in the company.

We had a small office and a rehearsal space at Burwood Teachers' College (now Deakin University), and a mandate to create theatre for the people of the eastern suburbs.

Other areas had their own theatre companies. The Murray River Performing Group was based to the north of Melbourne, in Albury. There was a company in the western suburbs called WEST. South of Melbourne, Geelong had the Mill Theatre, an initiative of Deakin University. So it followed that we should shine our spotlight on the east. Once we had our little office, we defined our zone of influence: we traced the circumference of a large Nescafé coffee lid on a map in the street directory. The lucky people who lived or worked within the circumference of that lid were now our flock, our Theatre Works family.

Unlike the other two VCA companies, Murray River Performing Group and WEST, which were busy honouring and celebrating the people and culture of their communities, we didn't much like the region we'd chosen. Only one of us, Caz Howard, actually lived there. The rest of us schlepped every day from Melbourne's inner bosom, the places we loved and identified with: Fitzroy, Collingwood, Richmond. One day, Peter Sommerfeld was driving us to work along the Burwood Highway. We crested a big hill and surveyed the arid and sprawling suburban landscape riven with freeways. From the back seat, Peter Finlay growled, 'It's like Kafka country.'

The name and the feeling stuck. Existential despair hung in the air like smog. There was no street life, no coffee, no migrants. There were Chinese restaurants, and Greeks with fried chicken shops, but anything of cultural interest was invisible to us. I found the east lonely and soulless.

But that was exactly why it needed us, just as Kafka country needed Kafka. We rolled up our sleeves and started to make theatre. We toiled seven days a week and most nights. We had no leader. No artistic director. We five—Susie Fraser, Caz Howard, Peter Sommerfeld, Peter Finlay and I—were the 'artistic directorate'. We spent hours discussing and writing manifestos to describe our vision. What we finally came up with began:

> Theatre Works aims to create work which is pertinent to
> contemporary Australian lives, and which reflects the energies
> of urban life, building a symbolic vocabulary which will serve
> and sustain people in their search for meaning and identity.

We were very intense.

We five lived in each other's pockets. We went camping together in our holidays. We ate at each other's houses. Caz's partner, Paul Davies, joined the company after a few years, and regularly made spaghetti bolognaise for all of us. As far as I saw, that was the extent of his culinary repertoire. Often our numbers swelled with the extra actors we employed on shows. We drank red wine from casks and smoked. We knew everything there was to know about each other's romantic failures, sexual adventures and family troubles.

At night we went home alone or to our partners.

We were so ambitious to make good work. We never let up.

Our first show was *The Go Anywhere (Within Reason) Show*. We performed it 178 times. It involved a family, Dick and Dolly Dickens, their children, Daphne and Darryl, and Dolly's sister, Desdemona. The show kicked off with the Dickens family arriving at the performance venue—a shopping centre, a school, a community hall, a fete—where they would erect their tent. This ritual kicked off with an elaborate square-dance routine. When the tent suddenly sprang into shape, it was a reconstruction of a kitsch suburban house, down to the fence and pot plants.

It was a pretty snappy show, full of sight gags and pratfalls, singing and dancing. We employed every trick we'd learned at drama school and gleaned from our director, Robin Laurie, who was from Circus Oz. She had us skidding on skateboards, falling through deck chairs, or banging our heads on the plastic pot plants that dangled from the tent. At night, we were consumed with earnest discussions about feminism and Marxism. During the day, we were slipping on banana peels or whacking each other with pieces of wood.

I played goofy Daphne, the intellectual, myopic daughter. I was waging a sustained campaign to do all in my power to injure my sibling, Darryl.

The more we performed the show, the more the bookings rolled in. It became a cash cow for the company. It paid our wages. We pulled on our costumes and piled into Caz's kombi. She was Dolly, and she drove the van in a wig and a tracksuit ensemble she'd dyed a bright pink. She'd fill the tank at the service station, then totter over to the counter to pay, in all her glory. She never batted an eyelid. She was the least self-conscious person I have ever met. My abiding memory of her is the way she used to wear high-waisted cottontail undies that looked like they might have been WWI-issue. They were shot through with holes. This was teamed with a singlet of a similar vintage or a grey bra. She was lean and attractive and, for the whole time I knew her, she never appeared to give two hoots that she looked a fright.

The *Go Anywhere (Within Reason) Show* could have run forever. So any chagrin I felt about being Daphne Dickens was ameliorated by the satisfying whiff of modest commercial success. We'd started a small business and it was working. Sort of.

The boldest and most outlandish project we undertook was *Storming Mont Albert by Tram*. This was Paul Davies' idea, and it was to become Theatre Works' signature piece. We called it 'location theatre'. This was a lofty concept born out of necessity: we had to make a virtue of being a theatre company without a theatre.

Storming Mont Albert by Tram was a play set on an actual tram. The audience boarded the Number 42 tram, at the end of the line in Mont Albert, and took the journey into the city. The story unfolded as different characters joined the tram along the route.

The audience spent interval enjoying a drink at the Australia Hotel in Collins Street. Then they returned to the tram and we all rumbled back to the eastern suburbs. At the end, we repaired to a coffee shop, which stayed open for the tram-load of over-excited customers.

The season was originally scheduled for six weeks, but it ran for six months. We worked on those trams every night, with additional matinees on the weekend. It was relentless.

I played Samantha Hart-Byrne, from Surrey Hills. In the throes of marital mayhem, Samantha had ejected herself from her philandering stockbroker-husband's Mercedes and ventured onto public transport for the first time in her life. She was on her way to the Melbourne Theatre Company, which was staging a play at the Athenaeum on Collins Street. On board already were the conductress and an elderly dero, who was woken up as the tram clattered off from the terminus.

As the tram ploughed its way into the city, it moved through a diverse socio-economic cross-section of Melbourne. New actors clambered aboard at stops along the way. In working-class Richmond, for example, a punk boarded the tram with a plastic guide dog he'd just stolen from out the front of a chemist. The dog was dragging a heavy chain.

The stage manager, Graeme Stephen, drove an old Holden station wagon. We actors piled into the car, with the plastic guide dog and other props, and Graeme drove like the clappers along the road following the tramlines, dropping each of us at the prescribed tram stop to board the tram when it arrived. He would also collect any actors who'd got off or been ejected by the connie, as in the case of Danny the dero.

I learned more about acting in those six months than in my three years at drama school. A tram is a small space. The proximity to the audience demanded an authenticity that had to be sustained. Moreover, while the Tramways Board allowed us to perform on their tram, they did not allocate us a specific driver, so every show we had a different one. Sometimes, he would gun it down the hills and we would have to edit our dialogue to cover the necessary plot points before the next actor got on. Or he might amble along the route, and we'd be improvising like mad to fill in the minutes.

For the audience, the best bits occurred when regular passengers unwittingly boarded the tram, unaware that they were both witnessing and starring in a play. We only admitted one or two of these innocents, as most seats were booked by paying customers.

One of the characters, a tram inspector played by Paul Davies, wrote activist plays in his spare time for a fringe theatre company. When we reached the City Square, I alighted and flounced off to see the Melbourne Theatre Company's production. Paul hung from the tram, screaming at me at the top of his lungs: 'Go and see your state-subsidised bourgeois theatre, you complacent Camberwell enemy of the people!' I stood in the Square and shook my fist, screaming back in righteous bourgeois outrage. This always attracted a crowd. One night, a young constable was much outraged on my behalf and I threw my arms around his neck in gratitude. The audience on the tram cheered and hooted. As the tram clattered out of sight, I mumbled a rather formal thank you and tottered off in my ludicrous high heels, praying he wouldn't follow and arrest me.

Once, the tram was rerouted because of an accident up ahead. I was preparing for my scene with Cathy (an escort from Abbotsford), who was waiting to join us at the next stop, when suddenly the tram turned left and proceeded along an entirely different route. The final three performers dotted along the Number 42 route were left stranded. Graeme leapt into his trusty Holden and sped down the highway, collecting the performers and depositing each one at tram stops along the new route. He had to figure out where we might be in the unfolding of the story, so the new character could get on in time. There were no mobile phones in 1982. Those of us already on the tram had no idea what was happening. We just carried on.

Storming Mont Albert by Tram was such a success that Paul Davies went home to Brisbane in the summer of 1983 to see his parents and write the sequel.

This time, we were travelling on a boat up the Yarra River. The occasion was Samantha Hart-Byrne's divorce party. Paul called it *Breaking Up in Balwyn*. We sold four thousand tickets in the first week.

It was not a success. The script was a howler. Queensland was too hot to think and Paul was under too much pressure. Moreover, we were on a river at night. Outside, it was pitch black. So the interaction between audience and the outside world was not the feature it had been on the tram. That was the fun of it, in *Storming Mont Albert*— the audience's sense of collusion in the mischief-making.

There was another problem. I was the lead.

In my defence, I had mastered a pitch-perfect Melbourne private school nasal drawl. My world was full of Nigels and Fionas and Sebastians. I was very happy with the voice. I also had a divine cossie. It was a sugar-pink party frock with a sweetheart neckline, nipped in at the waist and then frothing with masses of pink tulle. I made my entrance by jumping out of a cake. My ex-husband crashed the party wearing a gorilla suit, and my new boyfriend—Nigel, from the tram—ran off with the maid. That's all I remember about the story.

But there is one performance I will never forget.

It was a warm and balmy March evening. The Yarra Princess, smelling vaguely of the onboard toilet, puttered up the Yarra. We pulled in at Como Park, where we had set up tables and chairs for the audience, who were plied with champagne and nibbles. This was interval.

After twenty minutes, it was my job to mingle with 'my guests' and herd them back onto the boat. So I drifted about in my frothy dress and urged the guests, in my braying voice, to drink up their bubbly and follow me down the carpeted path back to the boat.

This night, no one moved.

'Come on, sweeties,' I beseeched. 'Darlings, darlings!' I begged. 'Chop chop.'

Nothing.

A young man was sitting on the grass staring gloomily into the Yarra. I sat down next to him.

'Time to get back on the boat, sweetie,' I cooed.

He looked me squarely in the eye. 'I would rather swim.'

And the funny thing is, I felt the same way. I was also hoping I might drown.

In that moment, I made a resolution. I would never act again.

The sad coda to this story is that, of the gang who worked with Theatre Works in those early years, nine people are dead.

Caz Howard died at thirty-seven of cervical cancer. Peter Sommerfeld died of cancer. Peter Oyston, Danny Nash, Taya Straton, John Wood-Ingram, Lynda Gibson, Rosie Lalevich and Susie Fraser's husband, John Barbour, all died prematurely.

But Theatre Works endures, now in its new home in St Kilda. It has been performing plays for thirty-four years.

12
The Fruit Shop

IN 1978, politics was a relatively simple business. You didn't have to get your head around the current account deficit or its relationship to globalisation. You just had to understand that good and evil were matters of gender. All things male were suspect and all things female illuminated the path to world peace, social justice, creativity and care for the environment. Boyfriends were acceptable if they had a very developed feminine side. This meant that they were open to having deep and meaningful conversations late into the night. They could pick up a packet of tampons from the chemist unabashed, and they could do things with chickpeas. Good men were hard to find. Ones who'd grown up with a lot of sisters and a politicised mum were the best. They sat quietly at the kitchen table and nodded sagely when we discussed how useless they were.

I was twenty-one, and learning about the imperative of being ideologically sound. One night, I went along to the Cultural Palace in Moor Street, Fitzroy, for an evening of women's films. There were two hundred women. No men were allowed. Some twenty minutes after the advertised starting time, the screen was still blank. The crowd started to get fidgety. The projectionist and a huddle of serious women were deliberating at the back of the hall. The projector was whirring away merrily, but producing no image. As it happened, my boyfriend Jaems was around the corner at the Standard Hotel, having a drink with some mates. He was a cameraman. Could he be of any help?

No!

No. No. No. Boyfriends who thought they knew more than us

about technical matters were not welcome or needed.

Forty minutes later, the crowd was turning nasty.

As the temperature rose, I smuggled Jaems into the projection booth with his parka over his head. Two minutes later, we were watching our film.

When I got home, I asked him about the technical hitch.

The projector was working fine, he told me.

There was a box in front of the lens.

A decade later, I was writing for film and television in the independent sector. This meant writing the scripts for education and training videos, and working with the Australian Film Commission on its recently established women's program. We were committed to challenging stereotypical representations of women. We wanted to create drama in which powerful and complex female characters instigated the action. We didn't want subservient women—secretaries or maids or the hero's girlfriends. Women had to be in leading roles. But we didn't want them to be too flawed. In the fight for gender equality, we had a responsibility to create women who were just that much smarter than men.

Power was what we wanted, because power in the hands of women wouldn't corrupt. It would bring peace and equitable childcare solutions and good will to all personkind.

I shared an office space with three other writers above a fruit shop in Smith Street, Collingwood. Two of them moved beds into their offices. Their marriages had imploded. There was a kitchen, where we drank tea and smoked and whinged. It was all very companionable.

One morning, I came into the kitchen to find one of the blokes slumped over the table, head in hands.

'I can't get my women to talk. I have been at that computer for three hours, and they refuse to open their mouths.' He looked up. It was a pitiful sight. 'What do women talk about, for godsake?'

Having been out to dinner the night before with two women

friends, I generously recapped the conversation for his benefit. 'Gynaecology. Thrush, to be specific.'

He stuck his fingers in his ears.

'My friend Nell was in a bus,' I ploughed on, 'going across the Nullarbor. She was so itchy, she wanted to climb onto the gear stick.'

The scriptwriter groaned. 'Lovely. Very useful.' He skulked back to his office in the back room where there was no natural light.

In the late eighties, the problem for male writers was twofold. First, the issue of plausibility—do women actually speak like this? But there was an additional concern: if I create a really flawed woman—nasty, bitchy, weak, manipulative, cruel—will my women friends speak to me again?

Women writers faced a different challenge in creating male characters. Men's conversations tended to be more public, and thus more accessible. The hard part was creating men's interior world: creating the subtext, the discrepancy between what is said and what is *felt*.

I had been known to write pages where the women got great chunks of dialogue, intercut with a male character saying *Uh huh?* or *Really?* or *Do go on*.

It was convenient to claim that this was an ideological choice. But, in truth, I was floundering with men. I didn't really get what was happening in their heads.

In the kitchen, at lunch, I volunteered to take a look at my colleague's uncommunicative women.

He was hopeful that I would unveil the mysteries of female small talk. He knew women could be witty. He just couldn't make them say witty things. As a result of my intervention, he was anticipating that he would be besieged by sexy actresses wanting to date him. He would be beloved by all women. Even radical lesbian separatists would smile and wave at him at the film festivals.

It was a weighty responsibility. With some trepidation, I sat beside him at his word processor.

After a few hours of discussing the characters and inserting and deleting bits of conversation, my colleague leaned back in his chair.

'I don't believe this,' he said. 'I solicit assistance from the great feminist upstairs and all you give me is this inane chatter. About shoes.'

This was true.

'I know what's going to happen,' he said. 'My producer will say it's fine, except for that piece of sexist shit in Scene Twelve.'

Next morning he came in, sheepish. 'My sister's just read the whole script. She says the scene about the shoes is fabulous.'

'Did you fess up that I wrote it?' I smiled charmingly.

'Are you kidding?'

My moment of self-congratulation was short-lived. I had three weeks until the deadline for my own TV script.

I lay on the floor and stared at the ceiling. I tried to think male. I imagined myself striding across a hotel foyer with my hand outstretched, ready to charm and vanquish a business competitor. I imagined hearty backslapping in a pub and loud dissertations about riotously funny incidents. I imagined being *an authority* on a range of topics and speaking *authoritatively* about them. I imagined having a pain in the guts, but refusing to consult a doctor. I tried to compose funny remarks about women with fat arses.

I was wandering aimlessly in the Gobi Desert of my second act. I cast a critical eye over my blokes. They were very shadowy figures indeed. But if my male characters were minor parts, so what? The history of Australian television had not served women well. It was time to redress the imbalance. If you want to hear men pontificate, you can arrange a dinner party.

It's not that my men were weak. It's that they were *absent*. In the heady emotion of this script, they were likely to be off screen, chucking the frisbee. When I tried to drag them back into the vortex, they didn't know what to do with themselves. They fiddled. They stared out of windows. They smirked. They found any excuse to get out of the kitchen.

I knew what my male characters were thinking. They were wishing they were in someone else's word processor.

Australian men are brilliant subjects, but they tend to keep a lid on their emotions. Reticence could be powerful on screen: it suggested mystery, profundity, strength. But, ultimately, if the character has no subtext he comes across as a boring dickhead and a cliché. The screen handles reticence better than the stage. In the theatre, it's very hard to make a silent character compelling.

The ocker accent doesn't help. It compresses the entire spectrum of human emotions into a narrow vocal band. An actor expresses intense joy or intense grief in the same register. He would use the same tone of voice, whether his wife had just been diagnosed with cancer or he'd backed Hyperno in the 1979 Melbourne Cup. In either case, his speech would be as flat and neutral as if he were buying a packet of Rothmans.

'How are you, son?'
'Aw, you know. Been better.'
'Sure.'
'Look after yourself, orright?'
'Thanks, boss.'
'No worries.'

My male colleagues returned to the office, after a very long lunch.
'What did you talk about, for godsake?'
'Nothing much.'
I slumped on the table.

When one of those writers moved out, Andrew Knight moved in. He is now one of the most successful writers and producers for TV in the country (he wrote *SeaChange* and *Rake*, just for starters), but back then, he was a lackey like the rest of us, whose major source of income was his Medicare rebate.

Andrew had a looming deadline. Maximum sensory deprivation was called for, so we put him in the basement.

I gleaned many tips from this basement dweller during his time at the fruit shop. This one is worth passing on: when it comes to those irksome character notes that must be completed with each draft, your standard astrology reference book is your best friend. I have one right here. Take the profile of a Taurus male: simply insert this in your character notes after you've written Paul, thirty-three, policeman.

> Paul is the type of man who strides defiantly onto the arena of life, but who says little.
>   When he is not on show, he is a man of simple needs and sensible ideas. Leave him alone and he'll bask in the sun. Challenge him and he will charge you down. Respect him—or watch out.

Invariably, your producer will read those lines and say, 'Okay, I know the type exactly. Good work.'

I was writing a new TV script when Andrew arrived. It was an episode in a six-part drama series about female sexuality. In my episode, I had to tell an improbable story about three lesbians: Sandra, Paula and Susan. The producers were hoping to sell the story to the ABC. But SBS was interested, so they revised my brief. My episode now had to be about three ethnic lesbians.

I resubmitted my draft unchanged, except for the names of the main characters. My story was now about Francesca, Dominica and Isabella. The producers found this cynical. I argued that it was radical and progressive. 'Are you saying Italian lesbians do it differently from Anglo-Australian lesbians?' I was so far out of my depth already, I figured I had nothing to lose.

SBS wanted a *migrant angle*. But as I told the producer, my best friend is a second-generation Greek. We don't spend our time discussing her migrant status, how her mother came to Australia with only one suitcase. We talk about boys and rooting, just like everyone else. The man from SBS was unimpressed.

Anyway, before my contract was terminated, he decided to give one of the characters a sex change. Paula became Paul and had sex with Sandra (before Sandra came to the realisation that she was a dyke and then an Italian).

I was busy on a fourth draft and I remember yelling downstairs to Andrew, 'How do you write the sex bits?'

'Just fade to black.'

As it happened the whole project faded to black, but the pesky problem of how to write the sex followed me to the next project.

Just how detailed are you supposed to get?

> JOHN puts his right hand on CELIA'S left breast, while his left hand is snaking up her inner thigh. CELIA sucks his fingers, while holding the edge of the table with one hand and his left buttock with the other.

Is this a sex scene, or have I just written the instructions for a game of Twister? (I've just realised I've given John three hands.)

Each of the writers in our office had a different view on this vexing matter. Bryan used to write:

> Scene 31, Interior, Howard's bedroom.
> They fuck.

In the fruit shop kitchen, I argued that sex and desire were as much a part of our emotional palette as anger and revenge.

'To write "They fuck" is no different from writing "They argue. Dissolve to Los Angeles earthquake footage."'

'That's a good idea,' said Andrew, and went downstairs to insert that into his script.

I rang my friend Andrew Bovell. He had only recently co-written a screen adaptation of Christos Tsiolkas's novel *Loaded*, about twenty-four erotic hours in the life of a young Greek guy. The film's depiction of gay sex is extremely graphic. If anyone had to solve the problem of writing explicit sex for the screen, it was Andrew and his co-writers, Ana Kokkinos and Mira Robertson.

Andrew told me they had taken their cue from the novel. 'The novel gave us the licence to be vivid and explicit.'

'Was it embarrassing talking about this stuff in a script conference?'

'One straight boy and two girls spending all day talking about cocks? It was fabulous.'

Part of the disheartening reality of the screenwriter's lot is that—initially at least—you are writing for an audience of men in suits. If you want them to imagine sizzling sex, you can't write, 'JAKE steals a kiss from the lovely GWYNETH.' You have to push GWYNETH up against the wall and JAKE has to thrust and throb.

Even if you close down your computer in the afternoon feeling smugly that you were the next Anaïs Nin, re-reading your efforts the following morning feels like finding your mother looking at pornography. Ew.

You can write a murder scene without being a murderer. But it's harder to write sex at a distance. Maybe I'm too self-conscious.

A weekday, for me, during my years at the fruit shop, meant shutting down the computer at 3 p.m. and making a dash for the school pick-up. After all that emoting, I could put on my coat and become a mum. Whoever I was pretending to be at the fruit shop got locked up in my computer overnight.

13
Let Me Eat Cake

AT 5 A.M. one summer's day, I was met at Charles de Gaulle airport by Jean-Marie Retby, the man who had translated my play *Hotel Sorrento* into French. Poor Jean-Marie couldn't remember where he'd parked his Citroën. He was awash with apologies as we roamed the car park: it was his first experience of being out in the world before sunrise. I understood perfectly. He was a nocturnal theatre animal. One of us.

It was June 1995, and I was one of six young Australian playwrights who had come to Paris to see our work showcased by the Comédie-Française. For a week, we reeled from one four-course meal to the next. Garden parties were followed by cocktail parties, dinners at fabulous restaurants and nightcaps at sidewalk cafés.

We were taken to dinner by the writer Jean-Noël Fenwick, whose award-winning play about Pierre and Marie Curie had been running in Paris for six years. Concerned that we wouldn't understand the finer points of the script, he performed the entire play for us at the restaurant, in English. Then the whole fifteen-member entourage had to run about two kilometres down the street to the theatre to see his show. And there was burly Jean-Noël, urging us through the streets of Paris like a flock of Australian sheep.

We got to know each other quite well. The doctor and playwright Ron Elisha became my particular buddy. He spoke of his wife, Bertha, so lovingly and rang her every day. Karin Mainwaring had intense encounters with the homeless *clochards* and sought existential truth on the night-time banks of the Seine. (Her play *The Rain Dancers* became the first Australian work staged as a full production by the Comédie-Française.) And Daniel Keene impressed the French audiences so much with his play *The Hour Before My Brother Dies* that his dark existential plays have continued to be produced in France ever since.

Our plays were performed at the Théâtre du Vieux-Colombier, a rather handsome three-hundred-seat theatre in the centre of Paris. These were simple readings, staged on six successive nights by some of the finest performers in France. We played to full houses. And if the thunderous clapping and stamping feet were any indication, the audience liked what they heard. We took curtain calls with the performers, clutched flowers, had our photos taken and swanned in the foyers.

I'd been to Paris only once before. Five years earlier, I had crossed the Channel with my friend Wendy Harmer, who spent the entire ferry crossing practising the phrase *Garçon! Apportez-moi plus de navets!* ('Waiter! Bring me more turnips!')

My most abiding memory of that trip, apart from the ubiquitous dog shit, was my humiliating attempt to have a facial. After all, wasn't that what you did in Paris? Apparently not. Having traipsed from one beauty parlour to another, I finally ditched the mission when a woman in the last salon stared at me with impeccable disdain, which she seemed to draw up from her ankles. She said, incredulously, 'You want *me* to clean *your* face?'

This time, things were different.

I was a person of standing. An *artiste*.

In fact, I became so ebullient about the whole business that I felt confident enough to establish a marvellous ritual for the opening nights of all Australian plays. The afternoon before the reading of *Hotel Sorrento*, I mentioned casually to one of our hosts, a professor of French literature, that I had been in Paris a week and hadn't had a cake. It was just a casual remark, making small talk in a car, as you do.

Five minutes before the play began, I was standing in the foyer beaming away in my party dress. My new-found Parisian friends were milling around and wishing me *merde* (shit)—the French equivalent of 'break a leg'. Just as the theatre bells began to ring, the professor appeared. The dear man presented me with a box with a big ribbon on it. 'Madame asked for cake,' he said, gallantly. I opened the box: it was groaning with delectable petits fours pumped full of cream. A wiser playwright would have said, *'Merci*, I will enjoy them later.' But *pas moi*. I said, *'Merci,'* and selected a cake. As the doors to the auditorium opened, there I was with my mouth full of chocolate éclair.

What was I thinking?

I rushed to explain. 'It's an Australian tradition. The playwright always eats cake before the curtain goes up.'

'Ah,' said the French. *'Merde, merde.'* They seemed delighted that such colourful traditions were so well established in the new world. They filed into the international debut of my play, happier than ever.

Cake, a pretty frock and an opening night in Paris.

Formidable.

14
Love and Writing

WHEN I was a teenager I would go to the movies with my mum to watch romantic comedies. We sat side by side in the darkness of the Elsternwick Classic cinema, and I was infused with longing for the moment when the hero finally overcame all obstacles and drew the heroine into an ardent embrace. But through this yearning, I felt sick with worry and pity for my mother. I thought: this is all over for her. She's married to my dad.

Robert Redford was never going to ask her to walk with him barefoot in the park. She would never drink a highball with Cary Grant, or have breakfast at Tiffany's. She would never have a farm in Africa. I imagined her despair. I was mortified for her. And sorry. She must be hating this reminder of her middle-aged-ness.

And now here I am. Half a century has skulked past. I have been writing for thirty years. Are you wondering: is she still in love? Is her prose still, you know, *sexy*?

One afternoon at the cinema, my mother gave me four pieces of advice.

Learn to like beer. Boys should not be expected to fork out their hard-earned money on brandy or fluffy ducks.

Never complain about your period. Everyone has them. What makes you so special?

When you leave home, the first thing you must do is develop a relationship with a butcher.

But the fourth piece of advice (and the only one related to the topic at hand) is this: to be successful in love, one must work at it. You have to put your shoulder to the wheel with marriage, and *labour*. At my cousin's wedding that same year, the celebrant asked, 'Will you take this woman to be your wife? Will you make the *daily effort to relate to her?*' Frankly, if you met my cousin's wife, you could believe that relating to her would be a daily effort.

For those of us growing up in the sixties and seventies, the evidence of the labour of marriage was in our kitchens and living rooms: marriage for us girls did involve a great deal of work in the form of ironing, vacuuming, making white sauce and deferring to one's husband. And the journey from sexy bride to frowsy matron seemed lamentably short.

But as my mother warned, love itself was also work. Lasting love required a real rolling up of one's sleeves. And as an American senator once said, 'You can't wring your hands and roll up your sleeves at the same time.'

The moralist in me will tell you that there is no mastery without discipline and work. That is true.

But my inner romantic will tell you that I cannot write unless I am in love with the writing.

I have tried over the years to marry for money, to dupe myself that I could be motivated to write for reasons other than love. I made corporate training videos, educational DVDs, episodes of this and that. I wrote countless film scripts and rewrote them, draft after draft, until I wanted to bash my head on asphalt. I've had arranged marriages, working to order, and ones where I have pitched my own stories. It's not as if my heart wasn't in it. I've always bled. But if you tango with television—know this—he is a brutal lover.

Once, we used to regard writing for money as the work of prostitutes. We turned up our noses and called it 'selling out'. Nobody thinks like that any more. Everybody knows that work is good. Work and work and work and work. You're lucky to have it.

But don't mistake it for love. Love is a journey of the soul.

If the long-term marriage between me and my PC, which has

produced fourteen bouncing baby plays to date, ever shows signs of being a dull and dragging thing, an obligation, a co-dependent bickering of two old dogs on the same leash, then my first duty as a writer is to have an affair. To flirt with another genre. And for me, that is invariably to write about travel. It may not be the sexiest thing to read, but it is certainly the sexiest to write.

Writing on a train. Writing in a diary with a pen. Writing what I see out a window. Naming the architectural form of a building, summoning the energy of a particular neighbourhood, the smell of a canal, the angle of a Greek fisherman's cap. There's so much to understand and express. So much tantalising detail to capture. I am free. I am a mere passer-by. What do I know of these lives that are being lived so far from my home in Fitzroy? But here I am, primed for adventure. Anything could happen, and everything or something does.

Writing in the sexy embrace of a diary is like diving into the warm waters of the Aegean. Or hiking up a French mountain where the air is cold and silent and laced with the citrus zing of the orange I'm peeling for my lunch.

I am alive. I am fresh. I am enlivened by solitude. I am in love. And like lovers the world over know, this has never happened to anyone else before. But what happens to the words I write in diaries? Mostly they languish. Mostly they are gifts I have bought for myself.

E. L. Doctorow says: 'Planning to write is not writing. Outlining, researching, talking to people about what you're doing, none of that is writing. Writing is writing.'

When I first came across that declaration, I felt castigated and exposed. I call all of it writing. I bundle it up and put it all on the tab. *And* I throw in walking and making soup and writing emails and reading.

Doctorow's definition, to me, feels like confusing sex for love. The actual time you are engaged in the business of sex—from a certain look to lying spent, heart thumping, in a tangle of bedding— is only a small fraction of the whole experience of making love. So many other things—small, seemingly unrelated things—are part of that same huge, significant, messy thing.

Doctorow is a bean counter. A pedant. I denounce Doctorow.

It's all or nothing.

When I was watching those movies with my mum, I wanted to be Julie Christie or Jane Fonda. I wanted to be the kind of woman who would come down into the kitchen the morning after, wearing only a lover's oversized shirt.

My love affair with writing is childish and profound, full of stings and jealousies, excitability and calm, tantrums and glittering happiness. I will work for a year for one exquisite insight, which may never come.

What my mother missed when she stressed to me that love had to be worked at was that you may work at it, but love can never be labour. It can only be love.

15

The Boxer

MY FATHER was gifted at making money, but he had no gift for keeping it. Our family finances were a yo-yo. Sometimes we were flush. Often we were not. Then an ill-judged property investment left my parents in significant debt. The yo-yo stalled at the bottom, and as hard as Dad jerked the string, he couldn't coax his good fortune back. He had to sell our family home.

Eight years later, at the age of fifty-eight, my father dropped dead mowing the patch of lawn outside their rented townhouse on the Mornington Peninsula. My dad had been in charge of everything. Mum had never even paid her own car registration. Now she was widowed and broke. She needed to return to the city. And she needed a job.

We gathered in my brother David's lounge room for a family meeting.

I asked quietly, 'What would you *like* to do, Mum?'

She was as ferocious as a caged cat—desperate and frightened and angry.

'I want to be a brain surgeon. What do you think!'

I was twenty-four and way out of my depth.

That night, David, a building designer, resolved to build her a house. Meanwhile, Mum found a job as a live-in carer for an elderly woman with Alzheimer's. Then she worked as a housekeeper for Miss Montgomery, the principal of the exclusive Presbyterian Ladies College. From there, she moved into the school's boarding house as a housemistress.

Seven years after Dad died, my mother and David purchased a handkerchief-sized block of land in inner Melbourne. He designed a natty little house for a single lady.

A young man named Andrew Smythe lived in the worker's cottage next door. He kept pigeons in a coop on the land that my mother and brother had just bought.

I am staring at several photographs of Andrew in old newspaper clippings that I've spread on my kitchen table. In the photos he is twenty-three, with a mop of blond hair that curls down to his shoulders. He has a gappy smile, revealing a missing front tooth. He looks a bit like John Farnham did at the time, in the late eighties, as if he's about to break into 'You're the Voice'.

Andrew and his girlfriend, Paula, used to sit out on their front verandah on a couch. Mum thought she'd better make herself known to them, even though they were 'roughies'. On several occasions, when she visited the block of land, she gave them a friendly wave.

On 1 October 1989, Andrew Smythe vanished.

It turned out that he was an amateur boxer. After a victory in the ring, Andrew had gone to the Fountain Inn Hotel in Crockford Street, Port Melbourne, to celebrate.

Later that night, he rang friends and, according to crime reporter John Silvester, 'expressed fears that a group of men might be looking for him'. He said he'd ring back in ten minutes, and if he didn't, they'd know he was in trouble.

He never rang back.

Andrew's friends checked his house and found that his clothes and dog were missing. His pigeons had been released. Inside the cottage, his waterbed was slashed, pictures were ripped off the wall and furniture was wrecked.

Andrew's Jaguar—his pride and joy—remained parked out the front. His brother Mark told the police that he doubted Andrew would have gone anywhere voluntarily without the car. Officially, Andrew Smythe was now 'a missing person'.

Meanwhile, next door, construction of my mother's new house was under way. David was in his professional element, supervising the process of clearing, levelling and grading the site. The builders were preparing the ground—forming it up, as they say—in readiness for pouring a concrete slab the next day. In the bottom of the excavated area, the concreter laboured in the heat, digging extra trenches for the concrete beams, which would hold the main slab secure in the sandy soil. After a job well done, the weary concreter knocked off. Later that day, a plumber arrived and laid the pipes.

The next morning, my brother got a call from the concreter. Apparently, the plumber had left the place in a mess. The carefully contoured ground was all churned up. Some of the wooden formwork had been kicked over. The concreter refused to continue the job.

My mild-mannered brother confronted the plumber, but he refused to accept any responsibility for making the mess.

David found a new concreter and, two days later, ten cubic metres of concrete sloshed into the foundations.

We all gathered for a glass of champagne to toast the pouring of the slab.

Nine months later my mum moved into her new home. She was as happy as a girl. The house had soft, pale-blue carpets throughout, large Italian tiles in the kitchen and a sun-drenched bedroom with views across parkland. It was modern and cosy. What's more, it was hers. She was in control of her life and her finances. She had a job and interests and friends, and she was studying part-time.

The missing boxer was all but forgotten. Occasionally, one of us might ask about that Andrew guy from next door, but Mum had no further information. New people had moved into his former house and life carried us all forwards.

Then, in August 1991, John Silvester wrote an article in the *Herald Sun* about cases of 'missing persons' that were really 'invisible murders'. Silvester paid particular attention to the case of Andrew Smythe. Anyone with information was urged to call Crime Stoppers. Neighbours speculated about drugs. No one knew anything for certain. Whatever the truth, it sounded as though Smythe had hung out with a pretty unsavoury crowd—and we thought no more about it.

Shortly after this, Detective Sergeant Tony Thatcher became involved in the case. Thatcher had worked in the western suburbs for several years before joining the major crime squad, where he was part of the Walsh Street taskforce investigating the deaths of two policemen. In 1993, he joined the newly formed Missing Persons Squad.

Thatcher is now retired from the force. I track him down through LinkedIn. I call a mobile. 'Is this Detective Sergeant Tony Thatcher?'

An ominous pause.

'Bingo.'

Thatcher agrees to meet me in Marios Café in Fitzroy. He's friendly and good-natured, what my mother calls 'a decent sort of cove'. He says he takes people as he finds them. 'People make mistakes. They do silly things.' He used to be the kind of copper who'd pull you over for drink-driving, but let you walk home and get your car in the morning. Old school.

Yes, he recalls the case vividly. He says that Victoria Police had become aware that every year a dozen or so murders were slipping through the cracks as missing persons. Homicide was not taking these cases on because there was no body. And the cases were too complicated for uniformed police, who had their work cut out for them keeping up with their day-to-day duties. The same was true of the CIB.

As Thatcher explains, these were usually cases where the killers had gone the extra mile to clean up the crime scene and to dispose of the body where it wouldn't be found. Sometimes, to be really smart, they reported the victim missing.

For the new Missing Persons Squad, there was no time to lose. Homicide was not impressed with these wannabes encroaching on their territory. Thatcher and his teammates needed convictions.

Around this time, Mum decided to lay on Christmas drinks for her neighbours. She asked my brother David and his wife, Sue, to come and help. The evening was progressing in a jolly fashion when one of the neighbours, with several glass of Christmas cheer under his belt, told the assembled gathering that the police had been snooping around about that bloke next door. The one who went missing. 'Maybe he's under your house, Jude,' he joked to my mother. Everyone laughed.

Later that night, in the car going home, David and Sue looked at each other. Sue raised an eyebrow. 'Remember all that mess the plumber made? Maybe it wasn't the plumber.'

The idea was too preposterous. Sue had read too many crime novels.

Shortly afterwards, David received a phone call. The friendly voice of Detective Sergeant Thatcher was on the other end of the line. He was calling from the Missing Persons Squad, which had reopened the case of the missing boxer. New information had come to light.

The police suspected that Andrew Smythe had been murdered, and that he was buried under our mother's house.

My brother gulped.

A picture was emerging. Police suspected that Smythe had knocked around his girlfriend, Paula. They believed her brothers had come over to Smythe's house to sort him out. The brothers were tradies, so it was not inconceivable that they would think to bury a body in the excavations for a concrete slab. Police did not know the extent of Paula's involvement. Was she a principal, an accessory or just a witness?

Thatcher told my brother that the CSIRO had been developing a new ground-penetrating radar. They wanted to use it to scan the earth under the house.

David and Sue drove over to tell my mum. Sue stared at the living-room carpet and shuddered. He was down there under their feet. My mother took that part on the chin. It was the idea of digging him up that worried her. Would they destroy her lovely, cosy house?

A week later, the police experts set to work with their gear. There were shadows down there. They could see that the ground had been disturbed. Thatcher gave them the all-clear to dig.

On the day of the excavation, my mother agreed to stay at my house. As my brother watched, they cut a hole in the floor and down through the concrete slab.

'How big is it?' I asked my brother by phone.

'About the size of a grave.'

When my mother returned home, she was satisfied with the excellent job the police had done in setting her house to rights.

Unfortunately they had not found a body.

They found some rusty springs.

In Marios, Tony Thatcher takes up the story. An ex-copper who ran a pub in Torquay had overheard someone bragging that they'd been involved in the murder. The Missing Persons Squad obtained a court warrant authorising them to install telephone intercepts and bugs in the houses of two brothers named David Bumpstead and Stephen McLeod. (McLeod changed his name from Bumpstead by deed poll, making matters a bit confusing). Their family ran a caravan park in Torquay.

Over the next month, officers from the Missing Persons Squad worked around the clock 'listening in' through a scratchy listening-device at the Torquay Police station. Thatcher remembers putting in a forty-eight-hour marathon stint, 'listening to these lunatics carrying on in their lounge room'.

But why would the suspects obligingly discuss the murder almost a decade later—at the very time that police decided to bug their house? 'You nibble away at the outside,' Thatcher explained. 'Nibble, nibble, nibble.'

Apparently, you let it be known through the suspects' networks that the case is being reinvestigated. You get the media involved. You ask the public for help. You offer rewards for information. You stir the suspects up. They get worried, and they start talking.

Even after hours and hours of recordings, Thatcher said, 'There was just not enough evidence to say, "Hooray, hooray! All solved! We can lock them up."'

Thatcher and his team decided to round up the brothers and bring them in for questioning. They arrested them both and the story tumbled out. Steve admitted that he had gone to Andrew's house to confront him about his poor treatment of Paula. This escalated into a scuffle. Steve grabbed the boxer in a headlock and in the struggle that ensued, Steve kept choking and choking until he realised he had gone too far and Andrew was dead. Steve then enlisted the help of his brother to bury the body. According to Steve, his sister was not involved.

Steve was charged with murder and pleaded guilty to manslaughter. There was no trial. His brother pleaded guilty to accessory to manslaughter.

And yes—Steve confessed that he had indeed buried the body on the building site next door. It was under Mum's house.

Details of this development appeared in the newspapers. I took Mum away for the Easter holiday. When we returned on Easter Tuesday, we found that her house had been pelted with eggs. Her bedroom window was splattered with yellow globs of yolk and the crusty slime of egg white.

That night, I rang my brother-in-law, a lawyer, and asked him to apply for a suppression order. We needed to prohibit publication of anything that might identify Mum or her address. And so, in the press reports, my mother became 'the elderly resident' identified only as ZZ, a fact which she found hilarious.

It never once occurred to Mum that a dead body could cause her any harm. She felt desperately sorry for Andrew Smythe, but she wasn't frightened of him.

In the dead of night, she did not lie awake and think of ghosts or hauntings or curses.

In fact, my mother said that if she felt lonely padding about in her house, she would sometimes say, 'Hello, Andrew.'

'It's only the living that are going to cause you any grief,' she said to me.

Life resumed its normal progress for another year. Then one day, the police arrived with a man in handcuffs. It was Steven McLeod. My mother waited upstairs. He pointed out where the body lay. It was not under the house at all, but in the garden. The experts returned with more equipment. They removed the giant tree at the side of my mother's house. No body.

It was in the papers. The body might never be recovered because police could not afford to excavate the entire site. A figure of fifty thousand dollars was bandied about. The Sunday *Herald Sun* report-ed that some senior police were 'concerned the expense would mean further cutbacks in the police crime squads'. The opposition police spokesman, Andre Haermeyer, used the case to attack the govern-ment, declaring that the police force was broke. 'If they were a public company they would be wound up,' he said.

But Mark Smythe, the brother of the boxer, urged the police to find the money. He and his family needed to bury Andrew. To know what happened so they could put their brother, their son, to rest.

Technically, the police didn't need a body. They had a confes-sion. But recovering the body was part of signing off on the case. Tony Thatcher told me they were also interested in the result of the post-mortem, in relation to the cause of death. If there were evidence of stab wounds, for example, it would show that Steve was lying.

Eventually, a date was set for one final excavation. The police had more sophisticated ultrasound technology now, which they were sure could locate the body under the concrete.

This time, my mother remained at home during the search.

It took them very little time to get a reading. There was something under Mum's kitchen. The team moved outside into the little courtyard, and began to tunnel under the slab, underpinning it with concrete blocks so that the floor didn't cave in. All the while, Mum was watching them from her breakfast table, eating boiled eggs on toast. Tony Thatcher stuck his head inside her kitchen.

'Wanna come and have a look?'

She'd rather not.

Tony Thatcher says that he remembers all too clearly what they found.

At the far end of the tunnel was a skeleton wearing runners.

Four years later, my mother was studying for an arts degree at Swinburne University. This was back in the glory days when university was free and education was a self-evident social good. She was pushing seventy. As part of a creative-writing unit, she wrote a murder story about an amateur boxer who went missing in suspicious circumstances. In her story a young professional couple named Diana and Mark were about to build their dream home. 'Architect-designed,' wrote my mother, 'to fit snugly between the two old established houses on either side.'

But ten years later, a detective informed the young couple that a missing boxer had been murdered and was buried under their house.

'It can't be,' cried Diana. 'Do you mean we've lived here for ten years with a dead man?'

In the creative-writing class, each student had to read their story aloud. When it came to my mother's turn, she stood and recounted her ripping yarn about Mick the boxer. He was a man obsessed with becoming a champion. But his girlfriend, Karen, a hairdresser from Werribee, came to realise that Mick was just 'a two-bit fighter with a lot of skite and a nasty streak to boot'.

My mum told the awe-struck class how Mick's brother had come to his aid in the boys' toilets at high school when bullies were about to flush his head down the lavatory. 'Fuck off, you bastards, if anyone's gonna flush this little prick's head down the dunny, it's gonna be me.'

Then Mick was killed—only to turn up a decade later, buried under Diana and Mark's house next door.

When my mother eventually sat down, tucking her neat Fletcher Jones jacket underneath her, the class clapped heartily. She got a High Distinction for her efforts.

What my mother left out, of course, was the fact that the story was true.

16
Next Doors

ONE WEEKEND, my neighbours Suzie and Dave demolished their house. It was a bit impetuous, really, but it was the kind of thing you came to expect when you lived in Collingwood in the eighties. The house was too small. So they took to it with an axe.

In those days, I lived with my partner, Jaems, and our toddler, Jack, in a house in Collingwood. When the back half of next door came down, the effect on us was dazzling. Sunlight poured in from the east and, instead of looking out at a huge brick wall, we now had a magnificent view of a bombsite. But the most significant impact on our household was that Suzie and Dave decided to move. Into our place.

Fortunately, they had exercised some restraint. They left their bedroom standing: one little room to brave the storms. It was a pitiful sight, really, but in the circumstances, a sensible decision. What with dogs and a small child crammed in with us, two more adults in our bed would have been a tight squeeze.

For the most part, their household contents were shipped off to various garages and attics in the outer suburbs. But the rest arrived like Christmas in our house. Suzie and Dave marched into our kitchen with boxes of appliances, wicked items that ecologically sound people were not allowed to own. Electrical things that whipped and diced and chopped. Gadgets that compelled one to make gigantic bowls of coleslaw that remained in the fridge for weeks after the chopping.

Suddenly, we had a drawer full of teaspoons. A CD player arrived. Tea towels, bathmats, oven mitts. The contents of their liquor cabinet.

Decisions had to be made. Could we honestly justify being a two-video household? Did we really need six jars half-filled with lentils? (What *was* the life span of a lentil? We could have been looking at genuine relics from the seventies here.)

But perhaps the most pressing issue was this: could I plug a double adaptor into another double adaptor so that I could operate the toaster, Magimix, juice extractor, electric knife and hairdryer at the same time? I am alive to tell you that the answer was no. But what the heck. Standing there, surveying the benchtops groaning with gadgetry, I knew I was in consumer paradise.

Another significant transformation occurred in the bathroom.

Prior to the arrival of Next Doors, I had a modest collection of girls' things—little bottles and jars and tubes full of make-up, shampoo, moisturisers, cleansers, nail polishes and body lotions. However, with the arrival of Suzie and *her* collection of little bottles and jars and tubes, we were in a position to open up a discount cosmetic outlet.

Jaems decided that this bounty deserved the attention of our friends. He herded a flock of them into the bathroom.

'If you will observe here. This six-inch by six-inch square contains all the toiletry needs of the men. And the rest...' He waved his hand theatrically over the groaning shelves, '...is for Suzie and Hannie. Now here, you will observe, we have an entire shelf devoted to blood absorption. Between them, they are equipped with every conceivable brand and variety available on the market.' He is warming up. 'Dear me. What will I wear today? The panty liners or the mini pads? Which one of the seven packets of tampons will I choose? The pink or the floral? Or perhaps one of these little boxes. So handy to pop into your handbag.'

Très amusing.

Three months later, the household functioned like a glorious, chaotic, all-embracing beast. I marvelled that nothing like an axe murder had taken place. After all, there were four adults and a child sharing one bathroom, one toilet and one living area.

There were other challenges. How could we ascertain the ownership of the many identical pairs of grey underpants in the laundry basket? Jaems took a stand. At dinner, he announced that he had decided to label his underpants. 'I know we're all close,' he said to Dave. 'But there's something about wearing your jocks, or thinking that I might be wearing your jocks, that doesn't really sit with me somehow.'

We and the Next Doors were ideologically (and economically) opposed to employing someone to clean our own house. And, to be frank, I'm still not entirely comfortable with the notion of paying someone to do your dirty work. But we sold out. We employed Voula. And I soon discovered the joys of coming home on Fridays to a beautiful, sweet-smelling, ordered house that had been cleaned by someone else.

The curious thing is that living in similarly close quarters in a student household was never this much fun. It could get a little tense. But then, in those days, we didn't employ Voula. Perhaps the communal living experiments of the sixties and seventies foundered, not because of an innate human drive to couple and live within a nuclear family, but because of the squabbles that resulted when someone forgot to hang up the bathmat.

In any case, by this stage, most of the caring-sharing people with whom I once shared houses were now living selfishly alone or in couples. One former housemate was appalled when she called in for a visit. She took me aside and whispered sympathetically, 'How are you coping? Honestly?' And my honest response was this: how would I cope when my Next Doors moved back next door?

It seemed to me then that the nuclear family was a ludicrous idea—conceived not by nature, nor by God, but by the people who wanted to sell us stuff. People who wanted us to crave their products because we were so lonely or so busy. Our son was growing up in a household where people laughed and talked and argued and shared all the details of their daily lives. At the age of three, he was already part of a public world, developing the capacity to be a happy, sociable creature. He would often initiate conversations with strangers: 'So, what you been doin' today?' One time, I found him crouched down on the street with a group of Vietnamese youths, his arm casually slung across someone's shoulder. 'Do you know I left my Peter Rabbit tape outside last night?' he was telling them. 'But I was lucky. 'Cos guess what? It still works.' I don't think they knew what had hit them.

There was always someone who would read Jack a story, acquiesce to being tied up with string and octopus straps while reading the paper, go and get him a drink and explain why the sky is blue. There was also more than one person who would tell him to shut up, go to bed this minute and quit being a pain in the bum. Of course, the buck stopped with me. I'm his mum. But it wasn't always just me, and that was the great blessing.

'When we're old,' Suzie said to Jack one night, 'will you come and visit us?'

'Yep.'

'Will you and your wife come over for dinner?'

'Yep.'

At this point, David was puking. 'Christ. Poor little bugger. He'll probably be gay.'

'Oh, well,' said Suzie. 'He can come with his boyfriend and their two dogs.'

As we sat there, surveying the building site from our dining room (there was no fence between the two houses), I began to envisage another possibility.

'We could create a beautiful garden, swimming pool and entertainment area on your block and build an upstairs on our place.'

Suzie was so fired up by the idea she couldn't wait to tell the builder. 'Listen, there's been a slight change of plan. Do you think you could just put whatever you were going to do at Number 72 on top of Number 70, instead?' He smiled wanly. It's a tough life, being a builder.

Meanwhile, there was change afoot in the house on the other side of Next Doors. The place was occupied by two Vietnamese families.

But they must have got a bit overcrowded in there because they did a swap with a Vietnamese household on the other side of the street. Jaems saw one of the blokes digging in the garden in that other house, and said, 'Didn't you used to live two doors up from us?'

The man beamed widely and explained that the families had swapped.

'And your landlord didn't mind?'

'Oh, we didn't tell him,' the Vietnamese man laughed. 'He doesn't know any different. We all look the same.'

Yep. That was Collingwood nearly thirty years ago, when the suburb was unfashionable and the houses were cheap.

Suzie and Dave still live in the house they built on their own block, not on top of our house. They are still my friends. We walked across England together, twenty years later—a plan we hatched back then. And even though I now live a few streets away from them, I still call them my Next Doors.

17
Real Class

I AM reading Marx. It is Saturday morning and my husband and I are sitting outside in the sun. MC is eating carrot sticks and reading the bestselling *The Liver Cleansing Diet*. His plan for the new millennium is to love his liver and live longer.

We are in weekend bliss.

And then Dom from across the street arrives with his three little kids. He is very rude about my reading matter.

'*Karl Marx: His Life and Thought*. Jesus wept.'

'Class is back on the agenda, Dom,' I tell him. 'Of course, you guys at the big end of town don't want to draw attention to this.'

Dom thinks ideas about class are stupid and outmoded. This is a culture in which anyone can make it. Life is a skyscraper. The lift is open to all. Dom himself is a case in point. His parents were Italian immigrants. His father was a concreter. Dom got in at ground level—from a high school in the western suburbs—and travelled up to the merchant banker floor. He has an office with a panoramic view, a land cruiser and a holiday house.

'What you refuse to face,' says Dom, 'is that the poor are poor because some people are born with the L-gene—for "Loser".'

'There are people out there who go to the ATM on Friday night and they discover their life savings are four dollars fifty.' I try not to get too worked up. 'Doesn't that bother you?'

'Nope.' He is laughing. 'The difference between you and me is that you don't live in the real world. Most people just want to do the best for themselves and their family.'

He is halfway out the front door. 'I'll see you later. Up the revolution!…See you, kids.' And he's gone.

His wife, Polly, is at Le Nails having a manicure. This was a Christmas present from Dom. He gave her the gift voucher sometime before the Boer War, but Polly hasn't been able to take time out of her busy schedule to drive up to Carlton and squander twenty minutes on getting her nails painted.

Polly calls: she's locked the keys in the car and needs me to bring her the spare set, please. When I arrive at the salon, Polly is sitting with her hands in a bowl, making conversation with the manicurist.

'What shade of nail polish were you thinking of?' the girl asks.

Polly looks at the nails of the ash blonde at the next booth. The woman is having her hands brushed with warm oil while her freshly painted toenails are drying. Cottonwool has been popped delicately between each perfectly tanned toe. The blonde is talking languidly about how hard it is, even at the most exclusive school, to be sure that the teachers appreciate the full potential of her children.

Polly leans across. 'Excuse me,' she says, pointing at the woman's fingernails. 'What colour polish is that?'

The blonde smiles orthodontically. 'Oh, you can't get it *here*,' she drawls. 'It's *Chanel*.' More teeth. 'You can only get it over*seas*.'

Polly is thrilled. As it happens, she is going over*seas* tomorrow. The woman writes down the name of the nail polish colour on a piece of paper and hands it across to Poll. It is called *Ironique*.

Meanwhile, back at home, the children have embarked on a free-market project of their own. They have set up an impromptu garage sale. Many of my possessions are out on the footpath, in front of our house. They are being displayed for sale. As I pull up, the littlest one, Rory, offers me a twenty per cent shareholder discount if I buy them back.

'How do you know what a shareholder is?' I say to Rory. He is four.

'Jack told me.'

'Jack!' I round on my kid. 'Just stick with telling him where babies come from, will you?'

Other kids in the street join in. An assortment of unappealing merchandise begins to accumulate on the footpath in front of our house. There are several broken toys for which Polly's children feel certain that other children will want to pay top dollar. According to the posters the kids are sticking on lampposts, there are CDs and books and much, much more.

The whole operation is coordinated by my son. His system of pricing and bookkeeping is rather elaborate, and inexplicable to all but the Chief Executive Officer himself.

What looks like collectivity and communality is really ruthless marketplace economics. The capitalist class (Jack) is appropriating the fruits of the other kids' labour. Polly and Dom's kids have become the proletariat. (Polly will be very disappointed to learn this. She's spent a lot of money on private school education.)

While the other kids are drumming up custom in the midday sun, Jack has slipped inside the house, where it is cooler, to work on the books. I fear revolution is nigh. The alienated workers are feeling bored and exploited. Lily wants to come inside and have a biscuit.

The entrepreneurial impulse is all well and good, but this acquisitive drive is of some concern to me. And they're not even teenagers yet. When I try to explain this to my brother Peter, he thinks I am being ludicrous. He reminds me that we used to collect bottles for cash. But that was to buy an ice-cream, I protest. These kids are trading for their own Learjet.

MC looks up from the *Saturday Age*. He points to an ad which reads:

OLD COLLEGIANS SINGLES
Singles of all ages who relate to private school life.
20s/30s Only—City drinks
30s+—Evening drinks in Kew
For details and bookings call Libby.

I expect Libby and her friends spent a lot of time finding the exact phrase to express just who they were looking for: people '*who relate to private school life*'.

I've long since given my copy of *Karl Marx* to the Salvos. But at night, there are still sad and lonely people in the streets of Fitzroy. There are more beggars outside Woolworths than ever before.

When I point this out to Polly and Dom, they have a solution.

'Do what we did. Move to the leafy side of the river.'

18

The Golden Mile

I AM alone and forlorn in Wally Groggin's Golden Mile of Used Cars.

Then a presence at my side. Not the great man himself, but another Wally. His name is written on a gold bar pinned to his shirt: *Wally Butler.* Why is it, I wonder, that the used-car business attracts so many Wallies? I momentarily lose the plot. And before I know it, I am staring into Wally Butler's hungry blue eyes: 'I need help.'

Before I set out on this journey of personal discovery, my best friend gave me one piece of advice: do not let on that you know nothing about cars.

Easy for her to say. There we are, Wally and I, staring into the Golden Mile of opportunity. He is making suggestions. There are 'beaut little Pulsars, t'rrific little Corollas, Celicas, Camrys, Camiras' or maybe a 'nice little Laser'. Very sexy. 'Or a Gemini. Now there's a good little car for a person like yerself.' The list goes on and on. It is, in fact, one mile long and all the while I am nodding like an idiot.

I can't tell a Laser from a cream bun. Please, I want to say, I just want a car that works. I'm thirty-two and I've never had a car that works. For the very first time in my life, I would just like to be confident that when I put the key in the ignition, the car—whatever make, size or colour, with or without a twin cam, fuel-injected engine, power steering or two-way sunroof with cruise control—will in fact acquiesce to taking me to my office in the morning. Am I asking for the impossible, Wally?

Instead, I break down. 'Wally, I know nothing about cars.' I've said it. It's out. Wally takes my arm. His voice is gentle and soothing. 'I know.'

In that instant, we both understand that I will be inducted into the Wally Groggin family before the hour is up. I will agree to part with a significant proportion of my income. I will pledge loyalty. I will return in years to come, wanting a trade-in. In return, I will inherit an engine that will turn over from here to the afterlife.

Before I bathed in the light of the Golden Mile, I had been singularly depressed about the prospect of buying a car. I thought, maybe, that I should have a lady's car. One owner. Reliable. Quiet and sensible. I wanted a clean, well-mannered, dull little car that someone else's mother had used for 'doing messages'.

But Wally is an inspiration. I can have anything I want, he tells me. The world's my oyster.

The scales have fallen from my eyes. I want to be hot in winter. I want to be cool in summer. I want something fast. Red. Sexy. I insist on a sound system. I don't want to be *transported* to my office: I want to be blasted there by sixties motown music.

In fact, I want that car right there.

With this new-found resolve, I tell Wally straight out that I want to solicit a second opinion from my friend Mark. I can tell Wally is disappointed. 'Who is this Mark? Is he a mechanic?'

Mark Shirrefs is a children's TV writer.

The next day, I return with Mark. Mercifully, he gives his nod of approval and we enter the inner sanctum. Mark watches on as Wally Butler and I sit facing each other. We are smiling. We make jokes. This is indeed a joyous occasion.

The time has come to talk about the precise proportion of my income that I am about to part with.

As it happens, I am paying in cash. This decision was made at 5 a.m. the preceding day. I was lying in bed, waiting to see if my Jaems would appear in human form. As a filmmaker often out of town, he seems sometimes to be only a figment of my imagination. The only solid proof of his existence are the notes I find on the fridge every so often.

'I am wondering if a small proportion of the sixty dollars I leave in the food jar every Friday may be earmarked for the purchase of a small tube of toothpaste,' a note asked.

Given that this is the only claim he makes on household commodities, it seemed a reasonable request.

'Certainly,' I wrote on the fridge, ever gracious. 'And as it happens I have a small request of my own. You remember the six thousand dollars we put in a bank account somewhere? I am wondering if a large proportion of it (in fact all of it) could be earmarked for the purchase of a small car.'

At four o'clock in the morning, I felt a tap on my shoulder. Jaems was sitting on the side of our bed. 'What do you want me to say?'

'Yes?' I proffered.

So, here I am, face to face with Wally. The money in the bag.

But Wally is not done. He's writing figures on paper and offering me the deal of a lifetime. The car is now miraculously two thousand dollars more than it was yesterday. He draws more figures. He draws a line down the middle, he adds and subtracts things. He starts to sweat. I am feeling decidedly queasy. I say nothing. Wally says, over and over, 'Hannie, what can I do to get your business now? Today? Hannie, what do I have to do?'

He's getting a bit desperate.

'Wally, all you have to do is lower the price.' The answer seems simple.

'What do I have to do?' He's screaming at me now.

Mark stands. 'Thank you,' he says quietly. 'You've done all you can. But, to be frank with you, Wally, it's getting a bit icky in here.'

Icky. I roll the word around on my tongue. Icky, it most certainly is. Mark and I lunge towards the door. We fall into sunlight and I start laughing. We walk briskly away.

But Wally is running. He is yelling my name. Beseeching me to return.

'Hannie, come back. Wally's here. Wally's got a deal you can't refuse.'

I stand still. The man is a maniac. He needs help. He approaches, puffing and panting. 'I've talked to Wally. Everything's okay.'

The penny drops. He means Big Wally. The biggest Wally of them all. Wally Groggin.

Two minutes later, I am sitting across the table again from little Wally. He draws $6000 on his pad. By now he can't speak. He merely turns the paper to face me.

I stare at it, my lips pursed.

'Are we talking on the road, Wally? Six thousand dollars all up, no hidden costs, nothing?'

He nods. A defeated man.

'Sold.'

We shake hands. There is a squelching noise.

I sign forms, hand over a cash cheque and we drive home.

I park outside my house. The neighbours gather to inspect the car. It is shiny and red and fabulous. Michelle, over the road, tells me I've brought down the tone of the street. But generally everyone is in agreement: I've made an excellent choice.

That night we are all celebrating in the backyard when another neighbour bursts in, breathless.

'Don't die, lovey. But someone's just crashed into it.'

A guy was riding along on a Vespa. Three drunks jumped out on the road and waved their arms, for a lark. The rider fell off the Vespa, which skidded along the road, right smash-bang into the side of my shiny red miracle.

Later in the backyard, I muse, 'There must be a moral in this.'

But I am at a loss to know what it is.

19

Billy Crystal and Me

IN THE movie *City Slickers*, Billy Crystal visits his son's classroom to talk about his job. Unfortunately for Billy, he is preceded by a beefy, tow-truck-driving dad. A typical working day sees this guy speeding to the scene of an accident and employing superhuman strength to extricate a woman trapped under a fallen crane. He has the kids on the edge of their seats.

Crystal is next. He sells advertising space on radio stations.

'Oh,' says the teacher effusively. 'You make the commercials that go on radio? (Wow, kids!)'

'No, no, actually, I...er...sell the space.'

Billy Crystal's son hides his head in his hands.

Jack and I are on our way to his primary school. In half an hour I will address twenty-five eight-year-olds on the subject of *My Job*. I tell myself it could have been worse. In another life, I might have had to explain the All Ordinaries.

Jack's father works in television. He has just blown up a car for a TV cop show. How come he isn't doing this? I think of Billy Crystal, and I feel sick.

'Listen,' I say to Jack, after we have cleared up the matter of why I am wearing jeans instead of the red cocktail dress he picked out. 'Listen. I'm not...you know...I may not be...um...Talking in front of...groups...it's not my strong point, you know.'

He is nodding in his wise, eight-year-old way.

'It's okay,' he says. 'I'll still love you if you're a failure.'

When did my son start talking like a kid in an American sitcom?

As we come in sight of the school, Jack is oozing confidence.

He is humming. He is creatively visualising the thundering applause: twenty-five small children standing on their desks yelling for an encore, demanding that playwriting be on the curriculum.

His confidence is unsettling. I haven't slept since I got the gig.

So here I am, standing in front of the class. I am introduced as a *real* writer. I run my finger over my laptop to prove it and the thought occurs to me that I must look like one of those blondes on TV game shows who run their red fingernails along washing machines and microwaves. I withdraw my hand immediately.

I ask them whether they have ever been to the theatre.

'When I was living in Cambridge,' volunteers a boy in the front row, 'I was *in* three plays.'

I stare at this kid. He sounds like Robert Morley.

'Two of them were about Jesus, and the third was about Mary Poppins.'

The child looks set to continue reminiscing about treading the boards in Cambridge for the rest of the period. Mercifully, the teacher leaps in.

'Thank you, Tarquin.'

I hear from several other children. It turns out you can pack a lot into eight years. The things they've done, what they've seen. I wonder if we've been dragging the chain with our kid.

According to my briefing with Jack's teacher, one of the points I am supposed to stress is that writing involves lots of drafts. She wants the children to understand it doesn't have to be perfect on the first go. Even *real* writers scribble and cross out and make blots in the margin. That seems fair enough: after all, Chekhov did not write *The Seagull* in class time.

The teacher has asked me to bring in my manuscript drafts, notes and scribbles, as well as the published versions of my plays. I have also brought in my diaries and notebooks, and I tell the class about the joys of copying down 'interesting things'.

I talk to them about listening to the way people speak, introducing the idea of idiom. What does your dad say when he hits himself with a hammer? We talk about angry voices and sad voices and happy voices.

Three-quarters of an hour has sped by and the kids have hardly wriggled, except for Tarquin, the Cambridge thespian. He has clearly been unimpressed by my exegesis of the dramatic process.

Class is over and my son kisses me goodbye. He isn't exactly swaggering, but then again, he doesn't look the other way when I call his name.

Then I go and do what real writers do. I have a strong coffee on Brunswick Street.

The next day is Saturday. Outside, the weather is wet and cold. We make a fire and drink chicken soup in mugs. We eat toast soldiers and pad around in our ugg boots. As the rain slashes against the window and the fire crackles inside, there it is, the Saturday afternoon activity to make your heart sing. The school project.

Who among us has not experienced a surge of wholesome excitement at doing a grade 3 project? Pick a country, any country. Population, climate, location on the world map, agriculture, rivers and mountain ranges. Major imports and exports.

We have a packet of freshly sharpened Derwent pencils and a new sheet of crisp white cardboard from the newsagent. What more could a heart desire?

There has been some discussion about which country he should do. I want Spain because I am going there in November. He thinks that is expedient and out of the question, especially since he is still smarting from not being invited. His choice: the United States of America.

Typical, I think. What do you want to do that dumb place for?

It turns out that you have to bring food from your chosen country as part of your presentation. He is hoping I'll supply twenty cheeseburgers from McDonald's.

'I will help you make a pumpkin pie,' I offer.

We agree to settle the matter of the food later. I am keen to trace the map and label the fifty states. I am forty years old and I don't know where Minnesota is. I get the baking paper from the bottom draw and lay it carefully across the atlas. 'I'll have a go first,' I say. 'But you have to make your own, okay?'

'Sure,' he says, not looking up from his copy of *TV Hits*.

The baking paper isn't perfect, but it will suffice. Soon enough I am tripping along the Gulf of Mexico with my pencil, humming happily. God, this is satisfying! My friend's mum, who is Austrian, recites the fifty states in alphabetical order to get to sleep at night. I vow to try this.

Meanwhile, my boy is learning about the Spice Girls' Pepsi ad in America. This is additional research.

I've just coloured South Dakota a lovely canary yellow. Against the red of Nebraska and the burnt orange of Wyoming, this is coming up a treat. I think about the breathtaking amount of trivia taking up space in my son's brain.

I pick up the *Children's Britannica* and read aloud. '"The animal life of Alaska includes the caribou, walrus, musk-ox, seal and polar bear." Make a note.'

'Sure, Mum.'

I can tell I've hooked him in now. He wants to go to the shop and buy a Violet Crumble. Oh, why not? Learning shouldn't be punitive. A walk. Fresh air. Good idea.

'Will you drive me?'

What is it with this generation?

So off he stomps, into the rain. 'I just hope I don't get mugged.'

I dip into the books he's borrowed from the library. I read about how the British settlers came to the raw new continent in bold groups, showing nerve, resourcefulness and energy. And how, lucky for them, the Indians were too backward and ignorant to be a grave impediment to colonisation.

I scribble, 'Says who? You white bigot!' in biro in the margin. I resolve to lie if I am accused of defacing a children's library book.

Jack returns from the milk bar.

I make him trace the map. The baking paper is constantly slipping. Texas is sliding back and forth across the lines of latitude. Florida slithers into the Atlantic and Wisconsin completely disappears. He only has thirty-five states. By now, he is gnashing his teeth. Muttering and cursing.

'The teacher said we could photocopy the maps.' He posts each word through a small slot between clenched teeth.

The paper rips. It has been torn by the pressure of the pencil and the futility of life and primitive cartography. Jack scrunches up the paper as hard as his fists can mangle and hurls it across the room.

Fury is crashing on the rocks between us.

I am thinking: You are so content-less, your generation. You're obsessed with surfaces. Presentation is everything.

The phone rings. It is my brother. Since it's too wet for a kick of the footy, maybe we'd like to go to the cinema and see *Romy and Michele's High School Reunion*.

My boy is on his hands and knees. *Pleeeeeaaasssse*. He has never wanted to see a movie more in his whole life. He will trace ten maps of America. He will vacuum his room and remember to close the drawers in his cupboard.

'Pleeeeez. It's all about America!'

I give in. We have two hours before my brother arrives.

I decide to make a beetroot cake.

I admit this is not an immediately appealing concept, so I take care to be clandestine when adding the pureed beetroot.

Eventually, Jack finishes his map—and the cake is ready to eat.

'Yum. Chocolate cake!' He takes a huge bite. 'Yuk. It tastes like dirt.'

This is true. Beetroot tastes like dirt. Interestingly, when you cook it up in a chocolate cake it tastes even more like dirt.

'Why don't you take this to your class for morning tea on Monday?' I offer, hoping to consolidate my newly minted social currency among the grade 3s.

'Why?'

'So all the kids can have a taste of a cake made of beetroot. I mean, that's interesting, isn't it?'

'No,' he says. 'It's just embarrassing.'

My brother and his kids come to the door.

'Come and have some cake,' my boy offers, as they all amble down the hall to the kitchen.

'Beetroot cake?' says my brother. 'Sounds disgusting.'

Then he remembers. 'Hey! How was your mum at school yesterday?'

'Good'.

'What did the other kids think?'

'Good.'

'They thought she was good, did they?'

'Yep.'

My brother's daughter says, 'Don't get any ideas, Dad.'

He promises he has no intention of explaining the economy to grade 3. But if he worked in the theatre, that'd be different.

'Actually,' says Jack, 'I thought Mum should have talked more about her computer. That would have been interesting.'

20
Mrs Lewis

WE HAVE a saying in our house: 'That'll do us, Mrs Lewis'. It puts the finishing touch on any task. When making soup, you add a pinch of salt, taste, add a bit more—then you say, 'That'll do us, Mrs Lewis.' The same applies to whipping cream. Whip it too much, and it gets buttery. You have to know when to stop. When to pull out. That'll do us, Mrs L.

But Mrs Lewis is not only an arbiter of perfection. She can also be summoned when near enough is good enough, like running a quick vac over the carpet before guests show up.

Or when you're helping your elderly mother—as I was yesterday—to park the car.

Picture us in busy Chapel Street in Melbourne. Trams are careering down the middle of the road. I am standing in the gutter, beckoning with my hand as my mother's little face peers anxiously over her shoulder. Somehow, she has to reverse her car into that tight spot between a Volvo and a Vespa. As she contemplates the challenge, she is obstructing an ever-increasing line of cars, which are banking up between Commercial and Toorak roads. Slowly, slowly, she edges backwards.

Bit more.

Bit more.

BIT MORE.

The car is barely moving. A small crowd starts to assemble on the footpath. Come on. Keep it coming. I make a more extravagant hand movement, rolling the air in more preposterous circles. More, more, come on, that's it. She lurches in reverse. My eye darts to the Volvo in front as she sweeps past with a kiss of air, then pitches backwards. *Stop*! I thwack the boot with all my might. She jams on the brake. And she is in. Parked. I affect a cheery little tap on the roof to recover some shred of dignity in the presence of onlookers and say, airily, 'That'll do us, Mrs Lewis.'

It was actually my mother who coined the phrase. When you use it—as you must—think of her, Judy Rayson, mopping her smart checkerboard linoleum in our 1960s kitchen. Once the surface was clean and dry, she would get down on her hands and knees and swirl polish over the black and white squares with one of my dad's old singlets. Next, she would lug the polisher out of the hall cupboard and glide it over the lino like a hovercraft with two twirling lambs-wool pads. The house would smell of wax and a job well done.

Then Mum would wind the cord of the polisher around her arm and survey her gleaming lino with a satisfaction that housewives must never speak of publicly. 'That'll do us, Mrs Lewis.'

Mrs Lewis, for the record, was a real person: an alarmingly white-faced lady with a Tudor hairline who lived in our street. She would wear an extravagant, knee-length fur coat while walking her dogs (two matching pomeranians). Both fur coat and dogs were a shade of burnt orange.

But the Mrs Lewis we invoke is not a person. She is a state of being. She is a time for every purpose under heaven. She is a decision: a state of grace that comes from drawing a line in the sand. Mrs Lewis doesn't brook regret. When something is over, it's over. You could end a relationship with Mrs Lewis. You could turn on your heel and walk away.

My partner Jaems and I had our Mrs Lewis moment, after fourteen years.

Jaems is called Jaems, not because he is Welsh, nor because his parents were wankers, but because he went to a progressive school and was too busy pursuing his own interests to have time for spelling.

Once I asked him, 'What did you actually learn at Preshil?'

'I learned how to be kind and thoughtful.'

As a teenager, he saved up and bought a leather satchel. He set about neatly carving his name into it. He looked down: Jaems?

Always good at problem solving, he resolved to keep the bag and change his name.

After Jaems and I decided enough was enough, Jack lived between two houses for ten years. Jack would often go to Jaems's various film sets after school. He described to me one night the staging of a car accident, which his father was shooting in a suburban street. Jaems was sitting aloft a crane, filming an elaborate tracking shot. The grip was directing two burly blokes as they pushed the crane forwards on its trolley. More. More. Further. Bit more. The grip's hands were rolling the air in circles. Jaems's lens was following the car driven by the stunt man. Then the grip held up both hands and called out, 'That'll do us, Mrs Lewis.' And the trolley stopped.

Our son was astonished.

Grandma Judy, that font of all wisdom and softness, that grandmother who made him walk for miles saying, 'Let's pretend we're Burke and Wills', was being quoted and memorialised by strange men in puffer jackets.

Not so long ago, Joanna, my funny, bossy ex-sister-in-law died after a gruelling ordeal with throat cancer. After an almighty struggle, she drew her own line in the sand. That'll do us, Mrs Lewis.

21
Arthur Boyd

TWENTY-ONE YEARS ago, I lost a baby in Arthur Boyd's studio.

I had an assignment for an art magazine to write about Arthur and Yvonne Boyd's 'gift to the nation'. The gift was Bundanon, a property situated on the south coast of New South Wales.

I flew to Sydney, where I met the photographer Tony Amos. We hired a car to drive the 150 kilometres south to Bundanon to spend the day with the Boyds.

I was fourteen weeks pregnant. No one would have known and I certainly didn't tell. I don't know why I adopted this professional-woman-doing-a-job attitude. It was so un-me.

Two hours out of Sydney, Tony and I were driving down the dirt road through dense bush towards Bundanon, through steady drizzle. The road was slushy and the smell of early morning rain and fresh eucalyptus was intoxicating. A river materialised at the side of the road and we were treated to a sight of creamy white sandbanks. The drizzle cleared and we got out of the car. We stood listening to the dripping forest, and to the birds as they wheeled in the air and called to each other across the water.

'What bird is that?' asked Tony.

'I really don't know much about birds. Sorry.'

Tony shrugged. A moment later, he asked, 'Is that a river she-oak?'

'Um. I really don't know anything about...um...*nature*.'

I didn't know diddly squat about art either. What the hell was I doing here?

We clambered back into the hire car and pressed on. Five minutes later, I spotted three kangaroos boinging across the paddocks into the bush.

'Hey, look!' I shrieked.

'Real ones!' he shrieked back.

We pulled up at the homestead, and Arthur Boyd came out to greet us. He was seventy-three, white-haired and brown-eyed, a kindly, crumpled sort of bloke. Softly spoken, shy, courteous, helpful, vague. It took him at least twenty minutes of pottering about in the kitchen to make coffee.

I assumed that, as a landscape painter, Boyd had always felt an affinity with the bush.

Yvonne chipped in, 'No, no. We're very urban people.' They had both grown up in Melbourne suburbs: he in Murrumbeena and she in the Caulfield/Glenhuntly area. They had also lived in London for more than twenty years.

In fact, in his first encounter with the Australian bush, Boyd found the landscape overwhelming, 'sort of difficult and alien'.

I'd read somewhere that despite happy and productive times in the UK and Italy, Boyd had said that Bundanon was his 'spiritual home'.

With an ironic raising of the eyebrow, Boyd sighed. 'Did I say that?'

Later—having obviously mulled over my comment—he said, 'What do you mean, *spiritual* home? I can't think of what other home one might have.'

Tony asked, 'Do you get annoyed with people asking you about what your work means?'

'No, no, no,' replied Boyd. 'I don't get annoyed. I just wish I was better at telling them.'

After lunch, feeling a bit 'talked out', Arthur took Tony out to the studio to take some photographs. Tony was keen to do a portrait. Arthur obliged by donning his painting gear.

I went off on my own, tramping around in the bush, gathering my thoughts. Arthur warned me to be careful of bulls. I remember feeling ineffably happy.

After about twenty minutes, I peeped through the window of the studio. Arthur was painting. Like a blind man, he was applying paint with both hands. I crept in and sat cross-legged on the floor. The studio smelled of oils and turps and cedar. Tony was setting up his tripod. Boyd was chatting away, while his fingers massaged a landscape from the canvas. It occurred to me that I should be pinching myself. I was sitting at the feet of Arthur Boyd, as he created one of his paintings.

Boyd turned to Tony and pointed at his canvas. 'Would you like a boat? Or what about a goat? An animal gives a bit of meaning.'

Tony was caught off-balance.

'Far be it for me to tell you what to paint,' he said.

'Why not?' said Boyd. 'I've taken orders from a lot lower down than you.'

I think that's when it started. The yawing pain in my gut.

The spotting.

I excused myself to go to the bathroom. Sometimes, this doesn't mean anything. A few spots of blood. Women get that in the early stages of pregnancy, I was fairly sure. But was this still early?

I had a spare T-shirt in my bag. I folded it up and crammed it in my knickers.

We got in the car to go. Arthur and Yvonne hovered like protective parents. 'Have you had enough to eat? Will you promise to stop for coffee to break the drive?'

How could I tell these gentle people that something terrible was happening? That in their beautiful sacred place, my life was unravelling?

Back in Sydney my cousin took me to the hospital and the remains of my baby were cleaned out of my womb. I flew home to Melbourne the next day.

As it turned out, this was the second in what became a series of miscarriages, until I finally gave up. I had one beautiful son.

That would have to be enough.

But at the time, the loss of that baby changed everything. A month or so later, my relationship of fourteen years was over.

Arthur and Yvonne Boyd are both dead now, but I think of them only with a sense of wonder and gratitude.

On the way to my house, I mentioned to the taxidriver that I had just interviewed Arthur Boyd.

'What a great bloke, eh? Only wish there were more like him. I s'pose he sees it as a repayment for having lived in this terrific country.'

Bundanon, the Boyds' gift to the rest of us, has become a retreat for artists and writers. Every now and then, I hear people talking about it. Friends send me euphoric emails about their writing residencies. They report amassing staggering word counts in three weeks. Their novels race ahead. Or I read an article in a magazine. There it is—that name again. Bundanon. The place where I sat at the feet of Arthur Boyd.

The sacred place where I lost a baby.

22
Stepfamilies

JAEMS AND I met in a car park. It was midnight, and I'd just finished a waitressing shift. I was twenty-one. I don't know what he was doing in the car park, but one of the other waitresses drove us back to his house, a renovated stable in Fitzroy. I noticed on the stovetop a casserole that he had made for his dog. He lived alone, having recently broken up with his girlfriend. Before that, he'd had a fling with the writer Helen Garner, which she documented briefly in her novel *Monkey Grip*. This gave him huge status in my eyes.

A short time after that night, Jaems flew to Darwin on a job. He was making a documentary about uranium mining in the top end. He sent a flurry of telegrams to my drama school. At first, Brenda, the school secretary, ran them down to my classes and knocked anxiously on the door. After the eleventh telegram she was blasé. By the seventeenth, she was fed up.

Upon Jaems's return, we quickly became partners. His small, hairy dog Chai formed an attachment to me very early on. She followed me each day to drama school and waited outside the classrooms. I loved wandering about with that little white dog skipping behind. I felt like Gertrude Stein.

A decade later, I fell pregnant. In the weeks leading up to the birth, it was *de rigueur* for new parents to attend classes at the hospital. Jaems asked so many questions, I had to warn him: 'If you don't shut up, we won't be allowed to keep it.'

The following week, he took a job on a nature doco, hundreds of miles away in the scrub. He was camped on his own, waiting for the eggs of a malleefowl to hatch from a pyramidal mound. I remember the producer telling him it could take a hundred days before he captured this miracle on film. Mercifully, the first little hatchling burst through the mound four days before Jaems's own little hatchling was due at the Royal Women's Hospital. Jaems hot-footed it back to Melbourne just in time. I resumed speaking to him.

We separated after fourteen years, when our son was five. He's now twenty-eight, and for the last few years he's cooked a birthday dinner for Jaems and me at his apartment in the city. Just the three of us. No step-parents. No half-brothers or half-sisters. Our son has the old wooden dining table that used to be in our house in Collingwood. He has some large handpainted bowls that once belonged to his dad. This year, he made pasta sauce with black olives and capers (his dad's recipe) and served them in those bowls. To my mind, this is the most perfect pasta sauce. I had not eaten it for twenty-one years, not since we all lived together under the one roof. As the three of us raised our glasses, I felt utterly happy.

Jaems comes from a big family where almost everyone is divorced, but no one is discarded. Birthdays and Christmases expand to embrace the exes and their new partners. When I first joined this family, I thought they were marvellously modern. That said, I suspected the former spouses were bunging it on, pretending they were totally cool about celebrating Christmas as one big happy family.

Looking back, I don't think it matters if they were. Now, I understand that making an effort for the sake of the children, even if they're grown-up, is what matters. I don't believe it benefits children for their parents to stay together doggedly in an unhappy marriage, but *for the sake of the children* you should try to divorce well.

Easy talk.

Post-separation, our son lived between houses, week-about, for the first ten years. In the hours outside school, he moved between the film industry and my world, the theatre. The advantage of being on good terms with your former partner is that you can come clean about being a bad mother.

'Not a single vegetable has passed our son's lips this past week. Could you please make amends?'

Or, 'Where are his frigging singlets? I've bought two dozen since January and there is not a single one in this house!'

When we were separating, some wise soul—maybe it was Jaems's dad—said, 'Sort the money early.' This we did. After that, we divided every expense down the middle. Neither of us ever felt we were paying for the other's lifestyle. No lawyers, no court, no custody. Even stevens.

Easy talk. When there's one child. And you both have jobs.

Eventually, Jaems and I both married other people. Jaems filmed our wedding. Our son went to the birth of his half-brother, Cam, and then his half-sister, Alice.

So as you can see, the whole blended family business was no big deal to me. Then, through my work, I came to know several people whose lives had been turned upside-down by divorce. The steps in the stepfamily, which my lot skipped down so lightly, were hazards for these people. They were stumbling and falling, and no one was noticing.

In contemporary Australia, thirty per cent of all marriages fail. But the really alarming statistic is that, according to the most recent census, your marriage is *twice* as likely to fail if you are on the second. The issue seems to be stepchildren.

Last year I was at a family barbecue watching two nine-year-old girls practising handstands on the grass. I got to talking with their father, who told me that he sees his daughters every second Thursday and alternate weekends. When his wife drops their daughters at his house, she hugs them and says earnestly, 'If you're scared in any way, just ring me, okay? If he starts to touch you in inappropriate ways, you must call me. Even if it's in the middle of the night.'

I thought: you wicked, wicked woman (whoever you are). But there is no point saying that people need to learn how to divorce well. Because they can't. When some perfectly nice people get divorced, an alien invades their body: an ugly and vengeful alien who holds them captive to its every whim. We've all heard stories about the kind of rage and hate that make a man say to his lawyer, 'I don't care how many times I have to fight her in court. I'd rather *you* have the money than she does.'

In one in five Australian families, at least one of the parents has a child or children from a previous relationship. This means that there is an epic Russian novel playing out behind the front door of one in five Australian homes—a tale of passion, jealousy, blame or regret.

My friend Bernadette Wood works in the same building as the guy from the barbecue. She sees him in the lift, passes him in the corridor, but knows nothing of the trauma he is experiencing after hours: the trips to the family court, the lawyers, the hearings, the panic and fear he lives with. Not to mention the persistent aggravation of having to organise his life with a person who is committed to obstructing any kind of schedule he makes. To Bernadette, he is just another guy in a suit.

For a while, I entertained the possibility that Bernadette might be some comfort to him, as she herself is a veteran of internecine stepfamily warfare. But the barbecue man is just starting out. What solace is there in knowing that he could be looking down the barrel of twenty more years of this shit-fight?

This is Bernadette's story. She was on the way to her wedding in Sydney. It was a second marriage, both for her and her husband-to-be, Greg. Alongside her in the bridal car was her three-year-old stepdaughter, their flower girl. She looked up at Bernadette and said sternly, 'You've already broken Mummy's heart once. Please don't do it again.'

Twenty years later, Greg's ex-wife has remarried. But her wounds have not healed. She does not want her daughters to feel affection for their stepmother. Ever. As for Bernadette and Greg, they are still deeply in love. They now have five children. The tsunami of passion that made them leave their respective spouses, move interstate and disrupt the lives of many people has stood the test of time. It is a love story, but not just for the lovers.

Sitting opposite me in a café in Melbourne, Bernadette is tearing up. 'I love my stepdaughters. No one can ever take that away. No matter what their mother does to try and change that or turn them against me, I love them.'

There's your problem in a nutshell. When children are involved, divorce does not spell the end of the parents' relationship. They do not politely excuse themselves from each other's lives. Too often, an unhappy couple is transformed into a toxic ex-couple, who go on tormenting each other for decades.

My friend Jen is sitting opposite me in the Builders Arms. We are sipping salty dogs and talking about the endless rancour between Greg and his first wife.

'Do we ever really question the priority we place on falling in love?' Jen wonders. 'Maybe that's the problem—the idea that we can ditch our current partner because we have a *right* to be with someone who ticks more of our boxes.'

I sigh. I fell in love with my husband and within a week I knew he was *the one*. But he came along five years after I had separated from my son's dad. We were both free. Unencumbered. Lucky. Had he introduced himself to me on the Town Hall steps five years earlier, it would have been messy. Messy = Strife. Messy + Children = Nightmare.

Would I give him up because I thought it might ruin my son's life? No. Never. Why not? I hear you asking. The answer is simple: love makes you an optimist. If divorce makes demons of us, love elevates us to the side of the angels. Love makes you certain, or at least adamant, that you and your beloved will defy all odds. You *will* make it work. At least, that's how it was for me.

'When you first fell in love with Greg,' I ask Bernadette, 'did you ever think, "I have two children, he has two children, this is not a good idea"?'

'No. Never.'

I am confronted by the realisation that when it comes to

stepfamilies, love may not conquer all. You can't make your step-children love you. What's more, you can't keep on loving a child who steadfastly refuses to love you back. That way lies disappointment, grief, anger and murderous thoughts. In truth, it's not easy to love someone whom you may not even like.

'I wanted my various step-parents to like me,' my friend Margaret told me. 'But they didn't.' Her father married four times. 'It was a litany of disaster,' she said. 'They don't want to like you. Sometimes the new wife competes with you, or sees the "other woman" in you, or treats you like a spy from an opposing settlement.'

Perhaps love is too much to ask for. Perhaps the key to being a successful step-parent is simply to get on with the kids. To enjoy their company. Love may come. But it's not essential.

MC, who has been a stepdad for sixteen years now, offers this weird analogy: being a step-parent is like being an emergency teacher. You don't need to be responsible for the kids' education. They have their regular teacher for that. You just have to ensure that everyone is safe and has a good time while you're filling in.

This is not as off-the-wall as it sounds. I remember how often Michael would say, 'I am not Jack's dad. He *has* a dad. I'm just another adult who loves him.'

It is a strange dance the stepfather must learn to perform. Understandably, if you put in the effort, you hope to be loved for it. Otherwise, you are merely an onlooker in the relationship the children have with their mother, which is what many stepfathers report. After all, the stepfather is the newcomer to the household. In a traditional nuclear family, the relationship between the parents has a kind of authority over the children, simply because the parents have been part of the team for longer. But a stepfather does not have 'founding member' status. He is an interloper in a world where the child feels as though he and his mother are the original (and therefore more entitled) inhabitants. This is true for stepmothers, too.

It's no secret that one of the bitterest causes of conflict is the payment of child support by the absent parent—usually the father. I am reminded of that line in the movie *Kenny* when he is giving advice on getting married: 'Cut out the middle man; find someone you hate and buy them a house.'

Bernadette told me, 'My husband felt he was lining the pockets of two people he despised. Not only did he lose his wife and kids, but he had to pay for someone else to reap the pleasures of having a happy family life. I get that.'

The logistics of children living between households also adds to the stress of life in a stepfamily. Clothes, toys, school projects and other possessions are spread between two houses. Busy parents hurrying to get to work can find it hard to suppress their frustration when a little voice wails from the back seat, 'I left my bathers at the other house and we've got swimming this morning.'

Or, 'I'm not going to school because I haven't got any socks at this stupid dumb house.'

But these complex arrangements can have an upside. Living between two houses can make children more adaptable, more socially competent. Some also enjoy the feeling of being part of a mob. (Some hate it, of course.)

The origin of the word stepfamily is revealing. It derives from the Old English *steop*, a term used to describe a widowed parent who had remarried. The word *stepbairn* was synonymous with orphan. Historically, it was death that caused people to remarry. Today, most people remarry because of divorce. And divorce itself is a kind of death—the death of love.

Family therapist Irene Gerrard has written a study of what she calls 'disenfranchised grief in stepfamilies'. Stepfamilies, she writes, are 'born of loss'. She explains:

> The loss experienced after separation is often expressed as anger, whereas the loss experienced after the death of a spouse is usually expressed as grief. However the complex feelings emanating from both divorce and death have their source in loss.

My friend Loren has a recurring dream: 'I'm sitting in the dark in the cinema. My dad has just made a film. The credits roll and my stepmother's name comes up, then my half-brothers' and -sisters' names. But my mum and me, we're left off. We're not thanked. We're not acknowledged. My dad has just moved on.'

Many people I know who have lived through their parents' divorce and navigated stepfamilies express a fierce determination to stick at their own marriage through thick and thin.

'You get one shot at falling in love cleanly,' my friend Margaret explains. 'If you want another crack at it, there has to be some form of devastation or loss. You wreck stuff. You wreck other people.'

As we go about the business of normalising separation and repartnering, dissolving and forming new family groupings, there is an expectation that we will all soldier on—business as usual.

But it's not business as usual. Not when grief and resentment, revenge and loneliness become partners in family life.

I cannot say why Jaems and I survived with our friendship intact. We don't see each other very often, except for family parties, birthdays and farewells, to which the Grants invite me with unfailing kindness. When we separated, a psychologist I was seeing at the time said, 'You have to find a way to *emotionally separate*: cut the ties.' Even in the midst of misery and bewilderment, I believed that to be wrong.

At a family barbecue at Jaems's house recently, I asked him if it was okay to include in this book that he'd had a little fling with Helen Garner.

'It wasn't little.'

'Okay, your great big affair with Helen Garner? Can I put that in?'

Standing there in his barbecue apron, he burst out laughing.

Inside the house, his wife and his kids were there, with his father and stepmother. My family were also there, so were MC and his mother.

If you had to make the choice to *emotionally separate* or be friends for life, I know which one I'd rather make.

23
Staging a Wedding

EVEN AS a young girl, I didn't dream of becoming a bride. I dreamed that I would be a glamorous secretary in a navy-blue suit with my own apartment. When I was older, I thought people only got married because they were frightened of change. Shoring up the known against the unknown. Better the devil you know. That sort of thing. Staying married—year after year after year—sounded like purgatory or cowardice. As one journalist pointed out to me the week before my wedding, there was not one happy marriage in my entire body of work.

Then I met Michael Cathcart and within a week I wanted to be married to him. 'Forever' became a radical and optimistic adventure.

So there I was, walking into a bridal shop. The shop assistants referred to me in the third person. 'When is the bride's happy day?' It was six weeks away. The shop assistants were scandalised. Apparently it took at least twelve months to take up a hem.

I asked to try on a dress. The price tag was $3900.

'I don't suppose you have anything under a thousand dollars?'

The saleswoman smiled. 'You'll be wanting our budget range.' She pointed to a rack of dresses that looked like rejects from the Playbox costume department.

'Then again,' she said, fingering the pearls on the $4000 dress, 'this is a very special day in a girl's life. And you only get married once.'

A week later, I tried another establishment. The saleswoman said, 'You look like a woman in love.' I warmed to her instantly. I wanted to spend money in her shop.

We found our wedding celebrant in the phone book. Driving to her house to meet her and sign the Notice of Intended Marriage, I said to MC, 'If she's that big fat woman in the loud pink suit, I can't go through with it.' MC agreed. We'd both seen the Barbara Cartland of civil celebrants at other people's weddings. You know her—the kind of person who has a Desiderata poster in her toilet.

In fact, our celebrant turned out to be perfect. She gave us a Wedding Pack, which contained everything we needed to know, and we fixed the date.

With a week to go, everything was in order: the frock, the hair, the shoes, the perfectly timed leg wax. (The beauty regime had been nothing if not gruelling.) Now MC and I were engaged in the most difficult writing assignment of our lives: we were composing the words for 'the solemnisation of matrimony'. The celebrant was on our backs. She needed our vows by 9 a.m. the following day, so that she could get them printed.

MC was quite specific. 'There are two things I don't want,' he said.

'First, I don't want people to bang on about what a struggle it's going to be.' That's what other people said at their weddings: they acknowledged that married life would be an uphill battle. In the years that lay ahead, there would be almost unendurable suffering, and the only way through was to put your shoulder to the wheel and grit your teeth. Curiously, some couples want this to be made very clear on the happy day.

His second condition concerned the ever-popular Kahlil Gibran. No wedding, it seemed, was complete without a reading from his book of poetry *The Prophet*. MC was particularly allergic to the stuff about allowing 'spaces in your togetherness'.

'You should stand together, but not too near,' says the Prophet. 'For the pillars of the temple stand apart.' So too do the strings of the lute, he says, though they 'quiver with the same music'. If there was any quivering, MC said, he wanted to be close to the source.

We were in our study, at separate desks. Our computer screens were glowering under the pressure as we each tried to come up with the perfect set of vows. My prose was on a par with 'I've been to paradise, but I've never been to me'. Clearly, the muse had gone out for a beer. I gritted my teeth and tried again. Unfortunately, I now seemed to be going through a Barry Manilow phase.

The Wedding Pack contained examples of what other couples had said in their vows. 'X, will you take Y to be your wife and lifelong partner? Will you make the daily effort to relate to her?' People—apparently—were keen to promise 'to communicate openly and honestly', 'to grow as individuals' and 'to boost each other's self-esteem'.

Time was running out. If we didn't come up with something soon, I was going to have to stand before my friends and promise to help MC reach his full potential as a unique individual. I might need to say, 'This time called life was meant to be shared', or, 'I've walked many paths and met many different people. They were all beautiful if I took the time to allow their beauty to flow.'

MC's printer lurched into action. He was waving sheets of paper in the air, triumphantly.

Eleven-year-old Jack traipsed in from school with two friends, pushbikes squeaking and scraping down the hallway; school bags were flung into rooms. The small people were *starving*. The phone rang. Amid the chaos, MC read aloud the lines he had written. I was buttering Boston buns and pouring glasses of orange juice.

MC's version of our vows was lyrical and elegant. We were moving forwards. I rang the celebrant. She was a tower of strength. She told us not to panic. We had all night.

Jaems rang. He volunteered to give me away. MC alerted him to the baton-change connotations of that image. We all agreed: great idea, unfortunate lapse in taste. I saw in small print that the groom could be given away, too. Call me old-fashioned, but the thought of the groom being given away by his mum was deeply irksome.

We dispensed with the giving away. Instead Jack would be 'the bride's best man'. That would give him a role in an event that, we knew, was not entirely to his liking.

We also decided that we would like a mother's blessing. But we had to be careful. We had too many acts.

'This is not so much a wedding as a family eisteddfod,' MC said, when I tried to find a little something for my brother to say.

The best man, MC's brother, Jim, agreed. He was having a beer at our house perusing *Wedding Ceremony: Draft Three*. 'This is shaping up to be like a Friends of the Earth benefit concert,' he said.

Nonetheless, we persevered with the mothers. We scribbled and scrunched and paced and drank.

'Your mother has more lines than my mother,' said MC.

We added, we rewrote, read and discarded until finally we acknowledged we had written something utterly magnificent. We poured ourselves large glasses of wine and basked in the sheer scale of our combined talent.

At half past ten, I couldn't wait any longer. I rang my mother and read aloud her bit over the phone.

'Over my dead body,' she barked. 'I wouldn't say that flowery, poncy rubbish if you paid me.'

She volunteered to write her own script.

My mother's rewrite arrived on the fax in the morning. It was good. We decided to run with it.

Now all that remained was to wait for opening night. And pray that the actors, especially the leads playing the bride and groom, could deliver the lines. With feeling.

At 9 a.m. on the Big Day, the groom and I courted disaster by swimming together in the sea at the Sorrento back beach. 'Swimming' is perhaps a bit of an overstatement. I was keen not to get my hands wet in case my nails came off.

We had decided to learn our lines off by heart. This involved taking every opportunity to practise. It was like being pregnant and reminding myself to do pelvic floor exercises while waiting at the traffic lights.

MC shouted at me in the surf. 'With this ring I thee wed.'

I shouted back, 'I will rear this wing.'

I began to see the folly in this plan. I did not want to succumb to hysterics during the ceremony and I certainly did not want to cry.

My friend Hilary had been adamant. 'When you're twenty and you cry at your wedding, it's sweet. When you're forty, you'll just get puffy and it'll be embarrassing.'

MC and I did a little practice of the bridal waltz on the sand, slapping at March flies, and then I slipped away to undergo the final stages in the gruelling beautification regime.

Reading back over my diaries I realise now that we instinctively conceived of our wedding as a piece of theatre. MC, who has directed a lot of theatre, was preoccupied with the space, as theatre directors are. Months earlier, we had stood together outside the tearooms on the foreshore at Sorrento.

'You should arrive by boat,' he said, 'at dusk. Sail around the point and then walk down the jetty as though walking down the aisle. And we'll have a cappella singers and their voices will drift across the glassy water as you make your way towards us. We will wait for you here, on the verandah of the tearooms. And then the warm February sun will sink gently into the sea.'

And that is how it happened.

The bride and her son set sail from nearby Point King, with our friend Kate Baillieu at the tiller of her beautiful couta boat, which was adorned with a white ribbon. As it turned out, this was also the day of the annual Sorrento to Portsea swim. As the bridal boat rounded the point, five hundred swimmers dived off the Sorrento pier accompanied by a flotilla of bobbing craft, there to cheer on the swimmers. As we sailed through this choppy swell of thrashing arms and bobbing heads, I sat in my bride's dress and sandshoes wrapped in glad wrap. Kate at the tiller called out to people on the other boats—'I'm taking her to the church'—and they honked their horns and waved.

I so badly didn't want to wave.

'Wave,' hissed my little boy. 'Smile and wave.'

So I did. After a while, it was easy.

Just before coming into view of our party on the beach, Jack unwound the plastic wrap and I stood up at the prow, feeling disturbingly like the Moomba Queen.

As I glided across the water towards the waiting throng, the RAAF Roulettes roared into view. The six aircraft zoomed and dived and pirouetted in the sky overhead.

When all this was just a plan, I had imagined 'the arrival scene' with an actress playing the part. Cate Blanchett, perhaps, or Emma Thompson would sail around the point. She would walk down the jetty. And waiting there at the altar would be Colin Firth—with his best man, Orlando Bloom.

But it was I who climbed up to that jetty—to the same spot where the British actress Joan Plowright had sat alongside the Australian actor John Hargreaves and delivered the opening speech of the film *Hotel Sorrento*.

Jack and I walked down this aisle on a perfect February afternoon at dusk. The girls sang. And MC was waiting at the far end with our families and friends.

And if you ask either of us, 'What has been the best day of your life, so far?' we will both say: 28 February 1998.

24
Seville

HERE WE are in the south of Spain, heading for Seville. This is a city with a reputation for sex and danger—the city that inspired *Carmen*, *Don Giovanni*, *The Barber of Seville* and *Don Juan*. The perfect setting for a urinary tract infection.

'*Qui non ha visto Sevilla non ha visto maravilla.*' 'He who has not seen Seville has not seen a marvel.' MC and I are on a fast train, hurtling south from Madrid. We are travelling at speeds faster than an aeroplane, sitting in luxurious seats with little fold-out tables. There are women, like flight attendants, who take your tickets and hand out headphones.

Outside, the country is arid. Olive trees march across sandy hillsides as dry-looking as the Mallee. According to *Let's Go*, the budget guide to Spain, Seville is notorious as '*la sartenilla de España*' ('the frying pan of Spain').

I need to go to the toilet. This is the second time in an hour.

'The Arabs arrived in this region in 711 AD and stayed on for eight hundred years.' MC is not listening. He has fallen asleep. I muse about the way couples travel, how we often assume the other to be the source of all information. So you hear people say to their spouse, 'Is that the chapel of the royal Bohemian martyr St Ludmilla, over there?', or, 'Would you say the basilica predates that Romanesque church we saw yesterday?'

To which the only reasonable response would be, 'How the fuck would I know?'

When I used to travel with an ex-boyfriend, we developed a shorthand to deal with questions of this nature. He would simply answer, 'Forty-one per cent' to any question I asked. But MC is pretty good at this stuff. He's the kind of person who would clean up on *Who Wants to Be a Millionaire*.

Down the far end of the carriage, a couple of boys are loitering near the luggage racks. I keep my eye on our backpacks. They are stuffed with saggy shorts and T-shirts, cameras, velvet soap and suntan cream. MC and I are discovering how alike we are: we have both brought stretchy clotheslines we've strung up in youth hostels and pensions, from Galway to Jerusalem, over twenty years of travelling.

I lie back and gaze at this tender sleeping person. I am so happy I could skip.

MC has been floating the idea of staying in a youth hostel. His argument is that when you travel overseas you expect to 'meet people'.

'We've been away two weeks and we haven't met anyone,' he says. 'You don't meet people in hotel foyers.'

'Maybe people don't like the look of us.'

I ruminate on this as the scenery rushes past: a school, a village clustered around a church, a man herding goats up the side of a hill. These give way to vast olive plantations spread like a gigantic net across the countryside.

MC is awake now, reading out the description of the Seville Youth hostel.

'The problem, my darling,' I say, 'is that the people you meet in youth hostels are nineteen, which is not a bad thing in itself. Except that you and I are forty.'

'So?'

'So,' I say, 'remember when you were nineteen in a youth hostel? Did you want to meet forty-year-old couples? No, you did not. You wanted to meet nineteen-year-old Swedish girls. Let's face it, forty-year-old couples in youth hostels are creepy.'

I win. We'll try a pension which boasts 'Guests socialise up on the terrace'.

We ring from the payphone at the railway station, juggling the coins and the guidebook, which lists accommodation and telephone numbers. In addition, the Spanish phrasebook has to be held aloft, open on the 'Useful Phrases When Checking into Your Hotel' page. I am concerned about the possible lack of a 'water particular' (private toilet).

I am so relieved to have been understood I can only be cavalier about the torrent of words at the other end. I take it to mean 'Yes, yes, come on over. Private toilet, the works! Everything is marvellous. The view from your room is breathtaking. And we'll have the gin and tonics waiting for you.'

I hang up and reassure the other member of this party that negotiations have exceeded all expectation. 'HOSTAL GOOD SLEEP', here we come.

In the narrow streets, the air is hot and ancient. We find our place in an alley jammed with hostels. 'Welcome we spik English' the sign proclaims—a highly exaggerated claim, if ever there was one.

The owner directs us up a winding marble staircase to the third floor. There are plastic flowers in the hallway and cheap paintings of bullfights. Our room is cool and white, with a little wrought-iron balcony filled with ferns and geraniums.

In the plaza nearby, we find a table at a restaurant, under the orange trees. We choose from the blackboard menu propped up against a tree: white garlic soup garnished with peeled grapes, gazpacho with Catalan country bread, grilled sardines and mountains of *ensalada*. We talk expansively and throw back *tinto de verano* (chilled red wine blended with bitter lemon) in *tubos* (long glasses). Then we wander back to the coolness of our *hotel pensión*, close the shutters and make love under the swish of the ceiling fan. Afterwards, we sleep wrapped in deep ancient dreams, to wake again at dusk.

At night, we wander through the puzzle of narrow streets and alleys. The locals shout, children squeal. Taxis toot and rumble down the cobbles. Tourists stare in bewilderment at their maps. We overhear snatches of conversation in all the languages of Europe. Walking past the back of restaurants, we hear the jangle of crockery being washed.

And everywhere the throb of Vespas, powered by youthful sexuality. This is intensified by a flagrant disregard for safety. Beautiful long-limbed girls wrap themself around their men as they roar through the streets, helmet-less, hair flying.

The night air is cool on my bare skin; the stone of the buildings is warm on my back. We hold hands.

On our fourth day in Seville, I have mentally packed up our house in Fitzroy and moved into an apartment in the old maritime *barrio de Triana*. In fact, I have moved my whole family here. There's my mother, picking over fruit in the market, arguing with fishmongers. We have all become fluent Spanish speakers as we ride around on Vespas with our hair streaming behind us, our limbs smooth and brown.

And that's when I face it. The urinary thing. Day Four.

There is a strange knowledge about these things. A hint that something is not quite right, which develops steadily into unease, which slides into certainty. Yes, something is up. Something is definitely up. After a day of denial and exertion of willpower (*there is nothing wrong with me, I'm only imagining it*) the time has come to concede that I will need to see a doctor.

MC goes downstairs to the English spikker at reception.

'Where is doctor?' he asks.

'Doctah?'

'*Médico!*' he clarifies.

'Ah—*médico*. Why you say doctah? Not doctah! Doctorrr!'

We go to the hospital. I give my name and age. I hold one hand up and flash it four times. She writes down twenty. MC, who is good at the numbers, reminds me that I need to use two hands. Naturally, I am thrilled that the receptionist did not bat an eyelid. I point out my mistake. She shrugs. What does she care?

We wait in a waiting room on hard white plastic seats, watching two orderlies in white boilersuits lounging in the corridor, chain-smoking.

Eventually, I am called by a man in white pyjamas—'Arrnie?'

—and we push through a blue door with a round hole, like the entrance to a restaurant kitchen. MC stays in the waiting room. Four doctors sit facing me, hands folded on the table. This is like doing a French oral exam in HSC, except the nightmare element is that you are not sure in which language you are being tested. Spanish? French? German? English?

'English,' I say enthusiastically, but unfortunately no one speaks it. A fat Arab doctor is assigned as my translator. My major concern is to communicate that I am allergic to penicillin. If at all possible, I would rather not die in the name of clearing up a minor infection.

I hold up my notebook in which I have copied stuff from the dictionary.

'*Tengo una infección in me orina.*' (There was no way I was going to do *pee pee wiss wiss* acting.) Then I listed a range of synonyms which might mean 'burning'. We rejected *incendiar*, which I think means burning as in bushfire, and *ardiente* (burning ardour). 'Too much *ardiente* got you into trouble in the first place,' says MC.

I am ushered into a cubicle. The Arab appears with a big needle. He says 'Sit! Lie!' I am submissive. I sit. I lie down. But just as I am about to raise a small objection to the big needle—Why do I need an injection? What is he giving me?—there is a cry from next door.

The Arab disappears. He takes the needle. Two orderlies burst into my room. They begin peeling on plastic gloves. *Christ, they're going to give me an internal examination. Both of them!* I start to sweat. They rush out again. I lie perfectly still, straining to listen. There is whimpering. I sit up and creep over to the curtain. I want to go home. I want MC in here. I peer into the next cubicle.

Lying there in the bed is a beautiful, dark-eyed, dark-haired man, about thirty-five years old, who has slashed both his wrists. He is staring in a kind of wild calm at the ceiling, as two pads stream with blood and gushing water into a bucket on either side of his bed. I avert my eyes, but it is too late. The shock has bolted through my body.

I retreat to my cubicle. I sit meekly on the edge of my bed. The

Arab returns. 'Sorry,' he says mildly. He lifts my dress and feels my tummy. He takes another needle. This time, I can see the sealed plastic case. He takes a blood sample. The nurse gives me a bottle for the urine sample. This is how it's supposed to be. I am sent to wait in the waiting room. Half an hour for the *resultados*.

Back in the waiting room, MC tells me he has seen the whole thing: the mad sweep of the taxi to the entrance, the man dragged from the back seat, the trail of blood and the wife—the haunted, stoic wife.

We watch her. She is fortyish. She makes some phone calls. She smokes. She paces. What is it about this woman? This hardness that has closed in a tight fist around her? She is young and suburban and ancient. She has seen it all before: suicide, pain, trauma, suffering, poverty. She is helpless and unimpassioned.

Finally, they wheel him out, in a wheelchair with a drip. Both arms are bandaged in big white wads up to his elbows. The black matted hair and wild brown eyes make him look strikingly like a Christ figure in a seventeenth-century painting, *Jesus de las Penas*, or the famous Juan de Mesa sculpture featuring the marks of torture on the body of Christ.

I tell MC I can't go into any more galleries or churches. I have taken to dreaming about those two—the husband and wife. I see the bleeding wrists and the contempt of the orderlies as they spit after him in disgust: sinner, deviant, scum.

I feel the cold fingers of Spanish darkness and I shiver in the blistering heat.

25
Bangkok

MY FRIEND Susan has a brother, Jim, who travels regularly for business.

On one such trip, Jim arrived in Bangkok, feeling achy and sore after a long flight and the fourteen-hour days he'd spent crumpled over his computer in preparation for this business meeting.

Jim decided to have a massage. He found a shop, in a back street near the hotel, that advertised massages for two hundred baht, considerably cheaper than what was on offer at the hotel. So he went in, and a pretty, young Thai woman ushered him up two flights of stairs and into a small cubicle. She indicated that he should take off his clothes and lie on the bed, face down.

Jim looked around. It looked clean. Aboveboard. He did as the young woman instructed.

After a few minutes, a very short, ugly and elderly woman entered the room. Without speaking, she got to work. She slapped warm oil across Jim's back and shoulders and began to knead.

Her hands were strong and commanding. Jim felt the tension ooze from his body like a slow leak. His muscles, cramped and stiff, began to loosen with each roll of her thumb and the ball of her hand. The creaks and knots of middle age that were pinching into his back, neck and shoulders started to release. He felt his strength flowing back. His skin was warming and returning to its old suppleness. He felt it become brown and sun-kissed. He was lying on the sand after being pounded by the ocean. He felt warm and happy.

The masseuse tapped his bottom. He was stretched out on the beach at Lorne. He felt himself being shaken gently. His arse was wobbling. Where was he? Bangkok. The cubicle. She was indicating for him to turn over.

Jim turned onto his back. He had a massively hard cock.

Before he had time to feel confused and embarrassed, the masseuse put her hand on his thigh and barked.

'You want wank?'

Jim had heard about these services. These 'specials'. He was far from home. Who would know? It would only be a wank after all. Not sex. Not breaking any real trust between him and Ginny, his wife. She wouldn't care anyway. He was pretty sure.

Fuck it. Why not?

'Sure,' he said to the woman. 'Why not?'

He closed his eyes.

'Okay,' said the masseuse. 'I leave you. Five minutes.'

And with that, she pulled the curtain back and left.

26
Blood Ties

'SO, HOW was Madrid?'

Polly has perfected the act of listening attentively, but I can tell when she's counting. Polly is an obsessive counter. She counts her teeth with the tip of her tongue. She counts the palings on picket fences, the tiles in the bathroom. She admits it. She can't help herself. She's always been like that.

'The matador stabbed the bull and the crowd rose up like...' I follow her gaze. 'How many slats are there, Poll? On my wooden venetians?'

'Sixty-four,' she says. 'Sorry. I *was* listening.'

Polly and I have been friends since uni, and our comrade in arms is Freya. She's lurking in the doorway, enveloped in smoke. Whenever she comes over, she takes up the same position at my back door, one foot in and one foot out of every conversation. So it is with smokers: they hover on the periphery, committed only to the luxurious inhalation of blue air.

My first mistake is to seek their advice. A few days ago, Michael noticed that we were badly in arrears in the dinner-party stakes. To my delight he went on a rampage of largesse. He has bestowed dinner invitations upon nearly everyone we know. An obscene number of people have accepted.

Michael is already planning what he'll cook. Something simple. He is more your Margaret Fulton man than, say, your *Vogue Living* type. He's a man who enjoys a nice chop.

Now, this is just the sort of challenge Polly adores: the large dinner party. The moment I mention it, she starts counting and making mental lists. Her eyes light up and her tongue taps happily at her teeth. She is planning a menu, working out a seating plan, packing her station wagon with things I will need to borrow from her house.

Freya, on the other hand, finds our interest in entertaining to be embarrassingly conventional. Where Poll and I will spend a Saturday afternoon making apricot chutney, Freya will go to a festival of Taiwanese experimental cinema. Her major criticism of Polly is that she has two sets of cutlery. She calls her Mrs Thurston Howell III.

On the rare occasions that Freya talks about food, it's in terms of proteins, anti-oxidants, fats and cholesterols. She is also obsessed with toxins. Avoiding them. Purging them. Having them banned from processed foods. Yet she has survived all these years on a diet of Doritos and cigarettes.

And then there's the gender politics of this whole arrangement.

'How come Michael isn't doing the cooking?' Freya demands. She is beginning to construct him as some kind of Wilbur Post, out there in his study talking to a horse.

'He is!' My eyes blaze. 'He is planning a barbecue.'

Polly is quietly alarmed. 'You mean like a sausage sizzle?'

My second mistake is that I commit to Polly's ludicrous menu. Before long, she has spread my cookbooks on the table and has drawn up a series of lists. Michael is responsible only for making a green salad and getting ice. I will be making salmon rolls in shark's fin vinaigrette and a ginger zabaglione with poached guavas.

Freya is scandalised. She is smoking with her mouth open. I am edgy. My friends are running my husband's dinner party. Polly is already *exhausted*. I find myself apologising for putting her to all this trouble.

She rings me the next morning to arrange a meeting at an Asian supermarket during her lunch break. She can only spare fifteen minutes. This is a big favour. I get confused. I comply. When I emerge from the shop, I am carrying a load of exotic foodstuff.

When you have two hundred grams of superior shark's fin (wet) in your string bag, there's no turning back.

I apologise to Michael. For twenty-five years I've been out-manoeuvred by my well-meaning friend and I still haven't developed a strategy to fight back.

Then again, I am a little keen to try out the shark's fin.

So there we are, Michael and I, chopping and dicing the night before the big event. That's when I make my third mistake. And this is a significant one. It's getting late. We decide—sensibly, we think— to nip up the road and grab some Indian takeaway.

Unfortunately, the refrigeration unit at the Indian takeaway has broken down. We learn this later because the resultant bout of food poisoning is so bad I feel compelled to report it to the Health Department. When they send their people to investigate, that's what they find.

By 9 a.m. on the day of our dinner party, I have been vomiting liquid curry for twelve hours.

'We have to cancel,' says Michael.

'We can't,' I bleat. I am thinking about the Japanese radish and the enoki mushrooms languishing in the fridge. 'We just can't.'

The plan, valiantly hatched, is that I will remain in bed and Michael will soldier on. He will cook, he will serve, he will pour drinks, make small talk and generally be witty and attentive and marvellous.

By seven-thirty, the Javanese fish in banana-leaf packets is ready to be barbecued. The chicken phanaeng is in the wok. The calamari are stuffed and baking. The guests are tucking into our homemade crab sui mai and fresh Vietnamese spring rolls. I am propped on a chair, made up like a drag queen. It seems inappropriate to fess up that I have been sick.

'So glad you could come over to eat. I've had such shocking diarrhoea, you wouldn't read about it.'

So I just sit. Every now and again, I go to check on the children: Jack and Maudie, his friend from school. This is the first time Maudie has been allowed to stay overnight. They are holed up in the lounge room, gorging on free-range telly and potato chips.

At nine o'clock, I have to go to bed. I excuse myself and slither away. Maudie and Jack are dancing to the Spice Girls, bouncing on the mattresses they've laid on the lounge room floor. They are *ooh–aahhing* into their hairbrush microphones.

It does occur to me that our guests might think it a tad strange that the hostess is going to bed an hour after the food has been served. Maybe they think I have a little alcohol problem. Frankly, I'm too sick to care. I take off all my clothes and slip between the cool sheets.

Half an hour later, Jack is shaking my shoulder. 'Mummy. Mum. Michael says to wake you up. *Maudie's got blood coming out between her legs.*'

I leap up. 'What?'

I pull on a T-shirt and some trackie pants, and slip across into the lounge room. There is Maudie. Sobbing. Michael is sitting next to her on the mattress rubbing her back, making gentle, consoling noises. He looks up at me and mouths the words 'Help! Help!'

Someone else's daughter has got her period for the first time at our house. There are twenty people outside laughing and drinking and arguing.

Maudie thinks she's got blood clots. Michael feels he should try to make this a cause for celebration, but he has never set eyes on this little girl before this evening. She has a mum of her own, who isn't here. Maudie is sobbing. Michael is working overtime, slipping, sinking.

'No, it's a beautiful thing. It means you've become a woman.'

He is waving, not drowning. Maudie is clutching the sleeve of his shirt.

Eleven-year-old Jack is always good in a crisis. He has brought the tampons from the bathroom cupboard. Michael didn't think they were the thing. They had also found some sticky pads.

Jack tells me later, 'I didn't know whether the sticky part goes on your bottom or your knickers.'

Ever helpful, Jack explains to Maudie that her egg has just cracked inside her. This is not exactly a source of comfort for Maudie. The thought of things cracking is a bit much. Tears dribble down her face.

There they are: my open-hearted son and my kind and gentle husband. This little girl is being inducted into the mysteries of womanhood by two fine men. Nonetheless, I feel it's time to take over. This is women's business, after all.

I am buoyed by the nobility of the sentiment. It gives me the strength to repress the urge to start vomiting again. I move over and claim my place next to Maudie.

Unfortunately, no matter how many times I've read about the biology of menstruation, when called upon to explain it, I am suddenly a little hazy on the details. I can't really remember. Exactly. Fortunately, Michael can cobble together a reasonable explanation.

But, honestly, it's not biology this girl wants. It's her mother. 'Let's ring your mum, eh?'

Maudie considers. 'She'll be asleep. And there isn't anything she can do, is there? I'll be okay.'

I lie with her on the mattress on the floor. Eventually, she goes to sleep.

I crawl back into my own bed. I can hear balloons of raucous laughter coming from outside. At 3 a.m., Michael crawls in next to me.

'I think we sort of pulled it off,' he says.

For some reason, we are both euphoric.

27
The Good Citizen

I HAD a penfriend in grade 5. She lived in Chicago and she signed her letters in big loopy writing, 'from Your Penpal'. She had white teeth, a blonde ponytail and large ears. She kept a pet rabbit and she went on about that rabbit, ad nauseam.

I, on the other hand, went to the library to find *interesting facts* about Australia. I wrote about the population, the importance of sheep, the variability of our rainfall, the height of the tallest mountain, and our parliamentary system. Dead interesting. She wrote back with more details about the rabbit.

My brother agreed she was a moron, despite the news she'd just been elected class president.

'That's America,' said my dad. 'Morons get to be president.'

My teacher told us this was a way of becoming citizens of the world: sign up for penfriends. Tell them about our country and you will learn about theirs. Clearly, the president of the Rabbit Club had been briefed differently.

As a parent, you want your children to develop notions of citizenship. At its simplest level, this involves acting with respect for others and concern for the environment. My own child was nine and burning with moral ire about many of the big issues: price hikes at the tuckshop, people who smoke in his vicinity, mandatory attendance at Phys. Ed. and being forced to sit next to a boy in class who farts.

Justice, freedom of choice, fair trading, the rights of the individual. As I recall, these were the topics we wrote essays about when we were in school, but were never encouraged to translate into our own experience. We most certainly didn't imagine we had a right to complain.

Jack didn't get the memo. We are walking down the street behind a man who lights a cigarette and throws the empty packet over his shoulder.

Jack says, 'Did you see that? That's littering.' He picks up the packet and says, 'Tell him he's a litterbug.'

I have no intention of doing any such thing.

Jack says, 'Go on. If you won't, I will. That's disgusting.'

I shove the cigarette packet in my pocket. 'The most important thing is that you and I put our rubbish in the bin.'

My son is dogged. 'But if someone doesn't tell him, he'll keep doing it.'

Part of the pleasure, I imagine, for a nine-year-old in this situation is that sensation of power that comes with occupying the high moral ground. Especially when adults are the wrongdoers.

My problem is that I can't think of what to say. 'It's not our place to tell other people what to do'? 'He might turn around and slug me'? Or should I have hurried after him, tapped him on the shoulder and said, 'Excuse me, but I think you inadvertently dropped your empty cigarette packet over your left shoulder'?

In the end I opt for that indispensable parental defence tactic: deflection. 'Chill out. You're beginning to sound like Fred Nile.'

Citizenship is also about participation in the democratic process. At my son's primary school, they had a Junior School Council, and every grade elected a representative. My boy was dead keen. The whole idea was awesome, especially given the possibility that meetings might be scheduled during Phys. Ed. classes. Jack was opting for politics in a big way.

The first challenge was to compose a policy speech.

This involved him sitting at the dining-room table, pen poised, while his mother paced up and down, dictating.

'Are you sure other kids get their parents to help?'

'Sure, sure.' Jack waved a nonchalant hand. 'Anyhow, even real politicians have speechwriters. Daddy told me.'

Which was a fair point.

So there I am, cranking up the rhetoric. *A vote for me is a vote for progress. I stand before you as a person of integrity.* The oratorical flow faltered a little; I had to stop to spell every second word, as he copied furiously.

Pumping him for his own ideas, in the way that liberal humanist mothers do when they are trying to make the dinner, I got him to volunteer an angle.

'Maybe I should say "I will listen to the ideas and concerns of the people of my grade".'

'Excellent!'

Then a terrible thought occurred to him. I could see it forming on his brow.

He might actually have to do this.

He was thoughtful for a moment. 'Do you think they'll remember I said I'd do it?'

I wanted to explain to him that the way politics works is that you get in first with wild promises and deal with the fallout later. But I opted for integrity.

'They'll remember.'

His solution was quite simple. He would set a time limit. 'I will listen to the ideas and concerns of the people of 4M for five minutes at lunchtime.' Honest, but not exactly persuasive.

The day came to deliver the speech. He'd secured the spot as final speaker because he'd figured that was the way to make a lasting impression. 'They'll have forgotten the kids who had to go first!'

On the way to school that morning, he said, 'You don't think I'll sound like a ponce, do you?'

I was heartened. I like a bit of self-doubt. Great faith, great doubt—therein lies wisdom. But not politics, I suspect.

Back at home I sat at my desk, staring out the window, unable to concentrate. Like a parent in an American sitcom, I was asking myself earnestly how I was going to cope if he lost. But not only that. He had practised his speech on the phone to every friend and family member, and they were ringing me anxiously. Has he done his gig yet? Did he get in?

Three-thirty came and I tried to act casual in the playground.

'Well?'

'Well what?'

'How d'you go?'

'Oh, that. I got to be emergency. Can we stop at the milk bar?'

Later, when I asked him if he was disappointed he said, 'Nah. Tran only got in 'cos he's a suck.'

Another test of moral fibre came when I was dragooned into participating in the forty-hour famine, the annual fundraiser run by World Vision. I could hardly eat in front of my boy if he was fasting for a worthy cause. But I wasn't truly committed. By the day of the famine, I'd raised less than ten dollars. Jack, on the other hand, had managed to extort $218 from captive shopkeepers and other children's parents.

He was so keen. He couldn't wait to stop eating food and stock up on barley sugar. But at the twenty-hour mark it was another story. He and his friend were pale, headachy and had lost the plot entirely.

'Food. Give us food. We're only kids. Please. Mum. Food,' they whimpered and wailed alternately. Ever the creative problem solver, Jack suggested, 'Couldn't we just have time-out? Have something to eat now and then start fasting again after?'

The two of them ate a family-sized pizza. They ate and they ate and they didn't speak until it was gone. I was sworn to secrecy.

Several days later, I saw the report his friend had written for the school newspaper on the World Vision famine. It read, 'When it was twenty hours, Jack (grade 4) ate. But that isn't too bad he is only nine.'

'So, you fessed up?' I said. He shook his head. He hadn't written the article. He'd been outed. I noted privately that there had been no admission from the author that she had eaten the other half of the pizza. But from the humanitarian tone of her report, she was clearly prepared to forgive weakness in others.

(It would be sheer hypocrisy not to admit at this point that I caved in too. Just a little snack at midnight, which rapidly got out of control. A tip for would-be fasters next year: don't even think about having a little glass of wine.)

When I enquired about what had been the best part of being a citizen of the world, my son had no hesitation.

'I liked raising the money.'

28
Making a Splash

'WHAT DO fathers talk about, do you think, when they get together?' I ask a group of ten-year-old boys.

A sandy-haired boy puts up his hand.

'Fathers talk about the cost of Persian rugs, and how you can pay too much.'

'What about mothers? What do they talk about?'

'They talk about how dreadful other people's children are.'

I love these kids. 'My dad is an energy ifishant archetect,' writes one boy. 'He drives a Michibishy and reads novels on the toilet.'

Apparently, when it comes to fathers, this is their most irritating habit. One girl volunteers that her dad reads books *and drinks coffee* on the toilet.

This is met with howls of 'Yuckk!'

I am at the North Fitzroy Primary School, taking writing classes with grades 5 and 6. This material will become the basis of a play, which we will perform over two big nights at the Fitzroy Town Hall.

Some years earlier, I had lunch with the comedian Campbell McComas, an old Scotch College boy. He confided to me that performing in the end-of-year play was one of the most joyous and profound experiences of his schoolboy days. He wanted other boys to have this opportunity, so he was embarking on a project to raise a million dollars to build a theatre at the Old School.

I was impressed. I understand the truly transformative potential of the theatre. But McComas's Old School is an exclusive place of privilege. I remember walking home from lunch thinking, 'There must be a way to do that for kids at the *local* school.'

So this is what we did.

MC is the director of the play, I am the writer and Jack has a big role. (Not too big, just appropriately big for a person of his immense talent and family connections.)

The play tells the story of the battle to save the Fitzroy Pool. Four years earlier, in 1994, Fitzroy was amalgamated with two neighbouring municipalities (Richmond and Collingwood). At the same time, the state government sacked the elected councillors and replaced them with three appointees—the commissioners. These commissioners announced that they had decided to sell the Fitzroy Pool on the grounds that there was another pool in Collingwood and that, since we were all now one city, this constituted a 'duplication'. Since both pools were always packed to capacity throughout the summer, a furore erupted. The pool users of Fitzroy embarked on a battle of astonishing vigour and intensity. The nine-week campaign became a major news story and ended in victory for the people. The pool was reopened and the poverty of economic rationalism was laid bare.

The children themselves were central to the campaign. On one memorable day, they marched to the pool and tied yellow ribbons to the cyclone fence.

Those who know the pool, made famous by Helen Garner's novel *Monkey Grip,* will remember that the wall at the deep end is emblazoned with a warning in misspelt Italian: Aqua Profonda.

So this is the name of our school play: *Aqua Profonda.* A heroic musical in which the sons and daughters of Fitzroy march on City Hall and change the course of history.

Apart from the challenge of writing a piece of political theatre for ten-year-old children, the other bracing reality is that there are one hundred and twenty of them.

As you might imagine, not all one hundred and twenty of these small children are keen on the idea of performing. However, in the tradition of nurturing each and every child's unique creativity, they are forced to join in. But theatre is a magical business.

There are three truths I want *Aqua Profonda* to communicate to the children. Firstly, I want them to see that the stuff of their own lives is valid material for art. So bombarded are these children by an imported TV culture, it is easy for them to grow up thinking that drama only occurs in Springfield or South Park.

Secondly, in a world where the winners are swinging from the chandeliers of profit and the losers are trudging along backstreets in growing numbers, we all need to be reminded that there are other questions to be asked beyond 'What's in it for me?'

Ten is a good age to start getting your head around what it means to be a citizen. A few months earlier I heard Chris Scott, the school principal, bawling someone out on the phone in her office. All the children were working on projects about Reconciliation. But some parent wasn't impressed.

'Don't tell me I'm being *political!*' Chris Scott was saying. 'I am teaching children about what is *right!*' I knew then that I had my boy at a marvellous school.

Thirdly, I wanted the children to experience the sense of intimacy and trust which develops in rehearsal, and to taste the intensity and thrill of performance.

One of the tricks of managing an all-singing, all-dancing cast of a hundred and twenty children is to adopt the maxim *Many grown-ups make light work*. A parent army must be enlisted. Mums come after work to black out the town-hall windows. Dads and step-mothers operate the follow-spots. Dad's girlfriend makes the props. Mum's girlfriend is in the stage crew. (Unconventional family arrangements are *de rigueur* in Fitzroy.)

My friend Amanda Smith, a former ballet dancer, choreographs 'The Flipper Dance'. (This is the show stopper.) A talented father puts together the band—Neil Kelly and his Aquatic Orchestra. Another father, theatrical agent Bob Burton, produces the whole event.

One of the grand things about being at primary school—unless you are prematurely cool—is that it's fabulous having your mum or dad doing stuff at the school. It is even okay having a stepfather on tap, as long as he doesn't prove to be a major embarrassment. That is the risk my boy has to take.

The media response is staggering. Admittedly, we have one of Melbourne's best known publicists, Miranda Brown, on the case. (She's another parent.) A week before the show goes up, I phone her to say we should call a halt to the publicity appearances. (We have just taken sixteen children to the ABC radio studios, where they sang immediately after the 7 a.m. news. Prime time exposure.)

'This is the first time a client has ever asked me to stop getting them media coverage,' Miranda tells me. Maybe it is a failure of nerve on my part.

'It's the grade 5 and 6 play,' I mumble. 'We don't want to get things out of proportion, here.'

On opening night, people are hanging from the rafters of the Fitzroy Town Hall. And unlike so much professional theatre, where a sort of ennui descends with the dimming of the houselights, this is an occasion where the roof is lifting with glorious anticipation.

'It's not enough that it's good for their self-esteem,' Michael says to me. 'What a namby-pamby educational philosophy that is! They have to do things and feel things that they never believed possible.'

'You are more marvellous than I ever dreamed you could be,' he tells them in his director's pep talk. Then the lights dim, the orchestra strikes up the overture and the children burst onto the stage.

'We are the Children of Fitzroy,' they sing. 'The sons and daughters of Fitzroy. The length and breadth of Brunswick Street, you heard the sounds of children's feet. We made a noise. We girls and boys. We saved the pool. Aqua Profonda. We saved the pool!'

And they are marvellous.

More marvellous than we ever dreamed they could be.

29
Car Rage

THIS MORNING, as I came out my front door, I saw a note tucked under the windscreen wiper of my car.

> LEARN TO PARK
> ARSEHOLE

Admittedly, the wheels of my Subaru were not strictly within the lines painted on the road. This is annoying, granted. But they weren't really *outside* the lines either. Percentage-wise, *most* of the car sat within the boundaries of the parking bay. You could still park in the space next to me—if you were driving a thin, socially responsible car. Of course, if you were driving an oversized car, like an SUV, then suck it up, arsehole.

You see how this inappropriate aggression causes retaliatory hostility?

Moreover, I think 'arsehole' is a truly horrible word. This is one instance where I think we should adopt the American term. 'Asshole' is eminently preferable. It suggests mulishness—obstinacy or stupidity—rather than somebody's anus.

How much better it would have been if I'd come out this morning and found a note that said,

> LEARN TO PARK
> YOU SILLY DONKEY

I am meeting MC for a quick lunch in our favourite Vietnamese phở shop in Richmond. I have disposed of the offensive note and am in the car, pulled up at the traffic lights in Brunswick Street. In my rear-vision mirror I see a woman behind me in a white station wagon, consumed with rage.

I begin to feel irritated with her for being so irritated with me, because she has a horrible little mouth and it is turned down in a dramatic thin arc painted with a mean stripe of coral-coloured lipstick, and I think, You've made your mouth look like that. You've moulded it into that fingernail moon shape over decades of tenacious malcontent. Okay, I forgot to flick my blinker. So what? This is a small misdemeanour, lady, in a world where people are wilfully blowing up other people because of irreconcilable religious differences.

Do you know anything, you miserable old biddy, about what's going on in the world?

I can hear the hatred in the sneering of her engine.

I'm afraid people like you—nasty, small-minded coral-coloured, suburban naysayers—need to be taught a lesson. I am now going to drive slowly in front of you for several kilometres in this single-lane road because you deserve to have your expectation of dissatisfaction renewed.

Honestly.

Yesterday I was in my car and a woman in a creepy black Mercedes Benz wound down her window and mouthed obscenities at me for some transgression—the actual nature of which I'm not entirely sure. Suffice to say, she was very put out indeed. I watched with a kind of grotesque fascination as decades of resentment and class hatred welled up inside her and she threw her hands in the air and then beat the steering wheel. But on that occasion, I was overcome by a profound sense of human charity. I thought, How awful to be so rich. Probably stuck in a loveless marriage. To a philandering stockbroker called Kenneth. Having to live in one of those mock-Georgian houses in Albany Road with manicured lawns and preposterous topiary. And doing all that valiant work to raise money for the Red Cross. Having to eat luncheon rather than lunch.

In my heart, I reached out to her. I felt awash with compassion. I smiled and gave her a friendly wave and drove on.

Today my heart is hardened.

MC and I have our delicious bowl of phở—chicken and tofu.

On the way home, he wants to dash into the discount chemist, so I park across the road, turn off the ignition and promptly fall into a deep sleep.

I awake with a gasp to a loud and insistent rapping on the window near my head.

A ginger-moustached man is looming over me.

I wind down the window. Despite my disorientation, I know instinctively that this man represents menace.

I start the car.

'No you don't,' he says. 'I have to ask you a few questions. Why are you asleep in a No Standing zone?'

It's two o'clock in the afternoon. I don't know why I'm asleep. Why are your eyebrows a lighter shade of ginger than your moustache? Some things are a mystery.

To be frank, I am a little shocked that I should have fallen into such a torpor. Perhaps I've been working too hard.

Do parking officers work hard? You don't think of them in the normal sense of the word, *working*. You think of them doing something a bit furtive and shameful—for money. You think of personalities that are blighted by a deep contradiction: conformist yet antisocial. My sense is that all people who work in the punitive industries probably share this quality.

My sister-in-law kicked one once. In the shin. He took the matter to the cops and reported her for assault. Some weeks later, she took an envelope crammed with fifty-dollar notes down to the police station. That was the end of it. I know you don't believe me, but it's true.

It was in a fancy suburb, too.

One of my fellow writers, Andrew Knight, says that when he was a kid, his family never went on outings because his father was convinced you could never find a park. Another writer, Matt Cameron, says his mother could not do a right-hand turn, so they could only go places that involved turning left.

You can tell a lot about a person by their attitude to parking. Mine is simple. When asked, 'Where are we going to park?' my response, even in the CBD, is 'Out the front.' Where else?

When my husband drives, he begins to look for a spot about ten kilometres from his destination. When it comes to parking, he is a glass-half-empty person. More accurately, he is a glass-without-water person: a man without hope. This predisposes him to the more environmentally sustainable option: he walks. And with that, he claws back a modicum of moral superiority.

I, by contrast, am a true believer in parking destiny. I set off to the theatre wearing my party frock. Let's say it's the Princess Theatre in Spring Street. It is dark and rainy. In my mind's eye I visualise the line of parked cars curving around towards the Parliament. I see myself approaching and then up ahead, *voilà!* Someone's indicator light flicks on and he or she pulls out, just in time for me to slip in. Thank you very much. A quick dash across the road and I'm in the foyer. *Grazie mille!* No need for a brolly. *Muchas gracias!*

I am prepared to concede that this method is not one-hundred-per-cent foolproof. There have been times when creative visualisation has failed me. When, despite my best efforts to pre-ordain success, parked cars remain stubbornly and selfishly stationary. On these occasions, I am forced to drive around and around, aimless and unblessed. But curiously, this never shakes my faith.

This is what it must be like to believe in God. The other God, not the parking one.

*

Some years ago, I decided to do some serious research into traffic infringement. As luck would have it, I shared a house with an Italian woman who worked in Aged Services. She managed to pull some strings and get me into the parking and dog-catching department of our local council.

So it was that one afternoon I found myself alone in a carpeted room with a filing cabinet. I am not sure if I had permission, as such, to open the filing cabinet, but these were the days before local government became an efficient streamlined machine. These were the days when waste management, for example, was run by garbos: blokes in shorts and beanies called Stretch and Waxy.

Today, our local councils employ front-line professionals in the waste and resource recovery industry. And when they're not collecting our bins, they go to conferences. This year, there's one in Italy: the Sardinia Waste Management and Landfill Symposium. They also hand out prizes through their peak body, the Waste Management Association of Australia. The winner of the 2013 Landfill and Transfer Stations Award was Dial-A-Dump Industries.

Anyway, back in the bad old days before local councils amalgamated and reformed, before they became customer-focused organisations that strive for best practice and build collaborative partnerships to achieve effective infrastructure, sustainable growth and leadership, a person such as myself could sit cross-legged on the floor and read letters that people wrote to get out of parking fines.

I read a filing cabinet's worth of these letters: missives sent in the belief that the universe is a benign place and goodness and kindness will prevail. I found them touching.

Mostly, the letters were prosaic. While the authors were reaching for the heights of Greek tragedy, they usually landed somewhere in Victorian melodrama. In Greek tragedy, the protagonist—usually a man of importance and outstanding personal qualities—crashes to disaster due to the intervention of fate. In melodrama, the good-but-not-very-bright hero is duped by a scheming villain, played in this instance by the parking officer.

There was a lot of split-second misadventure. Drivers returning to their parked car, sixty seconds after the meter expired, held up by circumstances beyond reasonable human control. A lot of grandmothers were terminally ill. Or their deaths had recently occurred. These incidents were linked in various but complex ways to the necessity to park illegally.

The human impulse to gild the lily was often in evidence. I felt a powerful urge to edit. To remove excessive sentences. To caution the supplicant: unnecessary detail leads the reader to think—perhaps unfairly—that you are engaging in a little jiggery-pokery. Telling porkies.

In the course of my life, I have written three letters seeking absolution from parking fines. Only on one occasion did I get a stay of execution, and that was when I parked outside the Royal Melbourne Hospital when I thought I was having a heart attack. I decided it would be very sad to die driving around, looking for a park.

When I wrote my letter, I included a report from the emergency department on hospital letterhead. It was very persuasive. The City of Melbourne parking authority extended its mercy and no one said, 'Well, aren't you a drama queen and a hypochondriac?'

The other two occasions? I was a student. I was poor. They were cries for help.

I think I should be appointed Traffic Appeals Officer for this city. I would be unfailing in my duty to read all submissions and let everyone off. Even the stupid. Even people who don't know the difference between *your* and *you're*.

Everybody deserves a little bit of good fortune. A lucky shot, once in a while. A bit of human warmth in the chill wind of the city.

The man with the ginger moustache delivered a much-deserved lecture on the consequences of my action: falling asleep in a No Parking zone warrants a $140 fine. On the spot.

But then he rose up on the balls of his feet (he was short) and, to demonstrate what a sterling chap he was, he reached deep into his heart…and—JUST THIS ONCE—he let me drive away, free as a bird.

Off I zoomed, down Smith Street. It was only when I pulled up outside our house that I realised I'd forgotten something at the discount chemist.

Poor MC.

30
Pigeons

MC AND I are in a Japanese restaurant in Fitzroy. There is a toddler called Sebastian at every table eating sushi. I hear one preschooler telling the waitress in a piping BBC voice, 'I'd like quail, please.' His mother hastens to explain he's mixing up his cuisines.

This is when I make the decision that we need to venture out beyond the sushi zone. My idea is that we drive 360 kilometres up the Calder Highway to Sea Lake, population nine hundred.

My fifteen-year-old looks it up on the net. 'It's got a grain silo and a railway line. Sounds great, Mum. You sure the weekend's going to be long enough?'

I have decided that teenagers need coercing. Left to his own devices, your average Fitzroy teenager is a highly urbanised creature. So when I come up with the marvellous idea that we might attend an international pigeon race in Sea Lake, the spirit of adventure is not fully evident at first.

But I am not to be dissuaded. Armed with my copy of the Australian Pigeon Fanciers Association newsletter, I am on a mission.

By way of explanation, this is research for my play *Inheritance*. My main character, Lyle Delaney, is a pigeon man. And there is much to be learned about what makes your average pigeon fancier tick.

We arrive at Sea Lake on a dark and rainy night. The publican shows us out the back to our rooms. We go down a dark linoleumed corridor with a naked bulb hanging perilously at one end.

'Just your basic pub accommodation,' he says.

We pass the gents' showers and the toilets. In our room, the fireplace has been boarded up by a piece of cardboard and the brown blind hangs at an angle across the window. My husband sits down warily on the edge of the bed.

'My character would have cleaned this room,' I say cheerily.

'Didn't do a very good job.'

In truth, it's like a cross between shearers' quarters and Pentridge Prison.

My son inspects the blankets on the bed in his room. There are big wet spots from a leak in the ceiling.

'Was this the only hotel?'

'It's character building,' says my husband unconvincingly.

I sense the onset of a profound malaise, *en famille*.

'Let's eat,' I suggest.

The dining room is aflutter with pigeon fanciers who've come from all over Australia. There are even men from Taiwan and Thailand. This is the Mallee Classic.

As 'the flyers' tuck into their dinner, their pigeons—all 454 of them—are huddled in baskets on the back of a truck heading five hundred kilometres north to Cobar in western New South Wales. At seven-thirty tomorrow morning, someone will open the back of the truck and release them. If all goes to plan, they will circle overhead until they get their bearings and then they will wing their way home through rain and wind and adversity. Back to their loft at the footy ground here in Sea Lake. There is an $8000 prize for the bird that makes it home first.

My husband gets talking to Gwen, who is wearing a navy-blue blazer bedecked with pigeon badges. She explains that this is a one-loft race. The flyers have entered their birds up to a year ago. A chap by the name of Barry Trewin has fed them and trained them for the sole purpose of competing in the Classic.

I find myself talking to Frank. He's a retired house painter from Queensland. He tells me that when you look a pigeon in the eye, you can see her soul. Frank is one of the most versatile flyers in Australia. He can win from all distances. His secret: a bird will come home if she knows she's loved. And his bird, Little Red, has got champion written all over her.

'How would you describe your average pigeon fancier?' I ask Gwen.

'Mad!' she chortles. 'We're all mad!'

'What you're looking for in a bird is the same thing you're looking for in a sheila,' according to Frank. 'You don't want the town tramp. You want someone you can be proud of, take home to your mum. The bird has to be proud, standing tall, bright-eyed and shiny as a new two bob.'

'You can't describe the feeling when you see a bird circling around up there and then it comes down, just to be with you,' says Jerry, a bricklayer from Shepparton.

On Sunday morning, the rain sets in. The birds are due back at lunchtime. We all make our way to a barbecue under shelter at the footy ground. The blokes seem to go in for the flannelette-shirt-and-beanie look. There are not too many women, despite the rhetoric that this is a sport for all the family.

A fierce cold wind has driven us all inside the clubrooms, where a big fire is roaring. We tuck into towers of white bread, sausages and tomato sauce. There are tubs of supermarket salads that nobody eats and plenty of beer.

'Where do you reckon they are?' asks my son.

'Little Red's so far out in front,' says Frank, 'he's had to turn back to egg the others on.'

My son and I venture outside to look up at the sky. There are only clouds, no dots.

The afternoon limps by. We wander up and down the main street. It is empty. Yawning with desolation.

By five o'clock, not a single bird has made it back. Pigeon racing, it must be said, involves a great deal of waiting. Waiting, waiting and talking about pigeons. The topic is inexhaustible.

My husband now feels he has acquired all the pigeon information he needs to live a full and rich life. Darkness is approaching and rain is sheeting down. The homing instinct is upon us. We can't wait any longer to witness Little Red's triumph.

We set out across the car park.

'Hey, precious!' Frank calls out. 'Gissa kiss for luck.'

On the way home, after four hours in the car, existential despair settles in.

'We went all that way and we didn't see a pigeon,' says Jack. 'Little Red probably got eaten by a hawk.'

We drive on in silence. I get an idea.

'What about if we go for Japanese when we get home?'

Everyone brightens considerably.

A week later, I ring Barry to get the results. On Monday at 10 a.m., three pigeons were seen in the sky. Little Red wasn't among them. The first bird to clock in was an entrant from Thailand. The Thais got third place as well. Second place went to a Melbourne pigeon.

And at this stage, Little Red still hasn't come home. Perhaps he broke away from the flock and flew north. Perhaps he went looking for Frank, because, after all, they return to where they're loved.

31

Jack Goes to Paris

MY SON whispers, 'Be brave, Mum. Be *brave*.' Minutes later, he's laughing and waving, and then he's gone. The big steel doors at Tullamarine close and I find myself sobbing in the arms of my ex-partner.

My son is fourteen years old and he's gone to Paris.

We drive back down the Tullamarine Freeway together, Jaems and I. We talk about the price of houses in Carlton. I am fighting back the urge to make him swing the car around and retrieve our boy. To prise open the steel doors.

'Sorry, everyone. We've made a ridiculous mistake.'

From Paris, Jack will take a train to Granville in Normandy. He'll be living with a French family for three months and will attend the local school. The family have two children, a rabbit and a cat. From his bedroom window, he'll be able to see the English Channel. 'We will roast chestnuts from our tree,' writes his French mother. She is the only one who speaks English. *Un peu*. With the aid of a phrasebook.

My son is travelling as part of a program organised by the Southern Cross Cultural Exchange, now in its eighteenth year. In 2001, the nine-thousandth student will go overseas with this organisation.

So I am the nine-thousandth mother to lie in bed and stare at the ceiling, imagining her son crying silently into his pillow. Lonely, homesick, scared. (Missing his mother.) The phone rings. It is 2 a.m.

'I'm here, Mum. I'm in Paris!' He is trilling with excitement. 'It's *really* awesome. I've just seen the Eiffel Tower.'

My heart leaps.

*

In Melbourne, my son lives between two houses. He has four parents. Together, we form his personal politburo. Where other children just have to manage two adult personalities in their nuclear family, our child has to go before a committee. Interestingly, there is rarely division between households. When it comes to decision-making, the differences occur along gender lines. Usually, the father and the stepfather line up against the mother and the stepmother.

We meet up with the step-parents, MC and Georgina, at Jimmy Watson's wine bar in Carlton after the airport. They are very pleased because in French they are called *beaux parents*—the lovely parents.

I am told firmly that I must not let Jack know that I am missing him terribly. MC says, 'You must set him free. He has to go with your full encouragement to have the time of his life.'

Jaems agrees. 'Don't let him worry about *you*. You mustn't do that.'

'I don't want him to feel abandoned,' I say lamely.

Georgina understands. 'I think it's okay in the beginning. Until he settles in.'

As a mother, I've never performed myself to my son. I've never pretended in front of him. I have never ushered him out of the room when the news was on TV. My motto has always been 'Don't protect, equip'.

I remember my neighbour coming to the door and bursting into tears. Her father had just died. Jack was three.

I said, 'Say you're sorry, Jack.'

He looked bewildered. 'I didn't do it.'

He has been party to the full gamut of life experiences. He's been to hospitals and funerals and law courts and weddings and the birth of two babies. He has learned that there is no more significant human response both privately and politically than the capacity for empathy. As a result, he is insightful about the meanderings of the human heart.

So now I must pretend. Apparently. And crack hardy.

It's not as if we haven't been separated before. The previous summer holidays, he lied about his age to get into acting classes at NIDA in Sydney. (He was encouraged by his stepfather, who said, 'Lying about your age is a great Anzac tradition. It's not an act of deceit. It's a show of pluckiness.') We all gathered at Spencer Street Station and ran along the platform, waving and waving as the train slithered away.

I was fine then. But this is different. This is character building of a different order.

I ring my friend Hilary. 'Do you think I've mollycoddled Jack?' 'Absolutely not.'

Two days pass. I am living in a time zone ten hours earlier. He is having breakfast now, I think. He is looking down at his plate. She is serving brains.

Jaems calls. 'I was awake all night,' he says. 'I was worried he might not be warm enough.'

The phone rings again. So far, Jack has sent two emails and made four calls. 'You can ring me, you know,' he says and I detect a little crack in his voice.

'What are they like?' I whisper down the phone.

He is silent.

'Can't you talk?'

'Not really.'

I hang up and replay the conversation over and over. There in all the cracks is uncertainty and strangeness and yearning. Perhaps I'll have to fly over there at Christmas.

I lie in bed and wonder: who is not coping here, me or him?

'Hey, Mum,' says the next email. 'Remember moles from Enid Blyton? The cat just caught one.'

I go to Coles feeling quite chipper. The mole story has cheered me enormously. I run into his best friend. 'I got an email,' she tells me. 'He says, "I'm safe. I'm scared. And I'm dealing with it".'

I hug Michael in the pharmacy aisle.

'This is why we sent him,' he says. He's dealing with it.

32

Where Do All the Moles Go?

IN THE seventies, women were encouraged to take a look at their vaginas with a hand-mirror. This self-guided tour was recommended by the Boston Women's Health Book Collective. Everyone I knew under thirty owned a copy of their book, *Our Bodies, Ourselves*. These Americans were really into the whole mirror thing. They suggested doing it in groups. Squatting in circles with other women, like some kind of Stonehenge Tupperware party.

I never got into it.

But then I discovered a black spot on my vulva. Well, in all honesty, I wasn't the one who made the discovery—it was my husband, who was in the general area. For all I knew, the black spot had been there since birth. My husband insisted that it was a recent arrival. He suggested I see a GP. He was casual about it, but I could tell he was anxious. The next day I saw in his diary: *Check H sees doctor*.

'Have you been googling "black spot"?' I asked, over breakfast.

'Just go to the doctor.'

The doctor rang the dermatologist.

'She has a suspicious, pigmented *lesion*,' the doctor stressed on the phone. This must have piqued the dermatologist's interest because she agreed to see me just two weeks later. (Halley's Comet returns to the inner solar system more frequently than my dermatologist has an available appointment.)

My GP hung up and smiled. 'It's probably just a freckle.'

It looked like a freckle. Or more like a Georgian gentleman's beauty spot. All my vagina needed was a powdered wig.

In the days before the appointment, I resisted the desire to self-diagnose online. Instead I googled around the topic and found a site called 'Nine Beautiful Women with Really Big Moles'. It included photos of Marilyn Monroe, Cindy Crawford, Angelina Jolie and Eva Mendes. The accompanying article was about a scientific study that showed that people associate moles with health and youthfulness. The more mole-y a woman is, the hotter she is.

'That's good,' I thought, unsure if it applied to vaginas.

Next, I found myself transfixed by a website called 'Genitals of the Day!' where readers submit extreme close-ups of their own penises or vulvas, as part of 'a daily celebration of the diversity and beauty of human genitals'.

I blame the Boston Women's Health Book Collective. If you are considering photographing your genitals and posting them online, my advice is to think about lighting. These rather unhygienic-looking photographs are accompanied by creepy affirmations from the person who runs the site. 'Thanks for submitting. I particularly like your hooded clitoris.' Or, 'I think your generous labia are very pretty.'

Eww.

Presumably, this website is intended to reassure us that genitals come in all shapes and sizes. But I reckon the people who post their happy snaps have good reason to suspect their parts are non-standard.

Off I go to the dermatologist, who asks me whether I would prefer a plastic surgeon to do the job. I hate it when doctors go all hippy and want to involve me in decision-making. Mind you, I didn't want a botch-job. I didn't want to feel compelled to seek reassurance on 'Genitals of the Day!'

Nora Ephron, in her book *I Feel Bad About My Neck*, says you should always get a plastic surgeon. She warns that, even if you wake up after surgery 'thrilled beyond imagining that it wasn't cancer' and promising never to complain about anything again, the day will come, all too soon, when you look in the mirror and think, 'I hate that scar.'

I mull this over.

The dermatologist hovers with her scalpel.

'Just do it.' I say. I am in a Civil War movie. Three fellow soldiers hold me down as I clamp my teeth on a stick, waiting for a drunken doctor to saw off my leg.

My dermatologist expertly removes the black spot and pops it in a jar.

She is kind, but noncommittal. It has to be sent off. But where?

Where do all the moles go? Will the person in the white coat who takes my black spot out of the jar with her forceps know that it's mine? Imagine the excitement were they to receive a celebrity black spot. 'Hey, I've got a David Williamson.' 'So what?' shouts another technician. 'I've got a Kylie.'

Or maybe it is more like the *Age* short-story competition, where the names are removed: the judges don't know if they are reading a Richard Flanagan piece or the work of a retired schoolteacher from Bairnsdale.

I ring the pathology laboratory. Dr Jill Magee picks up the phone. 'Hello! I've seen bits of you.'

I'm flattered. Fancy. Of all the gin joints in all the world, she remembered my mole!

When I tell her what I want, she laughs. Apparently no one has ever asked to be reunited with their mole. But, sure, I can come and look. They will keep it for two or three years. Then it goes offsite into storage.

As I drive to the laboratory, I have a dark thought. How come she remembered?

Dr Jill greets me at reception. She takes me up in the lift to meet Erin, the Irish lab scientist, who is meticulous in his explanation about the process which my mole has undergone.

About a hundred people work here. This is like the festival of all nations. Women in hijabs are peering down microscopes. There are Asians and Indians and Europeans in lab coats. Some work in histopathology, studying whole tissues under the microscope, and some work in cytology, looking at individual cells that might be scraped from, say, a pap smear or a fine-needle biopsy.

Dr Jill comments that my dermatologist has very dainty hands.

I feel pleased to have chosen a dainty dermatologist. If you need something suspicious sliced off your vulva, dainty is what you're hoping for.

Jill shows me how each specimen is preserved in formalin in a little jar and labelled with the patient's name, accession number and barcode. The chance of a mix-up is remote.

Erin starts poking at a bit of someone's tonsil. It looks like a shrivelled oyster.

'Do you think of that tissue as being part of someone?' I ask.

He admits that when you see a little flick of cervix, or a sliver of tongue, that belongs to someone who lives in your street, it's 'a bit weird'. But he tells me earnestly that you have to remind yourself at every turn that this shave biopsy is part of a person.

'It's what makes you careful.'

After the specimen is labelled, it moves to the cut-up station, where a young Iranian woman measures and describes it.

Here's what she wrote about my mole: 'Vulval lesion: a piece of mucosal tissue 6x5x3mm with a brown macule 4x5mm.'

With Dr Jill and me looking on, Erin continues explaining the process: they embed the skin tissue in a wax block, which is chilled and sliced into ultra-thin sections of, say, five microns (each micron being a millionth of a metre). Erin slices a block to show how it's done. It's like watching the Polish lady at my deli shave pieces of Bavarian ham. He neatly places a slice onto a glass slide. Then he rehydrates the specimen and applies a pink and blue stain. The bluer the slide, the more likely the tissue is to be malignant. What you really want is for your specimen to stain a healthy pink.

We repair to Jill's office, where we sit down together at a swanky microscope through which the two of us can view the specimen together. We both peer into our eyepieces.

'Hannie, this is your vulva!' says Jill.

I am looking down at a perfectly pink blob with little dots, ridges and rivulets. It is like an aerial shot of a pink country. There is no evidence of malignancy, says Jill. It is neither a melanoma nor a mole.

It is something called a benign labial melanotic macule with underlying telangiectasia consistent with chronic irritation.

What would cause chronic irritation, I wonder?

'Friction,' says Jill, as she peers into the microscope. 'Do you have a husband?'

Mystery explained. It's all his fault.

I notice that my mole is an almost perfect heart shape.

'Look at that!' I say to Jill.

She smiles.

The things you do for love.

33
Graffiti

MY SON lives in the epicentre of cool: a warehouse apartment in a lane in the middle of the city. And yet he dreams of returning to Fitzroy.

When I told him we were thinking of selling our house and moving across town, he was appalled.

'Fitzroy gives you hipster status.' He shook his head gravely.

The implication was clear. How else would we earn it?

'You are on kissing terms with the Marios, for chrissake.'

Marios is a legendary café in Fitzroy, so named because the two owners are both named Mario. Their status rocketed the day they turned down Jerry Seinfeld. His minder tried to make a booking for Mr Seinfeld. Sorry, he was told, Marios doesn't take bookings. Jerry Seinfeld will have to show up and try his luck, like everyone else. So Jerry went elsewhere.

The man who took that call was a flamboyant waiter named Andrew. When I asked him about the incident, he tucked his order pad into his black waistcoat, pushed his Buddy Holly spectacles up his nose, and said, 'Jerry Seinfeld wanted to work my room. Who does he think he is?'

I love that story.

Marios also doesn't make skinny lattes. It is an obduracy that their loyal clientele appreciate. Once I went there with the playwright Joanna Murray-Smith. She's a skinny-latte girl. We were meeting Sydney TV producer Ian Collie. They both thought the latte policy was perverse and annoying. They ordered tea.

Maybe they're right. Maybe it is just stubborn and snobbish to refuse to serve coffee with skinny milk. Maybe I'm part of an old guard that needs to get with the program. I feel the need to have a view on the latte rule, though it doesn't affect me directly. Even if the Marios succumb to consumer pressure and offer skinny latte, I will never order it.

Fitzroy was Melbourne's first suburb. It's two kilometres north-east of the city centre. It is small and densely populated. Tiny Victorian workers' cottages line the streets alongside grander homes and industrial buildings that once housed foundries, warehouses and factories. The largest and most imposing of these factories was built by the famous Chocolate King, Macpherson Robertson. Two streets up from my house is the birthplace of MacRobertson's Cherry Ripe.

These industrial buildings tell a textbook story of gentrification. The foundries, warehouses and factories have now been converted to provide 'bohemian urban lifestyles' for the middle class. Our federal member is the only Green in the House of Representatives. If you live here, you can cycle to work on bike paths. You can buy organic horseradish and gluten-free ancient grains in your local shop. You can call your children Ferghus or Finnbar and send them to school with kids from every nation on earth.

But, unlike the bayside suburbs, Fitzroy is still shabby. It still provides homes for hundreds of people in vast Housing Commission estates. And artists still live and work here, although many younger ones have moved out, or never moved in, due to soaring rents.

One gritty summer night, I was walking along our street with MC and Jack. A parked car had been vandalised and a side-window smashed: there was a pool of shattered glass beads on the footpath. MC looked at the glass and said, 'The tears of the poor.'

MC and I are probably more inclined to feel poetic towards thieves because it's been many years since our house was last burgled. There was a time when it was a regular occurrence. We were forever replacing windowpanes and DVD players and making cups of tea for cops.

They were testing times for arty Fitzroy liberal-humanists like us, more predisposed to blame the society than the thief. On one occasion, a burglar left a muddy footprint on the kitchen bench. Even though it suggested he was probably just a kid, the footprint seemed more menacing than humanising. It became a symbol of violation; a stranger was rifling through our lives, emptying our drawers. He was also smoking. As I opened the front door I smelled it immediately and felt a stab of fear. There was also a telltale log of ash in the bathroom basin. What kind of nonchalance is that? The burglar who smokes as he works. Was he also planning to have a gin and tonic?

It was hard to feel sorry for him.

After three burglaries, I rang a man from Pascoe Vale who installed a security alarm. We've had no trouble since. I'm wondering whether this is why we can sheet the blame to those neoliberals who seek to revile the weak and imprison the poor. The question of what sort of a low-life scumbag would break into your house and steal your priceless antique ring doesn't come up as much.

Then a woman was stabbed in the next street. As I am a professional stickybeak, I grilled one of the young police officers manning the roadblock. He wouldn't tell me much. Police have both professional and facial restrictions to their freedom of speech. Their lips don't move. But he did assure me that it was not a random act. The victim was known to the knife-wielder. This was a relief.

I know. Terrible. But that's what I thought.

Over the past ten years, every surface of Fitzroy has been scribbled over by taggers and street artists. We ask one man with a thin ponytail if he has permission to spray-paint the side of the brick house across the road from our place.

He lies with the steady gaze of a conman. Yes, he has permission. From the owner. And the Council.

'It's community art,' he tells us.

'Community art,' says MC, 'is by definition made in consultation with the community. I'm a member of the community and I haven't been consulted.'

We are standing in front of a massive spray of snarling faces and jagged, indecipherable writing.

'It's art,' screeches a banshee who appears from nowhere. She is the artist's belligerent muse.

'Would you prefer to have a Coca-Cola ad? Would you?' the artist scoffs, as if we are mindless apologists for advertising.

'No, I liked the colonial brick wall that was there this morning,' my husband replies.

'You wouldn't know art if it shat on your face,' spits the banshee.

MC hosts a daily art show on ABC Radio National. We don't mention this, although my desire to patronise this snivelling dullard is almost overpowering. If I were a method actor and needed to express rage, I would summon her sneering face.

'How come there is no graffiti in Malvern?' MC's sister, Sarah, asks a few days later. Malvern is one of Melbourne's spacious suburbs, where the smell of David Austin roses wafts over the French provincial furnishings and your chance of being killed by a BMW driver is high.

'Because people who live in Malvern can make their mark in other ways,' says MC.

I have to say that the defacing of Fitzroy was why I wanted to move. If you don't like the aesthetics of graffiti and tagging, it can fill you with a terrible despair. I know other people call it art. I experience it as white noise. Visual tinnitus. It is indifferent to the architecture on which it is imposed. It scorns urban form. It sneers at grace. To me, it merely says, *Dumb fucks rule.*

There is no choice but to adjust. Or move house.

Then, as the months pass, something lovely happens. Every morning, as I walk the streets at dawn, I begin to notice something on the pavement at random spots. Two words in red paint: *Hello Beautiful!*

I see it. I say the words. It makes me feel…happy.

Hello Beautiful!

I reply, 'Hello.' Softly at first. Then I say it gaily: 'Hello, you.'

I decide to find the artist. He is like the man who chalked the enigmatic word *Eternity* on pavements all over Sydney.

I see *Hello Beautiful!* in signature red in many places. I make a poster that says

> Desperately Seeking
> Hello Beautiful!
> Email me at hellobeautiful@gmail.com

I walk the streets of balmy Fitzroy one summer night and stick my posters to lampposts. A man comes out of his single-fronted Victorian terrace.

'Oh, I know him,' he says, before shooting me a querying look. 'You're not from…the government or anything?'

Within an hour I am speaking to a Mexican named Fonz. Yes, he's the person who drips *Hello Beautiful* onto the footpaths, Jackson Pollock–style. He won't tell me any more of his story. He says he will contact me when next he's in my hood.

But I never hear from him again.

When I call his phone, it rings out.

Fonz, it seems, doesn't want to be found.

What I know is that in the morning, when the light is pastel and crisp, I walk along the Fitzroy streets and a voice from the universe sings out to me, *Hello Beautiful!*

That's enough for me.

34
Paul Newman

A FEW years ago, a friend of mine travelled to Vermont, in the United States. After taking in the panoramic views, she noticed an ice-creamery. She went in and joined the queue.

There, standing about two metres away, was Paul Newman.

She thought to herself, 'Oh my god, that is Paul Newman,' (as you would) 'I am standing two metres away from Paul Newman.'

She bought her ice-cream cone and walked out onto the verandah to take in the view. There he was, eating an ice-cream.

'Beautiful day,' he said.

'Yes,' she said.

They both looked out for a bit more and then she said, 'Oh, what have I done with my ice-cream?'

He said, 'It's in your handbag.'

35

The Dinner Party

AMONG CERTAIN women friends of mine, there's a consensus developing that we may have wasted years of our lives hosting dinner parties. Over the summer, I get emails from several girlfriends, outlining their New Year's resolutions. Less cooking, more writing. Less socialising, more thinking.

My husband is appalled. This household will not comply with such meanness of spirit. We will continue to invite our friends for dinner. Even if he has to cook it himself.

His view is that people are suffering from performance anxiety at the prospect of entertaining their friends at home: the modern *fetishisation* of food has contributed to less conviviality rather than more. If only we were content to throw a few chops on the barbie and serve them up with a green salad, we'd all see more of each other.

I know this to be true. I just can't do it.

It's Monday morning. I am in my office, working on my book. Michael rings to say that Mr J—a famous theatre producer—is in town. He is free to have dinner with us tonight. So why don't we invite our friend Bob as well?

'Just buy some steaks from the butcher on the corner and I'll barbecue them when I get home.' Easy.

Steak and salad. Monday night. Perfect.

Then my eye is distracted by *Chin Chin*, a new cookbook my friend Nellie has just lent me. It's a recipe book compiled by the chef of one of the coolest restaurants in town. I begin to wonder. Why would you barbecue an indigestible lump of meat when you could serve tofu and shitake san choy bao followed by coriander and panko-coated fish with burnt chilli mayonnaise?

Why, indeed?

Sadly, the market is not open on a Monday. I ride to my fish shop.

(My former father-in-law told me that he thought it was a peculiarly Melbourne phenomenon to say *my* fish shop or *my* butcher. Perth people, apparently, just go to *the* fish shop. Are Melbourne people announcing their superior capacity for discernment? Personally, I don't think having a fish shop is so bad. I don't even object to a person having a relationship with the owner—*my* fishmonger. Where I draw the line is having *a little man*.)

My fish shop is closed. Gone fishing.

Mercifully, I have carried the Chin Chin book in my bike basket for just such an emergency. The gourmet butcher next door is open. Perhaps I could do a twice-cooked lamb neck with smoky eggplant salad and mint relish?

Now, one rule of dinner party protocol I have imbibed over the years is never inflict your diet on your guests. A less charitable reading of this rule might be: make every dinner party an excuse to eat like a little piglet.

As it happens, my husband and I have embarked upon a very sophisticated, scientifically tested and nutritionally balanced eating plan, devised by him. It is called controlled starvation. The guiding principle is simple: you will not lose weight unless you're starving. This doesn't strike me immediately as according with modern dietary dicta, but—

[Hello. This is the husband intervening here, while the Writer is popping out to the wine shop. In fact, my *guiding principle* is that we don't need the special little pre-dinner meal Hannie calls 'five o'clocks'—usually an assortment of dips and other treats served on massively overpriced crackers from the gourmet deli (baked by blind monks in some monastery in the

Italian alps). Nor is it strictly necessary to start every meal with 'firsts', or what Hannie calls 'Just something lovely that I'm trying out'.

But hush, I hear the clink of wine bottles on the front porch.]

Anyhoo, as I was saying, tonight we have guests! Why opt for a salad when you could have Chin Chin chicken dumplings with chinkiang black vinegar?

Of course, none of the Asian supermarkets stock all the ingredients I need. I ride around, burning calories and doing the necessary meditative preparation for writing my magnum opus, which is due shortly. I will get cracking on it this afternoon. Or maybe when the guests leave after midnight.

Perhaps Michael is right. We won't have nibbles. Who needs nibbles? We'll start with the chicken dumplings. The recipe says cook for eight minutes. I practise steaming one of the dumplings at five o'clock. I decide they might need a little longer.

Our guests arrive and we repair to the lounge room with glasses of wine. The conversation is lively. Bob and Mr J are marvellously entertaining. That said, it was a mistake not to have nibbles. Even a bowl of olives. Who doesn't serve nibbles? There is a social void that nibbles fill.

I nip out and put the dumplings in the steamer. I've bought one of those Asian bamboo steamers specially for tonight. It fits perfectly in the bottom of my favourite saucepan.

When I return to the lounge room, I embark upon the story about getting a urinary tract infection in Spain. Exactly why I decide to recount this episode in my life is unclear. I swear I've only had one glass of wine. Maybe my husband's eating plan is affecting my capacity to absorb alcohol.

It's quite complicated, this story, but I feel it's going well. My husband is chipping in with witty asides. I hear the stove timer ring. I've set it to eight minutes, but I know there's room to move.

I am explaining that in the hospital in Seville you have to go before a panel of doctors, none of whom can speak English. All six men seem totally bewildered by my attempts to demonstrate the sensation of *burning*.

I excuse myself to check on how our entrée is coming along— and laughingly open the door into the dining area. The whole back half of our house is engulfed in black acrid smoke.

I race to the stove, grab the saucepan, open the back door and hurl the whole thing into the garden.

The bamboo steamer is burnt black. It rolls out of the saucepan and onto the gravel. The dumplings, which should look like soft white pouches, look instead like triangles of grilled cheese on toast.

The smoke alarm leaps into action, emitting an ear-splitting shriek.

The men dash out from the lounge room. We throw all the doors and windows open. The high-pitched screeching eventually relents.

The English theatre producer is totally gracious. 'It was worth sacrificing the entrée for that story.'

Bob, a regular at our house, says, 'You are the only person I know who uses the fire alarm to measure cooking times.'

We sit down at the table, the night air blowing in. It is decidedly chilly, but what can you do?

I give myself a stern note. Do not apologise and lament. Move on.

The lamb neck—which is a vaguely off-putting concept at the best of times—is okay, but would have benefited from more faithful attention to the recipe.

The evening rollicks along. Mr J is regaling us with stories of famous actors. I am topping up Bobby's glass, encouraging Mr J to tell more, when, out of the corner of my eye, I see a mouse run across the kitchen floor.

I kick Michael under the table. I run my fingers across the table in quick mouse-steps. All the while I am smiling and listening to Mr J.

I start to wriggle my nose. Now I am doing mouse-acting.

Michael is mouthing: *What?*

Out it comes again. The mouse. This time, he doesn't scurry. He sort of ambles. As if he owns the kitchen. As if he lives here. I want to throw something.

I leap up.

Under no circumstances must the famous producer see the mouse. I have to get him to swap places with Michael. Yes. That's it. Mr J must be reseated with his back to the kitchen.

I decide to clatter about at the sink, to try to drive off the rodent. Michael follows me in. 'What in god's name?'

'You have to change places,' I hiss.

'What?'

'When he goes to the loo...'

'Don't be fucking ridiculous. He comes back and I'm sitting in his seat?'

I think the mouse might be making its entrance from a gap between dishwasher and cupboard. I give the cupboard door a kick. I need to create moral panic—send a wave of human terror rolling through the mouse corridor.

I grab a wettex and shove it in the hole. That's fixed it.

I return to my place at the table.

Later in the evening, Mr J is talking and I see his eyes widen in utter incredulity. But he barely misses a beat. Like a true theatre person, he carries on.

I, however, know with a terrible certainty that the mouse is back. And that Mr J has seen it.

The next day, Michael interviews the famous theatre producer on his radio program. After the show, he walks Mr J to the lift. Michael decides to make a clean breast of it.

'I know you saw the mouse.'

'It was very entertaining,' said Mr J. 'I saw it long before you and Hannie even knew it was there. At one point, it ran across the kitchen floor and into the toilet. Hannie went in shortly afterwards and I expected to hear a frightful scream.'

Mr J sent me a thank-you note:

'Thank you for a perfect evening. Hope the three of you are all well and enjoying a cheese platter together.'

36
Falling from Grace in Japan

IT IS a dark, rainy night, and MC and I are in a Boeing 737. The plane is taxiing around and around Sydney airport, looking for a runway. We are watching CNN, which is delivering the happy news that a typhoon will hit Tokyo to coincide with our arrival. The southern part of Honshu is flooded, and we see pictures of submerged houses and cars being swept away by raging torrents. Meanwhile, the Koreans have made an interesting decision to fire two missiles over the north of Japan. We are flying into a war zone.

There is a ping: it's our captain speaking. On account of all the driving around, we have to stop for forty-five minutes to let the wheels cool off. Airline regulations.

We watch more footage of trees flying through the air in the howling winds. Eventually, air traffic control allocates us a runway. We hare down it at full throttle. Just as we are about to take flight, the pilot hits the brakes and we screech to an almighty, shuddering stop. Engine trouble. Mechanics are called in to dismantle the plane, but they are too late. We have fallen victim to Sydney's airport curfew. All three hundred passengers have to abandon ship and be accommodated overnight.

I ring my agent from the hotel at 2 a.m. 'Help! What happens now?'

MC and I are travelling as guests of the Hyogo Stage Arts Group, who are producing my play *Falling from Grace* in Tokyo at the New National Theatre and then in Kobe at the Shin Kobe Oriental Theatre. We have now missed the dress rehearsal and a day of press interviews.

Ten hours later, we are on our way, high above Dubbo. The potpourri salesman sitting next to me says he has missed an important business meeting. He seems to have found the whole inconvenience invigorating. He orders another Scotch and belches contentedly.

MC is green; altitude does not agree with him. He tells me that he wishes he was home in his own bed.

'But then you wouldn't be with me,' I proffer cheerily.

He stares glumly out the window. 'I wish I was home in my own bed, missing you.'

We land in Tokyo without further incident. No cyclone. No evidence of missiles. We hop into a taxi driven by a man who has held up a card with my name on it. We hurtle along a freeway at two hundred kilometres per hour in the back seat of a taxi with no seatbelts. It is the anniversary of Princess Diana's death. MC is muttering about kamikaze driving. He knows he is being culturally insensitive, but so is the kamikaze driver of the cab. The meter clicks past $300 and still we have not reached Tokyo.

I am not sure who is supposed to pick up the tab here.

When we get to the hotel, I decide that now is the time to act like a celebrity. I get out of the car, smile graciously and walk purposely into the hotel, praying the driver won't call the police or drive away with our luggage.

We are shown to our room on the thirty-sixth floor by a cheerful bellboy who says, 'G'day!'

Next morning, we stumble downstairs dazed and excited, looking for breakfast. The foyer of this hotel is like the ground floor of David Jones without the merchandise: a vast emporium of glitzy lighting and mirrors, gleaming floors and leather couches. We pay sixty-eight dollars for two cups of coffee, a bowl of miso soup and a sad little croissant. In our room, a tea bag is 500 yen (six dollars).

I hate travellers' stories that drone on about the cost of everything, but really this place is staggering. We resolve not to do anything in the hotel except sleep and shower and have sex. Instead, we stock up at the supermarket, where I pay ten dollars for an apple. One of the saving graces in Japan is that tipping is considered vulgar—hooray, tipping *is vulgar*.

The subway closest to our hotel is Shinjuku, which is claimed to be the busiest place in the world. Three million people move through this one metro station every day. We stand in the midst of this maelstrom of human traffic, holding up our map, this way and that. A woman with a toddler in a pusher stops to help. We are at the wrong end of the station. She takes us up and down stairs, along corridors, through turnstiles and across the vast underground walkway to deliver us to our destination. She has taken us at least a kilometre out of her way.

Everywhere you go you cannot help but notice how exhausted people are. Japan—the ultimate capitalist project—offers a sobering lesson about the downside of corporate culture. Quality of life issues are clearly underrated here. People get one week of annual leave and work such long hours that, wherever you look, they are availing themselves of the chance to nap. On buses and subways, in lifts and taxis, on public benches, people sleep. One of the ways I calm myself at the prospect of having to address public gatherings on this trip is to remember that most of the audience will be asleep.

MC lies on the bed in the hotel room, testing me on the names. 'Okay. Artistic Director?'

'Masakazu Yamazaki,' I say, pacing up and down in my new frock, waving my freshly painted fingernails in the air. We have an hour to go before meeting the cast at the theatre.

'The actress who plays Suzannah?'

'Miyuki?'

'No.'

'Misuzu?'

'Yes.'

MC and I arrive at the theatre and I am treated like a pop star. I am so relieved to have a gregarious husband, because suddenly I feel shy. All small talk dries up. I can't remember who's who or, in fact, the title of my play. I smile and nod and shake hands with everyone from the lead actress to the 'hair make artist'. We are all gushing and laughing and bowing and nodding.

MC and I are shown to our seats. Behind us is the translator, with his mum and dad. It transpires that his elderly father is also a translator, whose version of the complete works of Shakespeare is the standard edition in Japan. 'He is the master,' says Oshi, introducing his father. 'I am the apprentice.' He says this not with formality but with real love.

Later, I find myself talking to his elderly mother. She discusses my play with intensity and intelligence. She relates her own experience. This is the first inkling I have that Japanese audiences might be viewing the play with some personal identification. This had never occurred to me. I had assumed they would be dispassionately observing 'the way they do things in Australia'.

The theatre is full. The lead actress is famous throughout Japan. This, I discover later, is the reason there are hundreds of bunches of flowers lying on the floor of the foyer. It is reminiscent of the gates of Kensington Palace on the day of Princess Di's funeral. Forty women occupy the front rows of the theatre. They are a sort of fan club, apparently.

The theatre itself is modern—big and yet intimate, robust, but beautifully finished. The design is so chic it's breathtaking. The lights dim, the audience fall silent and in the darkness, Michael is squeezing my hand so intensely I have to pinch his thigh really hard to make him stop. The three actresses enter. They look as though they are wearing couture by Christian Dior. What's more, they seem to change every ten minutes into something even more fabulous.

The play is the story of three women who run a magazine. These women are best friends and work colleagues. The world of the play is one where the demands of work, children, ex-husbands, lovers and ex-lovers are being juggled by three dynamic, funny, smart women. It is a play about the media and medicine, exploring what happens when professional and private lives collide over a matter of public morality.

We have been warned that Japanese audiences don't laugh out loud much. This is a little disconcerting for me, because the play is supposed to be funny.

But here they are, laughing. I am transfixed. What's more, I think I know what is happening. I even know what is being said. Perhaps you're thinking, 'What's the big deal, you're the author.' But I have seen my work performed in other languages before and had no idea what was going on.

The show finishes, the actors take their bow and I am called to take the stage. Bowing, bowing, clapping, clapping. Next to these tiny, fine little women I feel like some Amazonian.

'Tell me the truth,' I ask later. 'Did I look really, really stupid?' Bowing is not that easy when you're not used to it.

We all go out for dinner. We drink and eat and give gifts and make speeches, and Michael and I have fun. My gifts (which have created a drama of unprecedented hysteria in the week before) are accepted graciously.

One of the main movers and shakers in terms of cultural exchanges between Australia and Asia is Carrillo Gantner, former artistic director of Playbox. He was a key player in getting this project off the ground. Before I left, I rang him for advice.

'Gifts! You must have gifts!' he bellowed down the phone.

MC and I figured out we needed nineteen presents. There were so many producers and hosts and theatre managers, all of whom seemed to be important. Not to mention the cast and crew. This was like Christmas without knowing the family.

'Just get koalas,' people said.

I rang my friend Donald at the theatre company.

'Koalas!' he shrieked. 'My dear girl you will cause an embarrassing international incident if you do something so tacky.'

'That'd be right,' said a mutual friend. 'If it were up to Donald, you'd be distributing Cartier watches.'

So what do you give a middle-aged, sophisticated and urbane Japanese businessman you've never met, as a memento of Australia?

I ended up taking books and stationery and handkerchiefs, bringing home with me all the kitsch teaspoons and key rings people had suggested might be handy at a pinch.

One of the great things about working in the theatre is that, by and large, theatre people are the same everywhere. The formality I had anticipated and dreaded was entirely absent. Admittedly, the Japanese don't go in for the hugging and kissing and stroking and patting as much as we do. But most actors love intimacy, so it wasn't long before we were getting down to the nitty-gritty: boyfriend troubles, the insecurities of a life in the theatre, the trials of a disapproving parent, and so on.

What I did discover was this. An Englishman sat at our table after the show. He wore a monocle like Colonel Klink in *Hogan's Heroes*. He was 'our man out east'. He told me I was lucky to have a husband to support me (excuse me?) and expressed surprise to learn that MC was an historian. 'Australian history. Good lord,' he chortled. 'I didn't think you had any.' He was that sort of chappie.

Discussing our evening later, MC and I both had the same thought. From the isolation of Australia, the Japanese who seemed so exotic, so inscrutable, so foreign, were so very familiar. Their friendliness was reminiscent of Australian friendliness. Easy and generous. By contrast, the Englishman was a stranger.

Eventually, the party spilled from the restaurant to the street outside and we said our goodbyes. Michael and I were the last to leave. We walked home through the streets of Tokyo, laughing like children.

37

Greece

I AM sitting in a pall of thick, blue smoke in the non-smoking section of Athens airport. The Greeks are all puffing away. It occurs to me that no one has told them.

We have been awake since 4.30 a.m., when we boarded a train in Italy. It is now 10 p.m., and both MC and I have moved into that phase of travel where all people in airports look fat and ugly. The first time I came to Greece twenty-five years ago, I thought Greek men were Adonises. I mention this to my husband.

'Well, they've gone to the pack since then.'

We have just spent two glorious months at Paul Cox's rambling house in the south of France, quietly turning fifty. Now we are heading for the Greek island of Lesbos. Michael is finishing his book. I am writing a play called *The Swimming Club*. We are both planning to write every day for two months. We have one laptop.

As our tiny plane roars and vibrates across the Aegean Sea, I stare out of the window at the blackness—and see my own face, out there in the night, staring back. On that first visit in 1983, I crossed the same blackness by ferry, to spend a summer in the ancient village of Molyvos. It was a time before children, mortgages and global warming. A time when you could travel without a tangle of electrical chargers and adaptors. A time when you could ride a motorbike without a helmet. A time of bikinis, swimming and sex.

In the tepid pool of the overhead light, I read aloud our horoscopes from the back page of the *Athens News*. I feel this could be portentous.

Aries (Hannie): *Enjoy and relax. Expect good luck from slightly scruffy men. Be tolerant to their small sins.*

And Aquarius (Michael): *Avoid glory. Especially tomorrow.*
'Pity,' says MC. 'I was planning to slay the Cyclops.'

The next day, we wake up in the village of Molyvos. From our tiny bedroom, we can see across the rooftops to the sparkling waters of the Aegean. Achilles anchored out there, on his voyage to the Trojan War. We hug each other with sheer joy.

Lesbos is a mecca for gay women. As we walk along the paved roadway that leads down to the harbour, two square German women stride towards us in sturdy boots. They smile warmly at me. They direct ideological death rays at Michael.

We come to the little shop near the donkey station, where Roula sells souvenirs and guidebooks. Outside, there are international newspapers for sale on a wire rack: *Le Monde, Guardian, New York Herald Tribune, Die Zeit*—each of them over two days old.

'Do you have a map of the village?' Michael asks.

'No map. Why you need map?' In all her many lifetimes, she has never heard anything so idiotic.

Michael is stunned. 'What sort of place doesn't have a map?'

No map. My sort of place. I cite the American writer E. L. Doctorow: 'Experience comes from stumbling in the unknown towards meaning.'

'Experience teaches you to buy a map,' says Michael.

We eat lunch at an outdoor café in the harbour, alongside brightly painted boats and fishing nets. Cats mooch about. The owner's name is Stratos. He is tired and cheerful.

'Come, choose what you like to eat from the pots in the kitchen. You want a table outside, by the water?' He brings us a platter of octopus and calamari, fat olives rolled in wild oregano, spicy auber-gine, creamy fetta and olive oil with chargrilled bread, prepared by his mum. It is autumn. Stratos warns us that soon the tourists will leave and most of the cafés will close. It will be just us and the Greeks.

Alongside us, a fisherman is unloading his catch from a little blue boat called *Aphrodite*. A red bucket beside our table begins to wobble. A giant octopus climbs out.

Michael shouts, 'Mate!'

This is Greek for 'Excuse me, sir, you are losing your octopus.'

The fisherman jumps off his boat and bundles the tentacles back in the bucket.

'You want to look?' he asks. Before I know it, he has tipped the octopus into my hands. The suckers stick to my skin as the creature starts to crawl over me. The octopus I have just eaten begins to move in my stomach.

In Melbourne, we are always busy. Now we have nothing to do but spend hours walking around the slopes of this ancient island— where goats have grazed the rocky hillsides for thousands of years— and the modern world seems to exist in another dimension. We are on holiday—and we are both writing. But one of us has to use a biro.

In France, we managed to share the one laptop. But here we engage in married-people negotiations.

'You have it. Your writing is more important.'

'No it isn't. Don't be silly.'

'No, really. I am so happy with the biro. I love biros. I can transcribe my work when we get back to Melbourne. Honestly.'

Subtext: *all two-fucking-months of it.*

An American academic here named Carol intervenes and lends us her old laptop—so old that it doesn't have a USB connection. Carol assures us that Nikos at the computer shop will be able to help.

'He's a bit gruff,' she warns.

The little shop is filled with cigarette smoke, like some demented scientific experiment. (You place a man in a glass tank, pump it full of tobacco smoke and see how long he can survive.) The nicotine-coloured man at the counter looks up from his important work, scowling as though Jehovah's Witnesses have just walked in. He has a walrus moustache. Apparently, his public relations policy is to treat every customer as a pest.

'*Neh?*' he grumbles. Confusingly, this negative sound means

'Yes?' (It gets worse. The Greek word for *no* is *ochi*. When Greeks say it, they jerk their chins up—as if they're saying *okay*.)

Nikos opens the laptop as if he has a thousand better things to do with his time. The valiant little machine whirrs and hums as it boots up. A photograph of a white cat gradually scrolls down the screen. Nikos slaps the base of his palm on his forehead.

'Where you get this computer? Carol, uh?'

Yes. Guilty.

'You see this cat?' He pokes furiously at the screen. 'This cat is dead. Ten years dead. Like this computer. Dead. You tek this.' He points outside to the Aegean. 'You throw this to the sea. Feed to the fish. Understand?'

An hour later, Nikos is still fiddling with the laptop and giving Michael a dissertation about why he hates the French and the Spanish. By lunchtime, they are best friends. Nikos has revived the computer (a task, it turns out, he has performed many times, for many different users) and all my material is now on the hard drive. He gives us the computer and a box of floppy disks. He charges us just three euros, the cost of the floppies.

Our tiny house has just two rooms, an upstairs and a downstairs. Drama—my work—is undertaken in the bedroom upstairs. History—Michael's work—occurs downstairs on the kitchen table. We wonder if we will cope, living on top of each other like this.

Vangelis, the landlord, once lived here with his parents and eight children.

The Swimming Club started life as the true story of six friends who, one night, stole a crate of champagne and went swimming naked in Melbourne's Albert Park Lake. For each of them, it was a night of glory. They call themselves the Swimming Club. And every so often, they have a reunion.

But as I write in my little room in Molyvos, the play begins to take on a life of its own. My characters meet here in 1983, working in a taverna on the beach. They have just one reunion—thirty years later, when they are all fifty.

Michael and I have become friends with a Londoner named Karen, who comes to Molyvos for holidays at least once a year. Karen proposes that we walk to the village of Skala Sikaminia, where there is a restaurant under a famous old mulberry tree. The tree was immortalised by Stratis Myrivilis, widely regarded as one of the major Greek novelists of the twentieth century. He lived in our village.

We follow the road up to the castle that presides over Molyvos. Down the other side, our route leads us to a lonely white gravel road, which winds along the coast. It is a warm sunny day. On our right, there are wild mountains. We can hear goat-bells clanking high on the slopes. On our left, the sea is shimmering blue and slapping at the black-pebbled shore. Across the water, we can see the coast of Turkey, just seven kilometres away—so close that you can clearly see houses and roads on the Turkish mainland.

A group of three young men appears on a rise ahead of us. They walk towards us, silhouetted against the sky. As they approach, we see that they are in their early twenties and all dressed in a sort of shabby Sunday best. They have bottles of water in their hands. Nothing else. They pass us. Wary. Determined.

A kilometre down the road, four more men appear. They walk towards us. As they pass, Karen says, '*As-salamu alaykum*'—the traditional Arab greeting. Two of them mumble, '*Wa alaikum assalam*' and keep walking. This confirms it. They are asylum seekers.

After twenty minutes, we find a way onto the beach. The sand is littered with plastic water bottles, and everywhere there are old, deflated rubber rafts and paddles. Later, we learn how it works. These boys have come here from Afghanistan and neighbouring countries. People smugglers set them adrift out in the water between Turkey and Lesbos. They point to the coast and tell the boys that they are looking at Italy. In fact, they are on the easternmost coastal edge of Europe. Back home, their families have borrowed a fortune to pay the smugglers, in the vain hope that their brave sons will find good jobs in Europe and send back money. The result is tragic. Terrible debts for the families. And trouble for the boys.

In the *Athens News*, I see that thirteen thousand illegal immigrants have arrived in Greece this very month—and are now in detention centres. Meanwhile, my own son is spending the year at a French university. His quest for self-advancement is acceptable. Even laudable. But not these young men. If they are judged to be 'economic refugees', they will end up in jail.

A month later, the weather has turned wild. We shelter inside our little house as mountains of grey cloud mass over the Aegean. Dark thunder shakes the earth. Rain pounds the roof above our heads and courses down the steep cobbled streets. When the rain eases a little, we venture down to the harbour. All the cafés are closed for the winter. Except for Stratos's place.

'How come you're still open?' I ask.

'How could I close with you still on the island?'

Ah. Such charm.

Inside the café, the windows are all steamed up. It is Stratos's name day. He gives us sweet pastries to eat with our coffee. There are about ten local men in the café. Everyone is shouting. This is where we meet Tom.

'Where you from?' he shouts from across the room.

'Australia.'

The café falls silent.

'Ah. Aff-stralia. One thousand times more better than this country.'

That doesn't sound too diplomatic. But Tom's mates just watch, and click their worry beads.

It turns out that Tom lived in Sydney for twenty-two years.

'What do you miss the most?' shouts Michael.

Tom tosses his beads over and over in his big hand. It's a big question.

'You know what?'

'What?'

'Kentucky Fried Chicken.'

The other Greek men at his table nod solemnly. They have no idea what he's talking about.

'Three, four time a week,' says Tom, 'I use to stop on my way home from factory. I use to get the fifteen-piece pack. KFC. Ah.'

They are nodding. We are nodding. It's all very deep.

Christmas is coming. Michael has finished his book. I have written the first draft of *The Swimming Club*. It is time to leave Molyvos to the Greeks. Time to go home to the land of KFC.

38
Hotel

ON THE plane trip home, after we've been travelling, I always ask my husband, 'What was your favourite bit?'

He always says, 'The sex.'

I say, 'We could've had sex at home.'

'I know,' he says. 'I'm a simple person, really.'

It was his birthday. I considered buying him a power tool, or maybe a gift voucher from Bunnings so he could choose his own. Bunnings makes him immeasurably happy. He hums in the aisles. He denies this. He says the Bunnings experience is satisfying, but not rapturous. He says I have a misbegotten idea that he *likes* home renovation.

This puts me in mind of a very satisfying conversation he reported having at Christmas drinks at his work. He said that several of his male colleagues were discussing their holiday plans. Most were allocating time during their break to undertake necessary home maintenance. All agreed that their wives regarded this as an imposition. An act of selfishness. A commandeering of the family summer holiday as 'me time'.

Apparently, wives regarded their husbands' painting and hammering as wilful and self-centred, and to have the audacity to ask the womenfolk 'to hold something, like a ladder or a tape measure' was tantamount to wrecking things for everybody.

I can see the truth in this. I am that wife. So, to avoid any unpleasant stirring up of hostilities, I decide to steer clear of the power-tool option and go straight for the default sex.

I book a hotel room.

We don't live very far from the city; in some respects, it is odd to spend money on sleeping up the road from your own house. In view of this, not wanting to be wasteful, I opt for the discounted mystery hotel deal. What's the worst that could happen? It's only one night, after all, and seediness can have its own allure. Like a Graham Greene novel. We could pretend we are in Vietnam. Or India, in the Best Exotic Marigold Hotel.

Our mystery accommodation is standard and unremarkable, the kind of hotel where you might see John and Janette Howard coming down in the lift.

We meet in the foyer on a Friday afternoon. We kiss. We're a bit excited. I wonder if the receptionist suspects adultery. Hannie from Accounts and Michael from Sales, embarking on a tawdry assignation which will taint their lives forever. Surely she should intervene. Surely she should caution us, before one of us hands over a credit card.

Too late. She has taken a copy of my Visa and handed over the key to Room 1573.

We go up to the fifteenth floor and marvel at the spaciousness of our apartment. We make gin and tonics and eat cashews from the minibar and pad about in our socks. We make plans to sell our house and move in here. I flick through the recommended attractions in the plastic hotel folder. We could visit the Melbourne Aquarium. We could see the world's largest saltwater crocodile, in the state-of-the-art Croc Lair exhibit. We could marvel at the world's only display of elephant sharks.

'When they say *interactive animal encounters*,' I call out, 'what do you think they mean?' He can't hear. He's in the shower.

Suddenly, I am reminded of our real purpose in coming. How disappointing if we squander precious time viewing stingrays or brown leopard-spotted honeycomb morays.

Forget the fish.

I read a magazine article once where the comedian Wendy Harmer was asked, 'What do you most like about men?'

She said, 'When they come out of the shower wearing a towel.'

I completely love that answer. But I hasten to make a distinction between a white towel tied around the waist and the white towelling ensembles made famous by Bob and Blanche. Michael and I have a policy. Never wear a fluffy white bathrobe, even in a hotel fire. Better to rush out naked.

We rip the tightly tucked blankets off the bed and leap onto the crisp white fitted sheet.

It's Friday. We're stuffed. It's so beautiful to lie down. We both fall into a sweet, deep coma.

An hour or so later, the bedside alarm clock drones. Short, deep reverberations not dissimilar to the rumble of a dentist's drill. We shake ourselves awake, disorientated and slightly nauseated. My skin is ice-cold from the air-con. I feel strange.

'We could order in?' says my husband, hopefully.

I am reminded of Jane Fonda in *Barefoot in the Park*. She disappears into her sixth-floor apartment with her newlywed husband, Robert Redford. To show the passing of time, the neighbours on their floor note the daily accrual of milk bottles outside their door. Eventually, Jane comes out wearing Robert Redford's oversized shirt. Even as a little girl, despite not knowing exactly what they were doing in their apartment, I knew I approved.

So it is appealing to stay put. But do we really want to watch *Scary Movie 5* or *Swinging with the Finkels*?

No. We have made a booking at a Japanese restaurant. The night's a pup.

We stumble out into the humid evening. The city streets are pulsing with office drinkers. Bars throb with doof-doof music. Pouty girls smoke and flirt with nervy boys, engorged with bombast and longing. The pavement is hot. The air is wet with lust.

We walk through our own town like tourists. Savouring the lanes and nooks as if this is Venice, as if we are our younger selves, in Buenos Aires. Or Barcelona. We smile and lace our fingers together as we walk.

Married-people sex does not enjoy good press. And, after fifty, there is a certain unseemliness in mentioning it. This is one of the cruel imbalances in the life cycle. Just when we are in possession of the mysteries, we must act as though sexuality is a young person's game. Look at these callow youths. For all their carnal posturing, they know nothing.

The license to talk about sex depends on two factors. The first is what you look like. Fat people just mustn't. A fat person talking about sex invites the listener to consider the mechanics, and this induces a reaction ranging between derision and disgust. Given that sixty per cent of Australians are overweight or obese, and on average are seven kilograms heavier than our counterparts of thirty years ago, this suggests most of us should keep very quiet on the subject.

The second factor in talking about sex is getting the tone right. Bragging or lechery is unattractive at *any* age. But over fifty, forget it. The sexual predator is creepy.

The Japanese food is light; the wine, crisp. I know of a jazz club we could go to.

On the way, we pass David Jones. Could we just pop in and see what perfumes are on offer?

My husband has a different idea. He needs new shoes. I forget that tonight is his birthday. And, in my defence, he does not express his desire for shoes very *forcefully*. He does not say, 'Listen, it's *my* birthday and what I would really *love* to do is to try on a whole lot of brown shoes.'

He does not express this because in truth he hates buying shoes. But what is left unsaid is how ferociously he does not want to go to the perfume department. His desire *not* to go to the perfume department is intense.

So we go to the perfume department, because as my friend Matt says, every relationship needs 'a fricken stenographer', so there is a WRITTEN RECORD of who said what and when. In the absence of documentation, my recollection is that the decision to pop into David Jones is a mutual and happy one.

A lady sprays exotic, sensual fragrances onto small cards and wafts them across my nose. A helpful young man sprays scent on my wrists. On my forearms. On my neck. My husband (who is being genial and obliging) engages like a wine buff, swirling the bouquet in an attempt to detect the difference between a floral and a fruit scent. The lady talks about the complex base notes. My husband asks whether they have something plain. Like mandarine. No base notes. No 'gardenia finish'. Just something that smells like mandarines.

They don't. We decide to give the jazz a miss, and waft back to the hotel.

The first sign of trouble afoot is in the lift. Then in the room itself. My husband opens the door to the balcony.

'Men don't like perfume,' he tells me, as if he is a senior market-research expert with the Roy Morgan Group. 'We just like women to smell like a woman.'

He is finding it hard to breathe.

The scent on my body is so delicate. I don't know what he's carrying on about. If men don't like perfume, how come women have been wearing it for thousands of years? Honestly.

This is just a small performance to register his disapproval about the David Jones interlude. I ignore it.

We repair to the bedroom.

After a while, he says, 'Maybe you could have a wash. Or something.'

This is irritating. A trifle offensive, even. I ignore it.

I shove my arms under the covers, because the smell does appear to be intensifying.

When I see that his eyes are filling with water, I fling the covers aside and stomp off to the bathroom.

I stand in the shower, running the little round cake of soap over my body.

Wrapped in a big fluffy white towel, I am about to return to our king-size luxurious bed—when I smell the smell again.

I get back into the shower. This time, I scrub. But there is nothing

I can do to remove the dominance of the pong. It has permeated the core of my being with a cloying cocktail of flowers and spices and the musky aroma of a rotting rainforest. I am chemical. I am a concentration of aromatic compound in solvent.

I begin to feel sick and claustrophobic.

'You wanna make love or not?' I bark.

My husband is manfully fighting for oxygen.

'Let's go for a walk,' he suggests. 'In the fresh air.'

'No.' I don't want to walk. I am too miserable to walk.

'Do you want to just go home? You know—to our own house.'

'What good would that do?' Unless I sleep in the shed.

I'm too miserable to talk. I just want to sulk.

We fall asleep in our hotel room with the door open.

The next morning, we take the tram to the sea and we dive in and swim and swim.

Then we have bacon and eggs in a café overlooking the water and read the paper.

I don't come out of this story very well.

39
Carrie

AT A writers festival in Aireys Inlet, I heard the novelist Carrie Tiffany tell this story to an audience of about three hundred people. A week or so after her novel *Mateship with Birds* hit the bookshops, Carrie flew to Sydney to visit her father. In her rush to get to the airport, she had forgotten to pack a copy to give to him. So she popped into a well-known bookshop in Newtown. When she put her novel down on the counter, the young man at the cash register said, 'Don't buy that. That's bloody awful.'

Carrie was mortified. She rummaged in her purse for the money and mumbled, 'It's got a nice cover.'

The audience gasped and laughed.

My son, sitting beside me, whispered, 'She's adorable.'

My friend Nellie leaned over to me and whispered, 'Why would she tell that story?'

At the end of the session, both my son and my mother queued to buy Carrie's book.

Nellie works in the media. She has a favourite piece of wisdom: 'You are the story you tell about yourself.'

This is Nellie's golden rule. On every occasion, you have to *present* yourself as a success story.

You have to boast.

'My play has just finished a *massive* UK tour. *Utterly* brilliant. Played to *packed* houses every night. *Fabulous* notices.'

You don't mention that those theatres were in Booby Dingle

or Chipping Sodbury. Or that the hall in Barton-in-the-Beans was *packed* because it only seats forty. And they bussed in elderly folk from the Barking Hall Nursing Home to boost the numbers.

No. You must tell the good story. You must write the story of your life as if it were a press release.

My brother is a model example of this principle in action. When you call him up and enquire about his wellbeing, he says, 'If I was any better, I'd be arrested.' Always. Even after he rammed the handle of a squash racquet through his shinbone.

Naturally you don't want to go to the other extreme and succumb to the grievances of middle age, storing up examples of being overlooked and invisible and fat. Whingeing about the rudeness of Gen Y. (Even though they *are* rude.) Because when you meet those people, the disgruntled over-fifties, you know why life has failed to deliver on its promise. And in some cruel way, you know why successful people disassociate from them. Whingers are drainers. Purveyors of grievance risk suspicion that they brought it on themselves.

I am thinking about this because this morning, as I was waiting for a tram, I saw a poster in the window of my local newsagent. It read:

> Always remember
> You are braver
> than you
> believe
> stronger
> than you
> seem and
> smarter
> than you
> think

This, in a nutshell, is entirely the problem with the boy in the bookshop and his Gen-Y cohorts.

They don't need to be reminded of their status.

> Which is why
> they are
> more conceited
> than they
> realise
> more deluded
> than they
> grasp
> and more
> irksome
> than they
> know.

Suppose it happens to me. Suppose I put my book down on the counter of a bookshop and some self-important young cultural studies student glances cursorily at the cover, pushes his postmodern spectacles back up his nose and sniffs, 'Frankly, I wouldn't bother.' What will I do?

I *know* I will behave like Carrie.

Of course, I will restage the scene in the days/weeks/months that follow. In the reworked version, I will triumph with withering insult. I will have the bumptious little upstart sacked on the spot and the owner will send me yellow roses with a note, 'I cannot express how stupid I feel for employing such a simpleton in my shop.'

But in the sudden awfulness of the moment, I know I will forage and mumble because I *always do*. My first instinct will be to avoid embarrassment for all concerned. He, the boy, who I immediately assume has impeccable literary credentials, must not discover I am the author of the offending book, which frankly no one should bother with.

I must get out of this shop now, for both our sakes.

I was in a café with my older brother. A waiter spilled our coffees over the table. We both looked up and apologised.

Why? Because we have both learned that the most hideous and unforgiveable human act is *to make a scene.*

Unfortunately, I am a dramatist, which means that *not* making a scene is problematic.

I can't explain how he and I learned to avoid conflict. I can't imagine who taught us. My mother is *always* making a scene. She is eighty-nine and tough. I have to hose her down in Myer when shop assistants don't speak clearly enough. As for my dad, he was completely oblivious to what people might think. I can see him, back in the sixties, at the railing of the East Brighton footy club, shaking his fist and yelling at Peter, lying concussed on the field, 'Get up, ya big girl.'

We are having a dinner party at our house. I tell Carrie's story about the bookshop man. My friend Karen Hitchcock slaps the table with fury.

'I would have said, "I wrote that book, you little fucker. What have you ever done? You *Shop Sharon*!"'

I love Karen.

She is a senior doctor at the Alfred Hospital. Apart from having a swag of medical horror stories that make her a glittering asset at any dinner party, she is so *authoritative.* I feel the same when I see a sexy girl jump down from the driver's seat of a big truck. What is that feeling? Awe, I guess. And a bit of pride. You go, girl.

What is remarkable about Karen is that, in addition to being a doctor, she is also a prize-winning author. And she has a PhD in English Literature. A recent article she wrote in the *Monthly* magazine got half a million hits in three days.

She is also a westie chick who grew up in the suburb of Deer Park, notable for hosting the state's maximum-security female prison. So when Karen says, 'You *Shop Sharon*!', it doesn't sound patronising. It sounds tough.

I want that quality.

Oh, and by the way, the young man in the bookshop was so very wrong about Carrie Tiffany's book. That year, it won the inaugural Stella Prize and the Christina Stead Prize in the New South Wales Premier's Literary Awards, as well as being shortlisted for the Miles Franklin, the Prime Minister's Literary Award for Fiction, the Western Australian Premier's Book Awards, the Victorian Premier's Literary Awards, and so on and so forth.

My answer to Nell, who is incredulous that anyone would tell such a story against herself, is this. In a world where everyone is networking and promoting and selling, the authors I most want to read are the ones who are offering us their shining, guileless truthfulness.

40
Walking the Coast to Coast

THERE COMES a time when a playwright has to summon all the characters in her PC to a meeting on the desktop.

'I've gathered you here today to tell you that, despite my best efforts, you have all wilfully refused to contribute to any sort of plot. It's clear that you are not remotely interested in illuminating the human condition. Frankly, you'll never amount to anything, and as of today, I'm shutting down operations in this plant.'

That's when I decided to walk across England.

My friend Suzie said, 'We've been talking about doing this walk for years. If we don't go soon, my knees will give out and your feet won't hold up.'

This is the type of elite athlete you're dealing with here—my old neighbours, Suzie, Dave Flowers and me.

The walk, known as the Coast to Coast, is 320 kilometres across England, from the Cumbrian coast on the Irish Sea to Robin Hood's Bay on the North Sea. The trail wends its way across three national parks: the Lakes District, the Yorkshire Dales and the North York moors.

Before we set out, I imagined a sort of fifteen-day ramble, punctuated by nights in cosy pubs downing pints of Theakston Old Peculier, followed by hearty breakfasts in places like the Jolly Farmers. I saw myself ambling into a little hamlet mid-afternoon for a cream tea, having put in a cheerful day's walking, possibly spotting a red squirrel or two.

This is going to be a lark, I thought. Dorothy Wordsworth and I are going to be chums. I will be in conversation with the literary folk I knew at Melbourne University in the seventies: Coleridge, Shelley, Keats, mad-bad-and-dangerous-to-know Lord Byron and the Brontës.

In preparation, I read Daniel Defoe's account of his travels in the Lakes District, published five years after *Robinson Crusoe*. Defoe called this terrain 'the wildest, most barren and frightful of any that I have passed over in England.' The hills, he said, 'had a kind of unhospitable terror in them.'

I booked my flight. Then I took to the streets and trained. I became a Melbourne *flâneur*. I walked from Fitzroy to Port Melbourne, then to Hawthorn, then to Mordialloc. I wandered lonely as a cloud in Royal Park; I roamed the moors of Parkville with Heathcliff and those Brontë girls from Haworth Parsonage. I read accounts of plucky women heading off to the Dark Continent or 'out east' and I began to imagine myself as *splendidly capable*, a quality that, hitherto, might not readily be associated with me.

I no longer wanted to bash out words for a living. I wanted something I used to have. Something elusive, joyous and open. I wanted to be a girl with a notebook.

Before I left home, I made the first entry: a poem by the splendid Spanish playwright Antonio Machado:

> Wanderer, your footsteps are
> the road, and nothing more;
> wanderer, there is no road,
> the road is made by walking.

Already, I could feel the thrill of it. The sweet crisp air of an adventure.

Pass that pack, my good husband. Your wife, sturdy and without complaint, is off to walk the fells. Pass me my walking sticks and I will stride through Defoe's 'unhospitable terror' and, when the fog descends, I will shine a light into my own misty soul and see what lurks within.

Tradition dictates that those who walk the Coast to Coast, in the footsteps of pioneering fell-walker, guidebook writer and well-known curmudgeon Alfred Wainwright, must take a pebble from the shores of the Irish sea at St Bees and carry it across the country to fling into the North Sea, at journey's end.

So here we are—Suzie, Flowers and me. Day One. With our pebbles in our packs, we set out across the green carpeted cliffs that hug the Irish Sea. A fine mist of rain is perfuming the air. My legs are strong. My lungs fill with briny exhilaration.

The Coast to Coast walk can be undertaken in any number of days. We have scheduled fifteen days with one day off. This equates to around twenty-three kilometres a day.

It sounds easy enough, until you discover that a *fell* is actually a mountain. That *scree* is loose gravel scattered treacherously on the slopes of such mountains. That the paths and bridleways are rocky and awkward underfoot. That, thanks to *gills* and *spouts*, you slosh for kilometres through watery paths, mud and bog. And that England, blessed England, is cursed with weather from hell. (Who knew?)

And, oh yes, signposts are mostly non-existent. No other subject sorts the committed fell-walker from the rank amateur so comprehensively.

'You're like an American,' snaps a ropey-calved fundamentalist at breakfast. 'You want neon signs on everything!'

Given that up here on these mountains, a mist can descend so swiftly that, within an instant, you are shrouded in white (to the point where you cannot see your own outstretched fingertips), it does not seem too vulgar to this humble hiker to provide a discreet little arrow. But, apparently, a signpost is the first step on the slippery slope to Las Vegas.

So...you can spend a lot of time lost. On Day Four, a twenty-three-kilometre walk stretches into a thirty-three-kilometre walk. Then a forty-three-kilometre walk. I discover that being lost in the mountains is a little like passing through Elizabeth Kübler-Ross's five stages of grief: Denial, Anger, Bargaining (please god...),

Depression and Acceptance.

I never get to the final stage (I am at peace with what has happened)—I am marooned in Anger. Somewhere in a basin of drumlins (whatever they are), fear seeps into my pores like the relentless sting of rain. I channel Mick Malthouse: 'Get a grip. You're not lost. You're here. This is where you are. You're here.'

But then a more primal cry rattles the drumlins: 'Where the fuck is *here*?'

By the fifth day, I know that the training I have done—gym three times a week, plus fifty kilometres of walking each week—was not enough. The confronting truth is that the best walkers are lean and wiry. And many of them are old.

You know how you read about people who do extreme sports: the endorphins that are released and the euphoria they experience? I imagine endorphins like a brace of plovers. I wait for them to fly from my soul. Released into the great cosmos. This has not happened.

The upside is that I find myself in a most breathtaking, profound and pristine place. I live in the moment. I breathe a clean and ancient silence, and my world is coloured green. Lush, extravagant, soothing green. I had expected that I would be lost in thought; I would walk across England and think. But now, I realise, I am thinking only about walking. Mostly I have no choice. Concentrate on where you are putting your feet, Hannie, or you will fall off the side of a fell.

Descending a mountain goes like this: you are poised on a rock and you poke around with your stick for a secure foothold, then lower your foot onto it. Each step is like that. This particular mountain, Kidsty Pike, is 784 metres high. Apparently, if you look south from here to the deep cleft of Riggindale, there lies the eyrie of England's last golden eagle. Down and down we go. Step by knee-creaking step. Once at the bottom, we follow a trail for some hours. Then, way up ahead, another mountain looms. I see a coloured speck. With horror, I realise it's a hiker. That's the path. That's where we're headed.

By the time we have descended a second mountain, we are done-in, fatigued to a point of mania—but then we face a three-hour trudge on jagged rocks around the shore of a lake.

I cannot dredge up one dram of good humour.

Our instructions are to have a phone card to use at the red telephone box at Burnbanks, a remote hamlet some miles from our hotel. Late in the afternoon, Suzie announces that she has left the phone card in her suitcase. We won't be able to ring the hotel. I resolve the matter. I will not take one more step beyond that phone box. I will close the door and stay there all night.

Eventually, we round a corner and spot a red phone box. And there, waiting in his van, is our host, Anton. I could kiss him. He drives us to the hotel. Neither Suzie, Flowers nor I can muster the capacity to speak.

After the intensity of the Lakeland fells, we expect some easy walking, but this trail throws surprises at every turn. We start climbing the purple hills of the Pennines, the backbone of Britain. We are almost halfway. The hills are carpeted with heather. The wind lashes and the rain pelts down. Excited black spaniels are leaping about and the grouse beaters are smacking the heather with large flags. Shots ring through the air and I pray I will not become a news item. I see a black bird drop in a straight line to the ground.

Across these wild grouse moors we squelch over sphagnum moss, leaping between clumps of soggy reeds and tussocks, over watery stones and black mud. With our poles we poke about to test the depth of the morass. You could splosh down over your knees if you're not careful. We walk for eight hours through peat bog.

Strangely, I don't mind the rain. All togged up in wet weather gear I feel like my own toasty holiday cottage, listening to the rain on the roof (of my jacket). And at the end of the day, there is always a cosy pub and a hot shower (unless the thin, old people have arrived first and used up all the hot water).

*

By day eight, we have left Cumbria behind and we're in Yorkshire: James Herriot country. At Keld, where the Swale River swirls through green fields carved by dry stone walls and kissing gates, we are told by our host, Gary, that many Coast to Coasters booked to stay at his B&B don't show up. We learn of broken bones and crushed spirits. I am beginning to think that we three are made of quite stern stuff.

The most taxing day is our thirteenth, the twenty-nine-kilometre climb to Glaisdale in the North Yorkshire Moors. Dave, our B&B host, assures us there is only one long haul up a mountain for twenty minutes and then it is flat all the way to Beggar's Bridge.

What no one has factored in is the cyclone. From the moment we get to the top of Urra Moor, the mad wind roars into us. It is as if the Coast to Coast gods thought, what haven't we served up yet? Ah! What about a hurricane?

I am standing on this track with both poles jammed into the ground, knees bent, bottom out. Every ounce of my strength is devoted to resisting the shrieking gale. Suzie yells, 'You have to try and move. It's not going to let up.' Our wet weather gear slaps about our bodies like nappies on a clothesline.

As I cling to my poles, I am passed by a pink-faced Glaswegian. He yells, 'Exciting, isn't it?' We shout back our agreement. It *is* exciting.

The next morning I see a newspaper report: *Cyclone Katya Hits Northern England—Hurricane-force Winds 130 km Per Hour.*

Sixteen days after we set out, on a balmy autumn evening we arrive at Robin Hood's Bay and fling our pebbles into the North Sea. As we push open the door of Wainwright's Bar and sign our names in the Coast to Coast register, we note that several people who started out at the same time are not signed in. Two Americans, whose blog we read assiduously, have had to retire. Too hard.

Suzie, Flowers and I have little smiles dancing on our lips. Champagne, please!

At home, I turn on my computer. My characters claim to have missed me. The holiday, it seems, has been just what the doctor ordered. While I've had my mind on other things, they've had a few ideas of their own. Not before time.

41
Birth

MY SON is moving to London. His parental committee has made the journey to Tullamarine many times. Over the years we have waved him off to South America, to Israel, to various destinations in Asia and Europe. Jack is now twenty-seven years old and this time it's different. His ticket is one-way.

His father and I are helping him move out of his apartment. I have ruled a line through a page in my diary, assuming my time will be spent helping with the cleaning. But—oh joy—it's already done. Professional Gen Ys employ end-of-lease cleaners.

'Don't tell Dad,' says Jack. 'He'll hit the roof.'

His father is a roll-up-your-sleeves kind of bloke. He'll be pretty dark on the idea that you're too good to clean up your own place. In principle, I am of this school, too, but the fact that I'm off the hook is making professional cleaners look decidedly appealing. And Jack is busy. He puts in long hours as a lawyer and a party animal.

There's been a family gathering in Jaems and Georgina's house. The men of the family—father and stepfather—have said a few words. Jack is enrolled to do his Masters in Law at Kings College in London. We are all impressed. In his speech, stepfather MC has admitted he was the one who tried his hardest to dissuade Jack from a career in the law. I am reminded of my mother's hilarious cousin Margery, who taught Cate Blanchett at Methodist Ladies College. Margery loves to tell you that she once advised young Cate to give up any thought of acting and become a teacher.

*

At home, I have found a plastic bag in my camphorwood box. It contains a bundle of cards and telegrams, congratulating Jaems and me on the birth of 'baby Jack'.

'Sincere congratulations on your brand new "little guy", from Ray, Nigel, Frank and Shirley.' Who are these people?

'Congratulations on your special delivery,' from Edna and Max. No idea who they are, either.

'A Baby Boy? It's always nice to get a little male!' This is a card with a baby arriving in a letterbox.

My favourite is from my English literary agent. 'Congratulations on the birth of Jack. Hope the new year brings lots of joy and a success-ful new play.'

I can see myself sitting up in hospital reading that. A new play? In the new year? (Jack was born in November.) I'll be getting right onto that, Edwin.

Another from a colleague reads, 'Congratulations. You're no longer pregnant.'

There is a time in your life—usually when you are producing your own babies—when you are party to many tales, tall and horrible, of other people's birth experiences. Then you emerge from that little temporal tunnel and the topic never comes up again. It's like end-of-school exam results. For one year, those marks are what drive every waking moment. You hammer yourself until you crack. Then, very shortly after you've received your results, they become utterly incon-sequential. And even if you got ninety-six for English Expression, there is rarely an opportunity to brag.

Jack's birth is memorable because it occurred during the historic 1986 Victorian nurses' strike. This was a herculean struggle that lasted fifty days. A predominantly female workforce took on the State Labor government, defying an outmoded expectation they should perform uncomplaining service in the spirit of Florence Nightingale.

On 31 October, I was admitted to hospital with pre-eclampsia. This is high blood pressure and protein in the urine—a fairly common complication of pregnancy. That same day, five thousand nurses packed a stop-work meeting in Melbourne, voting to go out on strike indefinitely. Calls for a total walkout were defeated, but with heavy hearts nurses left their wards to a skeleton staff and joined the picket lines of most metropolitan hospitals.

My baby, sensing trouble afoot, decided to stay put. It was the first of many occasions on which he would display his capacity to avoid conflict and unpleasantness while cheerfully getting what he wants. I lay in bed at the Royal Women's Hospital, read books and waited. I read Gillian Bouras's memoir *A Foreign Wife*, in which she described giving birth to her third son in a hospital in Greece. I have spent time myself in hospital in Athens. When I was assigned a bed and pulled back the cover to get in, the sheets were bloody. After five more days in hospital in Melbourne, as the situation got steadily worse and the corridors were lined with temporary beds, it seemed as though the chaos of Athens had come to my home town.

Naturally, I supported the nurses' action. If I had not been lying in a hospital bed, I would have stood with them under their banner, 'Dedication Doesn't Pay the Rent!' But the government, like my baby, would not budge. As I understood it, John Cain, the premier, and David White, the health minster, were not so worried about the financial cost of a victory to the nurses, but more the precedent it would set for further industrial action.

On 1 November, the nurses walked out of all but critical care units. By 4 November, my baby started to make tentative gestures to begin ambling down the birth canal. I rang his dad. Get in here!

We had asked Jaems's sister Susan to be our support person. We learned this at antenatal classes: choose a calm and kind person to be there in case the husband faints or panics. Or in case the wife needs drugs and the husband gets it in his head that a drug-free labour would be best for everyone.

We also learned about the importance of installing a dishwasher and what to do if your dog gets jealous.

We did not, however, learn about how to fold a nappy, breastfeed a baby or what to do in the event of a full-scale nurses' strike.

Jaems and Susan came to the hospital and up we went to the Birth Centre on the eighth floor, all set to have a natural birth with a nice midwife and Keith Jarrett meandering through the key changes in the Köln Concert. (You were invited to bring in your own portable tape-recorder.) I'd worded up Jaems and Sue painstakingly beforehand.

'I want a baby, not a birth experience. Okay?'

This was not a popular position in my neck of the woods: my friend Nell told me that giving birth to her son was the closest she'd ever been to sexual ecstasy. When I told my mum this she said, 'That girl needs to change her sexual partner.'

My view was clear, as the spasms started to rip through my guts: 'If it were done when 'tis done, then 'twere well it were done quickly.'

My labour started in earnest at 11.30 p.m. on Monday 5 November. By nine-thirty the next morning, I was ready to throw in the towel. Gimme drugs. I was like a junkie, gimme drugs! Down I went, back to the labour ward to have an epidural. At the lift, I noticed that they were locking the Birth Centre behind me.

My mum finished her shift at the PLC boarding school where she worked. She drove past the hospital, saw the lights were on and came up to the delivery room. Outside, the pickets were stopping non-essential supplies to the wards. The premier announced that police would be used to break the pickets. My unborn son dug his heels in, in solidarity, and categorically refused to come out of his bedroom.

I dozed on and off, seduced into a calm, pain-free zone by the drug. Mum knitted and worried about getting a parking fine. Susan and Jaems made desultory conversation. I promised my mother I would hold off on giving birth while she went down to the street and fed the meter.

In the late afternoon, they introduced a hormone to dilate my cervix. Gradually, it reached its optimal dimension, but by six o'clock, still no sign of a baby.

The doctor arrived and said something had to be done. Jaems led the breathing. I pushed and pushed. Then, quickly, any semblance of hippy natural birth disappeared. Two doctors rushed in wearing operating gowns. The bed was rearranged and I was hauled up into the stirrups. One doctor took his position on a chair and applied suction to the baby's head. Another one began pumping on a pump as though he were furiously filling his bicycle tyres.

According to my mother—who didn't want to look, but didn't want to miss anything, either—the little head began to appear. Mum was horrified and fascinated in equal measure. She drew a small circle in biro in her diary, to indicate where the action was taking place. The nurse called out, 'Look, here come the shoulders!' and then the whole body plopped out.

The little creature was transferred immediately to a table and a paediatrician expertly sucked out his airways. The doctor said, 'It's a boy,' and I heard my baby make his first little cry. My mother sobbed. Susan howled. Jaems wept. The doctor wrapped my son tightly in a blanket and laid him in my arms.

I held him up and looked carefully into his eyes. Sam? William? Bill? Jack?

Jack Grant. There. He was named. A good union name, if ever there was one.

My mum left the hospital after twelve hours of nothing to eat. She went home to her house, made a cup of tea and a boiled egg, then got in her car and drove back to PLC to commence her night shift.

I know all this because she lent me her diary last week. In it she says, 'Han sank back with a beatific smile.'

Susan Grant left the hospital, too. We'd all been on a roller-coaster ride, but at the end of the day, as she told me later, 'You were the one who got the baby.'

Later that night, after Jaems had also gone home, a nurse shook my arm. She was cross. 'Your baby has been crying for ages.'

Horrified, I reached over and picked him up. Weren't new mothers hardwired to wake when their baby cried? I had no idea what to do. And there was no one to ask. I put him near my breast and, miracle of miracles, he sucked. He sucked and sucked and then he fell asleep.

The cross nurse returned. She put my baby back in the cot next to the bed and handed me a plastic bottle of Ajax and a wettex. She told me to go and have a bath.

'Clean it first.'

According to my mum's diary, I was a bloody mess and needed stitches. I have no memory of the procedure. I was just sore.

I climbed out of bed and followed instructions to find a bath. When I turned on the tap, there was no hot water. I cleaned and filled the bath, took off my clothes and climbed into the freezing water. I lay in there for a few minutes, thinking this must be what you do after you've had a baby.

The next morning, the doctor came by. He tapped me on the shoulder. 'You're fit and healthy. You're ready to go home.'

I gasped. 'Home? I can't possibly go home. I know nothing about babies!' I sounded like an indignant Penelope Keith in *The Good Life*.

An hour or so later, I took my precious creature home, only to discover that almost every service provider employed to assist new mothers to make the transition from hospital to home was also on strike. Even the garbage men were on strike.

My mother arrived with a brochure from the chemist. It showed a diagram of how to fold a nappy. Jaems and I pored over it. Mum, the only one with experience, was hazy on the details. It had been twenty-nine years since she had last given birth.

It transpired that breastfeeding was not exactly the intuitive business I had hoped. You need to have someone to show you how to do it. Jack was losing weight. In desperation I sought out Glad, an Infant Welfare sister who had a clinic on the ground floor of the Housing Commission flats in Collingwood. I walked into the waiting room and looked around at the women. They all looked like heroin addicts. Glad saw me come in. She leaned across her desk and called out, 'Oh, here's our little non-coping mother.'

I thought: six years of tertiary education and I have no idea what I'm doing. Humiliation. How does one be a mother? It is not natural. It's complicated and hard. At least being a playwright is *instinctive*.

Throughout all of this, baby Jack behaved as he meant to continue: good-natured, calm in a crisis, and always kind to his mother. Even when he was clearly starving.

So now we are at the airport, twenty-seven years later.

Jaems, MC, Jack and Jack's brother, Cam, sit at a plastic table under a fluorescent light. I order a Coke. Conversation is random and distracted. I take ugly photos of everyone on my phone.

A memory floats to mind. I remember a holiday Jack and I took together when he was six. We were headed to Magnetic Island. On the plane, I turned to my son.

'Hey, did you remember to bring the Panadol?'

He looked at me steadily before he said, 'Hannie. You're the mother.'

I'm the mother and my son is flying away.

To start a new life.

42
Slippery Street

WE ARE in Turkey making a radio program about the Istanbul Biennial for ABC Radio National. MC has just interviewed an artist whose exhibit was a bench with rulers laid end to end.

Yesterday, we looked at work by another artist, Mustafa Kunt. I emailed my friend Dave Flowers. He wrote back, 'I don't know Mustafa, but there are lots of Kunts in the arts.'

Because I am quite a juvenile person, I find this amusing. I am staring at my phone, laughing out loud on a bus.

Our work is done in Istanbul. We are headed to Gallipoli to make another one-hour program for Anzac Day. I am having a fab time, of course. I am the assistant/wife and the only thing that would make the prospect of this six-hour bus journey even more exciting is if I didn't have the shits. MC's brother Jimmy said of Turkey that he read an entire Robert Ludlam novel in a single squat.

Helen Garner has just sent an email: Keep up the fluids, old girl.

Yesterday, in Kuzguncuk, on the Asian side of the Bosphorus, I managed to get my hair cut and coloured for thirty-five dollars without a word of English spoken. One of the more enjoyable aspects of this hairdressing experience was that there was no small talk. Talk—small or otherwise—is impossible. MC and I cannot even manage the word for 'thank you', which has about five syllables.

My hairdresser, Rüzgar, pointed to those little curls of plastic hair they have on colour charts. I think he may have first used this chart in 1937. The choices were labelled as follows:

1. Intense blonde
2. Balkans
3. Central Europe

I mistakenly thought Central Europe might encompass Paris. I certainly didn't want to go Balkans, and there was no need to entertain discussion about the first option.

I watched Rüzgar ply my scalp with the dye using a thick paintbrush, the sort you'd use for exterior weatherboards. Slap, slap, slap. Quite a bit of dye was being slopped onto my face as well. I thought I might be acquiring complimentary Balkans black sideburns.

The upside was that a job that takes at least an hour in Melbourne was over in three minutes. I've seen men paint bollards on the St Kilda pier with more finesse.

Rüzgar wrapped my scalp in Glad Wrap and put me under the dryer, holding up ten fingers. I flipped through fashion magazines. Then came a fantastic head massage.

Rüzgar said, 'Sydney?' Then 'Sydney?' and after a while, I realised he was talking to me.

I didn't want to engage in conversation that might distract him from the important work he was doing on my head.

After the massage, Rüzgar hacked into my hair with scissors. Hack, hack, hack. Then, hackhackhack.

At home, hairdressers are fastidious about getting the hair parting right before they start to cut. This guy just kind of attacked. He didn't so much cut as scrape.

Scratch, rasp, scratch. Hair fell on the floor.

This was followed by magnificent flourishes with the hair dryer, and I was done.

I ventured a cautious glance in the mirror. Despite my pale-green complexion, on account of the aforementioned problemo, Rüzgar had performed a miracle.

*

Our shuttle bus arrives at the Otogar—the biggest central bus station I've ever seen. Nothing but buses, backing up, dodging, honking. Terribly important men in shiny suits are yelling, pointing and directing the seemingly chaotic movement of the buses. Our concrete section has 115 bays. The buses are operated by countless companies, so you can run along the line and find the best price. But finding where they actually go is a nightmare. This is the free-market version of Dante's Inferno.

I try to find where a bus to Çanakkale would depart from. The man at the desk points at MC. 'You. Take in backside.'

'Not today, thanks,' says MC, politely.

Gelibolu (Gallipoli) is every bit as intense as you might expect. We record hours of material. Our rapid immersion into the world of this place is aided as always by MC's fearless radio reporter persona. Two nights ago, we met an old bloke—a Western Australian farmer—whose grandfather played a key role here. Bill Hunter played him in the movie *Gallipoli*. You can watch it at the hotel if you ask them to put it on. MC used to lecture on the film at university. He has seen it a mere 256 times. He is not bursting to see it again.

At home in Australia, Gallipoli is all about us. Being here, it is about Turkey.

At Anzac Cove, we are so struck by how small the land area is. This little place. The unlikely alignment of events that would mean that so many countries would send their young men here.

All around us, people are quietly shedding a tear. MC cries. (I cry because he cries.) A man from our bus, senior partner in a Melbourne law firm, cries.

This whole peninsula is infused with melancholy. But the remote nature of what happened remains. What are we doing here? On this small strip of beautiful beach—the water is clear and blue—our country forged an identity? This beggars belief.

*

At last we are in Kas (pronounced *cash*) on the Mediterranean in the south-west of Turkey. This will be our home for the next ten weeks. Today we move from our pretty bougainvillea-decked *pansiyon*, Aphrodite, to our new lodgings—Ali Baba Otel Apart. We are upscaling to an apartment. Top floor, two balconies: one overlooks the harbour at the front, the other looks back at the massive mountain looming behind the town. We are paying 490 Turkish lire, which is about $250 per week.

We love it here at Aphrodite, even though the bathroom is so small that when you shower the water cascades onto the toilet. This is not uncommon in this country; it's a small but seemingly universal design fault.

In Turkey, too much tea-drinking is not enough. You can't have too much tea, too much food, or too many carpets. The lovely lady at Aphrodite comes over at five-minute intervals to bring more tea. This is not a financial transaction. This is concern for our hydration and happiness. We don't know how to make her stop. MC says she is like an ad for Duracell batteries.

We are both working on our respective projects. MC is writing a biography of the explorer William Wills (of Burke and Wills fame). I am writing a draft of a new play for the Manhattan Theatre Club.

Sometimes, when the sea is calling I think, '*Why do we always have to work?*'

The answer? Because this allows us to be in Kas. And when we knock off for the day we can swim at Big Pebble Beach, sip tea at Noel Baba's tea gardens and clamber along the hillsides lined with Lycian tombs. Not to mention bathing at the hamam.

It's a bit cold and drizzly here in Kas on the day I have my first traditional Turkish bath. Good weather for an indoor treat. We seek out our local hamam, but MC decides he doesn't want to be handled by the hairy Turkish man, so he goes for a walk instead.

I'm not sure I want to be handled by the hairy Turkish man either, but when I get there, he calls up his wife. She looks like a traditional Turkish lady from the village—all scarved and layered with florals and cardies.

Wearing my togs, I am led downstairs and into a marble room with a hexagonal slab in the centre. She instructs me to sit near an urn from which she ladles out hot water and sloshes it over me, head to foot. Then I hop up onto the heated slab. I am to lie there for ten minutes. It is like a hot morgue.

Ten minutes pass, and there is a loud drone, like a generator noise. The condensation on the ceiling is dripping. I begin to feel I am in some sort of weird torture chamber. Drip, drip, drip. There is nobody about. I hope I haven't been locked in. I resist the urge to get up and check. Finally, I hear the door creak open, and my village lady appears, totally naked.

Actually, she is wearing a small pair of undies, but nothing else. She has a fat little tummy, large breasts and an amazing scar from her armpit down her left arm. I try not to stare.

She sloshes me with more water, rolls down my bathers and slips them off, then puts on a mitt and rubs me all over, front and back, really hard. Something drops onto my hand. I think it's a spider, but it is actually skin. My skin. Like the rubbings of an eraser.

Then I am sloshed more. Great basin-loads of hot water buckets over me on the hot slab. After that, I am covered with the most delicious warm substance, which feels like fairy floss. It is a special soap, and the soapy massage begins.

Another sandpaper mitt treatment follows. She sloshes again and washes my hair. More sloshing. Then she hands me a towel and I am sent upstairs to sit. Her hairy husband dashes over with a glass of apple tea.

The wife returns, fully dressed, and sits next to me. She tells me her middle son plays on the computer and doesn't do his homework. I, on the other hand, had made the very sensible decision to have only one son. And a lawyer. Oh, a lawyer. 'A lawyer is a rich man,' she says, patting my arm with her warmest congratulations.

She stands up and takes my hand.

'What pity,' she says, in her funny earnest Turkish way, as if she had heard sad news. 'You so clean. Your husband. He so *dirty*.'

I am taken into another room, laid out on the bench and massaged all over with oils.

I can hardly be bothered walking home. When I finally make it up the stairs of Ali Baba, I just have to lie on the couch. I sleep for two hours.

MC is now convinced he has to have the hamam experience too. Especially since he is *so dirty*. But he won't get to be handled by the bare-breasted lady.

'Husband do husband,' she explained.

There is a famous hamam in Antalya, where we are going in a week or so. It was built in the thirteenth century. After I read that little detail aloud from the guidebook, MC was decidedly less enthusiastic.

'That's seven hundred years of human detritus!'

But my hamam lady told me that all Turkish people go. 'Rich lady, she come every week. Poor lady, she come two time every month.'

They come with their daughters and their grandchildren. The men come too.

My skin, I have to tell you, feels like silk.

Back in Melbourne, every weekday morning MC and I walk together from our house in Fitzroy to his work at ABC Radio National in Southbank.

Almost every morning, at some point along the way, he says, 'I wonder what's happening in Slippery Street this morning?'

Plan #57 for our future involves decamping to the top-floor flat of the Ali Baba Otel. Once ensconced, MC will buy a little traditional fishing boat and putter about, fishing and ferrying tourists. He will rent a stone barn across the road from the amphitheatre and, with his friend Corbs, will tinker with their boat and watch the footy online, supporting the rise and rise of their beloved Melbourne football team—the sole members of the Turkish chapter of the Demons Supporters Club.

I'm not sure exactly what I'm doing in this fantasy, but I think it involves cooking for vast numbers of tremendously interesting Australians whom MC has invited to visit us.

Do come. I will take you up the road and down some steps to Memet's secret garden. This is our swimming spot: a terraced garden leading to the sea. There are a couple of tables and sun lounges in among his plants and herbs and decorative mosaics. An old ladder descends into the water.

We go twice a day—morning and late afternoon. We swim way, way out into the Mediterranean. It is deep and warm, and out there you will feel calm and strong. In between, we can all tap furiously on our computers, trying to make progress on our projects.

43

The Butterfly House

I BEGAN my longing for summer too soon. October has been windy and churlish. I have been counting the days until I take possession of the famous Butterfly House in Dromana as its first writer-in-residence.

This is what I remember about Dromana from my childhood.

Once you see the Dromana sign on the Point Nepean Road, Sorrento isn't too much further.

On sunny days, the sea is striped with a band of iridescent aqua.

The water is clean and clear. If you close your eyes and swim towards the sun, you can breaststroke to Buenos Aires.

On a Saturday night, you can go to the Dromana drive-in and get pregnant.

We were Sorrento people. My dad worked with a bloke who owned a holiday house, which we rented. It was next to the Koonya Hotel—a hundred metres or so from the green and white bandstand on the Sorrento foreshore.

One afternoon, my father took us kids to the Dromana pub. He cashed two pounds into pennies and divided this bounty among his three children. We crowded around a table in the smoky Ladies Lounge and piled up our coins in front of us while he dealt the cards for Pontoon. As the rain lashed the windows, we played hand after hand, listening to jukebox hits: 'Good Vibrations', 'Help me, Rhonda' and Dean Martin singing 'Everybody loves somebody, sometime'. By afternoon's end, my dad had won back every single penny.

So here I am at last, ensconced in the Butterfly House, perched halfway up the hill under Arthurs Seat. It was built in 1956 as a holiday house for Nell and Gerald McCraith. In a gesture of incredible generosity, their daughter, Lois Dixon-Ward, and her two daughters, Bin and Kerryn, have bequeathed it to RMIT. In its new life, it is available to writers for residencies of up to four weeks.

Known officially as the McCraith House, it is listed on the Victorian Heritage Register as an architectural treasure of the 1950s. No wonder: it is a glorious statement of Australian modernism. The architects, David Chancellor and Rex Patrick, created an ingenious geometric construction, essentially two steel triangles—the shape of butterfly's wings. The house itself is small, perfect for a lady writer. And it opens its wings to embrace a spectacular view.

The Butterfly House and I are almost the same age. I am thinking about our parallel lives. She is a year older, built in the year of the Olympics in Melbourne, when my dad bought the first TV in the street and all the neighbours came by to watch.

For all her show of modernity, she seems to me to be exuberantly innocent.

In the centre of the room, among all the McCraith treasures, I have brought one of my own. It is my camphorwood box with all my stuff: airline tickets, telegrams, hundreds of letters, diaries, school reports, theatre posters, Bob Hawke buttons, a wedding bouquet I once caught, even the black and yellow sundress I was wearing when I first met my husband.

Two weeks have passed and I haven't opened it.

I am standing on the balcony, surveying the blue panorama of Port Phillip Bay flecked with white triangles—the sails of yachts. Directly across the bay is the hazy silhouette of Melbourne's skyscrapers. To the right, the coast sweeps around past Safety Beach to the leafy cliffs of Mount Martha. To the left, an expanse of water laps on the beaches of McCrae, Rosebud, Rye, Blairgowrie, Sorrento and Portsea.

Is there any coast road in any part of the world that smells of fish and chips for so many kilometres?

At night, the house floats in a vast black universe, smattered with twinkling lights. The ugly retail sprawl along the Point Nepean Road is gone. The dull, lurking suburbia is also erased by the blackness. At night, in the Butterfly House, there is only romance.

In June, there was a morning tea at the house, when the Dixon-Wards officially handed over their treasured holiday home to RMIT. Among the guests was the novelist Carrie Tiffany, who will be the next writer to take up residence here.

After the signing ceremony, Carrie and I were taken on a tour by Lois, whose late husband, Bryan Dixon-Brown, was a sea captain. Lois pointed to a ship that sailed into view and made a sharp left-hand turn towards Melbourne. She told us that when her husband sailed by, sometimes after being at sea for many weeks, he would sound the ship's horn several times. That was her signal to bundle the children into the car and hotfoot it up to Melbourne to collect him from the port.

When I first received information about the house from RMIT, the description said, 'the house remains exactly as it was in 1956—down to its exterior and interior wall colours, furniture, crockery, even the bed linen.'

'Gawd, Aggie,' said my mum, 'I think you'd better take your own sheets.'

In fact, there is no sign of the authentic 1956 bed linen. The RMIT property people have updated the sheets and the electrical appliances—but the heritage experts have been very exacting. This is a 'personalised memoir of a bygone Australia' and all the contents of the McCraiths' holiday house have been itemised in an inventory.

On Day One, I snapped a heritage plastic spatula while turning some bacon in a pan. I slipped it in the kitchen tidy. My sister-in-law suggested I pop into the Rye op shop to find a replacement.

I come from a long line of hardy women who love swimming in the sea. My grandmother pulled on her togs and flowered bathing cap and went for a dip the day before she died. Great-grandmother

Polly, settling in for a day at Aspendale beach, would send one of
the kids off with a billy to buy boiling water from the shop so they
could have a cup of tea after a paddle. My mother is eighty-nine and
still swimming.

Of all the beaches in the world where I've swum and imagined
calling home, this curl of coastline around Port Phillip Bay is where I
feel most tethered to my family.

The day before my sixth-form dance, my parents moved one hop
down the coast to Black Rock. We were one house back from the
beach road, above the craggy, reddish bluff of Half Moon Bay. This
was Clarice Beckett country, the painter whose misty beachscapes
captured the moochy years of my late adolescence.

In the 1920s, Clarice was caring for her ailing parents during the
day and sneaking time to paint, in the early hours of the morning or
at dusk. She died of pneumonia at forty-eight, after painting wild seas
off Beaumaris during a big storm.

When my father suffered a massive stroke, I felt enveloped by
the melancholy of Clarice's foggy coastline, wandering the cliffs of
Half Moon Bay.

My parents crept further down the coast, this time to Mornington.
Day after day, my mother kept her pecker up by swimming in the
friendly crescent of sea at Mothers Beach. My dad limped on for four
more years before he dropped dead one Saturday morning.

By then, I was living in Collingwood, and inner Melbourne had
claimed me. Summers came and went in the hot, gritty asphalt city.

I have my first swim of the season, here at Dromana, on a Saturday.
The sun is bearing down, but the water is winter-cold. Michael has
come down to the Butterfly House for the weekend. He is one of
those plunge-in, dash-out swimmers. I am a slow starter. You could
mistake it for procrastination. But once in and under, I can stay for
hours. After a few strokes in the general direction of Sorrento, I glide
about on my back, painted toenails to the sky, my hair swirling like

Medusa. It occurs to me that this is exactly the style of my mother and her mother, Mama.

This comes as a little shock. In the smallest unexamined actions, I am mimicking the gestures of my parents and my grandparents. Just when I thought I was entirely my own creation, here I am, performing this odd little action: breaststroking with my feet in the air in front of me, just as my mum does and Mama did.

Lloyd Jones, the New Zealand writer, has seeded this idea. He has come to the Butterfly House for lunch. Lloyd thought he was his own creation, too, until he started researching his memoir, *A History of Silence*. He watched his grandfather in a home movie and saw himself. Fleetingly, but recognisably.

I tell Lloyd that I've never been the least bit interested in writing about myself or my family until recently.

'It's as though I went to sleep one night and woke up with this new curiosity.'

It is a sparkling Wednesday morning at the Butterfly House. A phalanx of ibises fly across the pastel sky like the string of a kite.

I am at my desk early, but I have only written two sentences. I am a little girl trying to write a composition in class.

'You haven't written anything, Missy. You'd better get cracking,' admonishes my teacher, as she moves along the aisle.

'I'm sorry, Miss Box. I don't know what to put.'

I think of my journalist friends. I imagine their bylines in the newspaper and, underneath, a big empty square of paper with a disclaimer at the bottom: 'Sorry. Couldn't think of anything today.'

I have been a writer for thirty-three years. Will I ever stop feeling guilty that I'm out and about, doing my job, when other people have to be in an office?

A walk is in order.

I wander along the tideline, crunching on the shale under my thongs. The beach is dotted with those translucent jellies that squish through your toes in ways that are both thrilling and repulsive.

My dad didn't like the beach. He hated the feeling of sand on his feet. He preferred boating, fishing, doing things. My mum once said, 'I love him best when he's wearing his gardening clothes.'

I couldn't see it, myself.

But now I understand. A man messing about in his shorts and old jumper could make your heart swell.

In the shallows, I see seven huge dead fish. Like, really big. With clean, clear eyes. They are snapper. At first I think a fisherman has lost his catch. Then I see that each fish has a large fillet carved from one side only.

Who has committed this wasteful act?

I don't want to swim with dead things.

I decide to drive down to the Sorrento back beach and brave the icy blast of ocean rolling in from Antarctica. The waves are racing in to the shore, white foam flying, like brides with frothy veils. A boy is tormenting his sister, flinging wet sand into her shivery little back.

His mother barks, 'Give it a rest, Cooper.'

The peninsula telescopes to quite a narrow strip of land by the time you're at Sorrento, so there's not much between the front bay beach and this wild rowdy coast at the back. But how different they are. Even the seagulls are different. Here, they whirl and soar like proper wild creatures above the crashing surf, but in the gentle waters of the bay, they just waddle about and eat chips.

After my swim in the sea, I'm starving. It's 11 a.m. and I'm ready for breakfast. I stop at a café on the main street in Sorrento. I order a bacon and egg sandwich, but as I sit I become engrossed in Lloyd Jones's memoir. The waitress delivers my breakfast. It sits there for several minutes before a sudden movement startles me. Someone has thrown a white floppy hat at my table. No. It is a seagull. A seagull has swooped down and carried off my toasted sandwich. He wheels up towards the light pole, but he cannot hold it. The sandwich tumbles, and, as if in slow motion, it twists and opens out, falling through the air and landing splat, egg-side down, on the window of a BMW.

I look around hoping for someone who has seen it, so we can both enjoy this sweet and hilarious joke.

There is no one.

What happens if there is nothing interesting about my life? This is why, over these past thirty years, I have only ever opened the box a crack, to shove something in. This is why I have constructed an elaborate rationalisation that other people are always more interesting and that for me to write about my own life would be perilously close to vanity or professional suicide.

A vision of my brother Peter: he is staring at me, shaking his head.

'You want my advice?' he says.

'No.'

He persists. 'Get over yourself.'

The waitress comes over to ask if I would like a replacement sandwich. I am laughing. 'No. No, thank you. Thank you very much.'

I am going home to the Butterfly House. I'm getting over myself.

I am going to open the box.

Acknowledgments

I AM indebted to Hilary Glow and Amanda Smith for suggesting I write this book. One horrible winter's night, I sobbed my way through the sushi and sashimi combo at my local Japanese. I was miserable: the Melbourne Theatre Company had just knocked back my most recent play.

Instead of saying, 'It will be all fine,' which is the usual way you might console a sobbing woman in a public place, my oldest friends said, 'Forget theatre. Write a book. We'd buy it. Wouldn't we?'

So, that night, emboldened by an in-principle pledge of $32.99, I sent three stories to Michael Heyward at Text Publishing. He rang the next morning to offer me a book deal.

The rest is a story of pure happiness.

Michael nurtured this book with grace and enthusiasm, aided by Alaina Gougoulis, the editor from heaven. Jane Novak has been similarly encouraging and lovely.

Three of my writing friends, Charlotte Wood, Caroline Baum and Ailsa Piper, have written to me at least twice a week. Dear Girly Whirls...this correspondence has sustained me for the entire time I've been working on this book. Every writer needs a girly whirl to fill her sails, and send wise counsel, when, out at sea, her boat starts to fill with water.

My mother and my son, who feature in these pages, have been generous and gracious in their powerlessness.

Finally my love and thanks to Michael Cathcart, my husband. Any woman should be so lucky.